WCF 4.0 Multi-tier Services Development with LINQ to Entities

Build SOA applications on the Microsoft platform with this hands-on guide updated for VS2010

Mike Liu

BIRMINGHAM - MUMBAI

WCF 4.0 Multi-tier Services Development with LINQ to Entities

Copyright © 2010 Packt Publishing

First published: June 2010

Production Reference: 1020610

Published by Packt Publishing Ltd.
32 Lincoln Road
Olton
Birmingham, B27 6PA, UK.

ISBN 978-1-84968-114-8

www.packtpub.com

Cover Image by Sandeep Babu (sandyjb@gmail.com)

Credits

Author
Mike Liu

Reviewers
Yingwei Yang

Jeff Sanders

Acquisition Editor
David Barnes

Development Editor
Rakesh Shejwal

Technical Editor
Akash Johari

Copy Editor
Lakshmi Menon

Indexer
Rekha Nair

Editorial Team Leader
Akshara Aware

Project Team Leader
Lata Basantani

Project Coordinator
Sneha Harkut

Proofreader
Kevin McGowan

Graphics
Geetanjali Sawant

Production Coordinator
Adline Swetha Jesuthas

Cover Work
Adline Swetha Jesuthas

About the Author

Mike Liu studied Mathematics and Applied Software Engineering at Nanjing University between 1984 and 1988. After graduating with a bachelor's degree, he worked as a Programmer/Senior Software Engineer/Architect on Unix and DOS using C/C++, Dbase, and Oracle. In 1995 he moved to New Zealand and studied Business Computing at Auckland University of Technology. During the five-year stay in New Zealand, he worked as a Senior Software Engineer on Unix and Windows using C/C++, Java, FoxPro, Informix, Oracle, and SQL Server. He moved to the United States in 2000 and since then has been working as a Web Developer/Senior Software Engineer/Principal Software Engineer of various operating systems using various programming languages and database technologies. He studied Software Engineering at Brandeis University and graduated in 2005 with a master's degree.

Mike became a Sun Certified Java Programmer (SCJP) in 2000, a Microsoft Certified Solution Developer (MCSD) for Visual Studio 6.0 in 2001, and an MCSD for .NET in 2004. He started using C# for production development back in the year 2001 when C# was still in beta stage and he is now integrating a Business Process Management application with a WCF services backend system.

Mike had his first book—*MITT: Multi-user Integrated Table-processing Tool Under Unix*—published in 1993, and had his second book—*Advanced C# Programming*—published in 2003. The previous version of this book—WCF Multi-tier Services Development with LINQ—was published in 2008, with LINQ to SQL being used as the ORM in the data access layer of the WCF services.

Many thanks to the editors and technical reviewers at Packt Publishing. Without their help this book wouldn't be of such high quality. And thanks to my wife, Julia Guo, and my two sons, Kevin and James Liu, for their consideration and sacrifices while I was working on this book.

About the Reviewers

Yingwei Yang joined Microsoft in 2008. Before that he worked for ITG and Redcats USA. Yingwei enjoys working with .NET technology and is a big fan of Service Oriented Architecture, Silverlight, and High Performance Computing. He always thinks that Web Services/Software as a service brings endless opportunities and possibilities.

Yingwei Yang also helped review the book, *WCF Multi-tier Services Development with LINQ*, and he is reviewing *Silverlight User Interface Cookbook*.

Jeff Sanders is a published author and an accomplished technologist. He is currently employed with Avanade Federal Services as a Group Manager/Senior Architect and as the Manager of the Federal Office of Learning and Development. Jeff has more than 17 years of professional experience in the field of IT and strategic business consulting, in roles ranging from leading sales to delivery efforts. He regularly contributes to certification development with Microsoft and speaks publicly on Microsoft enterprise technologies. With his roots in Software Development, Jeff's areas of expertise include operational intelligence, collaboration and content management solutions, distributed component-based application architectures, object-oriented analysis and design, and enterprise integration patterns and designs.

Jeff is also the CTO of DynamicShift, a client-focused organization specializing in Microsoft technologies, specifically Business Activity Monitoring, BizTalk Server, SharePoint Server, StreamInsight, Windows Azure, AppFabric, Commerce Server, and .NET. He is a Microsoft Certified Trainer, and leads DynamicShift in both training and consulting efforts.

He may be reached at `jeff.sanders@dynamicshift.com`.

Table of Contents

Preface

WCF is the new Microsoft model for building services and LINQ to Entities is the new Microsoft ORM for accessing underlying data storages. Want to learn both? You may have already seen the huge reference tomes currently available.

This book is the quickest and easiest way to learn WCF and LINQ to Entities in Visual Studio 2010. WCF and LINQ to Entities are both powerful, yet complex technologies from Microsoft but this book will teach you both. The mastery of these two topics will quickly get you started in creating service-oriented applications and allow you to take your first steps into the world of Service-Oriented Architecture (SOA) without getting overwhelmed.

Throughout this book you will understand what's going on behind the scenes with WCF and learn the basic yet most useful techniques about LINQ to Entities. You will develop three real world, multi-tiered WCF services from beginning to end, with LINQ to Entities being used in the data access layer of the services. Various clients including Windows console applications, the WCF Test Client, Windows Form applications, and WPF applications will be created to test these WCF services. At the end of this book you will be 100 per cent confident that you understand WCF and LINQ to Entities, not only in theory, but also with sound real world experiences.

What this book covers

Chapter 1, Introducing Web Services and Windows Communication Foundation, covers the basic concepts of web services and WCF is also explained.

Chapter 2, Implementing a Basic HelloWorld WCF Service, discusses how a simple HelloWorld WCF service is implemented, hosted, and consumed.

Chapter 3, Hosting and Debugging the HelloWorld WCF Service, discusses various hosting and debugging techniques for WCF services.

Chapter 4, Implementing a WCF Service in the Real World, explains how to create a layered WCF service with an interface layer and a business logic layer.

Chapter 5, Adding Database Support and Exception Handling to the RealNorthwind WCF Service, explains how to add a data access layer and fault message handling to the previously created WCF service.

Chapter 6, LINQ – Language-Integrated Query, discusses LINQ-related language features such as anonymous types, extension methods, and lambda expressions.

Chapter 7, LINQ to Entities: Basic Concepts and Features, covers the basic concepts and features of LINQ to Entities such as LINQ to Entities designer, querying and updating a table, deferred execution, and lazy/eager loading.

Chapter 8, LINQ to Entities: Advanced Concepts and Features, discusses advanced concepts and features of LINQ to Entities such as stored procedures, inheritance, concurrency control, and transactional support.

Chapter 9, Applying LINQ to Entities to a WCF Service, covers how the data access layer of the WCF service will be recreated with LINQ to Entities.

Chapter 10, Distributed Transaction Support of WCF, explains how to add distributed transaction support to the WCF service.

What you need for this book

1. Microsoft .NET Framework 4.0
2. Microsoft Visual Studio 2010: Ultimate, Premium, or Professional
3. Microsoft SQL Server 2008, 2005, or Express
4. Internet Information Server 7.0 or 6.0
5. Windows 7 or XP

Who this book is for

This book is for C# and C++ developers who are eager to get started with WCF and LINQ to Entities and want a book that is practical and rich with examples from the very beginning. Developers and architects evaluating SOA implementation technologies for their company will find this book particularly useful because it gets you started with Microsoft's tools for SOA and shows you how to customize our examples for your prototypes.

This book presumes basic knowledge of C# or C++. Previous experience with Visual Studio will be helpful but is not required as detailed instructions are given throughout the book.

Conventions

In this book, you will find a number of styles of text that distinguish between different kinds of information. Here are some examples of these styles, and an explanation of their meaning.

Code words in text are shown as follows: "We can include other contexts through the use of the `include` directive."

A block of code is set as follows:

```
public bool UpdateProduct(Product product)
{
// TODO: call business logic layer to update product
if (product.UnitPrice <= 0)
return false;
else
return true;
}
```

When we wish to draw your attention to a particular part of a code block, the relevant lines or items are set in bold:

```
<?xml version="1.0" encoding="utf-8" ?>
<configuration>
<connectionStrings>
<add name ="NorthwindConnectionString" connectionString="server=your_
db_server\ your_db_instance;
uid=your_user_name; pwd=your_password;
database=Northwind" />
</connectionStrings>
<system.web>
<compilation debug="true" />
</system.web>
```

Any command-line input or output is written as follows:

```
C:\SOAWithWCFandLINQ\Projects\HelloWorld\HelloWorldClient>

"C:\Program Files\Microsoft SDKs\Windows\v6.0\Bin\SvcUtil.exe"
http://localhost:8080/HostDevServer/HelloWorldService.svc?wsdl /
out:HelloWorldServiceRef.cs /config:app.config
```

New terms and **important words** are shown in bold. Words that you see on the screen, in menus or dialog boxes for example, appear in the text like this: "clicking the **Next** button moves you to the next screen".

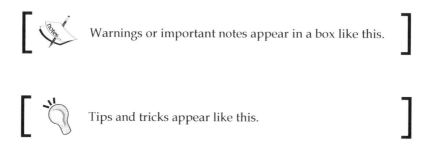

Warnings or important notes appear in a box like this.

Tips and tricks appear like this.

Reader feedback

Feedback from our readers is always welcome. Let us know what you think about this book—what you liked or may have disliked. Reader feedback is important for us to develop titles that you really get the most out of.

To send us general feedback, simply send an e-mail to feedback@packtpub.com, and mention the book title via the subject of your message.

If there is a book that you need and would like to see us publish, please send us a note in the **SUGGEST A TITLE** form on www.packtpub.com or e-mail suggest@packtpub.com.

If there is a topic that you have expertise in and you are interested in either writing or contributing to a book on, see our author guide on www.packtpub.com/authors.

Customer support

Now that you are the proud owner of a Packt book, we have a number of things to help you to get the most from your purchase.

Downloading the example code for the book

Visit http://www.packtpub.com/files/code/1148_Code.zip to directly download the example code.

The downloadable files contain instructions on how to use them.

Errata

Although we have taken every care to ensure the accuracy of our content, mistakes do happen. If you find a mistake in one of our books—maybe a mistake in the text or the code—we would be grateful if you would report this to us. By doing so, you can save other readers from frustration and help us improve subsequent versions of this book. If you find any errata, please report them by visiting http://www.packtpub.com/support, selecting your book, clicking on the **let us know** link, and entering the details of your errata. Once your errata are verified, your submission will be accepted and the errata will be uploaded on our website, or added to any list of existing errata, under the Errata section of that title. Any existing errata can be viewed by selecting your title from http://www.packtpub.com/support.

Piracy

Piracy of copyright material on the Internet is an ongoing problem across all media. At Packt, we take the protection of our copyright and licenses very seriously. If you come across any illegal copies of our works, in any form, on the Internet, please provide us with the location address or website name immediately so that we can pursue a remedy.

Please contact us at copyright@packtpub.com with a link to the suspected pirated material.

We appreciate your help in protecting our authors and our ability to bring you valuable content.

Questions

You can contact us at questions@packtpub.com if you are having a problem with any aspect of the book, and we will do our best to address it.

1
Introducing Web Services and Windows Communication Foundation

In this chapter, we will explain concepts and definitions related to SOA, web services, and WCF. We will discuss each of the following in detail:

- What is SOA?
- What is a web service and how is it related to SOA?
- What standards and specifications are there for web services?
- What is WCF?
- Use of WCF for SOA.
- WCF architecture.
- Basic WCF concepts.

What is SOA?

SOA is the acronym for **Service Oriented Architecture**. As it has come to be known, SOA is an architectural design pattern by which several guiding principles determine the nature of the design. Basically, SOA states that every component of a system should be a service, and the system should be composed of several loosely-coupled services. A service here means a unit of a program that serves a business process. **Loosely-coupled** here means that these services should be independent of each other so that changing one of them should not affect any other services.

SOA is neither a specific technology nor a specific language. It is just a blueprint or a system design approach. It is an architectural model that aims to enhance the efficiency, agility, and productivity of an enterprise system. The key concepts of SOA are services, high interoperability, and loose coupling.

Web services

There are many approaches to realizing SOA, but the most popular and practical one is—using **web services**.

What is a web service?

A web service is a software system designed to support interoperable machine-to-machine interaction over a network. A web service is typically hosted on a remote machine (provider) and called by a client application (consumer) over a network. After the provider of a web service publishes the service, the client can discover it and invoke it. The communications between a web service and a client application use XML messages. A web service is hosted within a web server and HTTP is used as the transport protocol between the server and the client applications. The following diagram shows the interaction of web services:

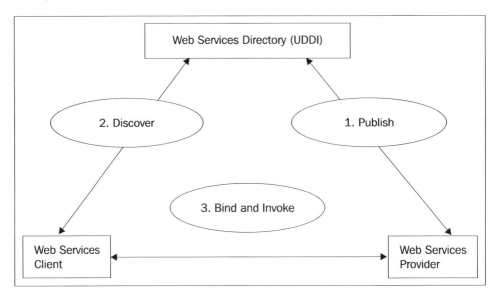

Web services were invented to solve the interoperability problem between applications. In the early 90s, along with the LAN/WAN/Internet development, it became a big problem to integrate different applications. An application might have been developed using C++ or Java, and run on a Unix box, a Windows PC, or even a mainframe computer. There was no consistent way that was standardized across the industry for it to communicate with other applications. It was the development of XML that made it possible to share data between applications across hardware boundaries and networks or even over the Internet.

For example, a Windows application might need to display the price of a particular stock. With a web service, this application can make a request to a URL and/or pass an XML string such as `<QuoteRequest><GetPrice Symble='XYZ'/> </QuoteRequest>`. The requested URL is actually the Internet address of a web service, which, upon receiving the above quote request, gives a response—`<QuoteResponse><QuotePrice Symble='XYZ'>51.22</QuotePrice> </QuoteResponse/>`. The Windows application then uses an XML parser to interpret the response package and display the price on the screen.

The reason it is called a web service is that it is designed to be hosted in a web server such as Microsoft Internet Information Server, and called over the Internet, typically through the HTTP or HTTPS protocols. This is to ensure that a web service can be called by any application, using any programming language, and under any operating system, as long as there is an active Internet connection and, of course, an open HTTP/HTTPS port, which is true for almost every computer on the Internet.

Each web service has a unique URL and contains various methods. When calling a web service, you have to specify which method you want to call, and pass the required parameters to the web service method. Each web service method will also give a response package to tell the caller the execution results.

Besides new applications being developed specifically as web services, legacy applications can also be wrapped up and exposed as web services. So, an IBM mainframe accounting system might be able to provide external customers with a link to check the balance of an account.

Web service WSDL

In order to be called by other applications, each web service has to supply a description of itself so that other applications will know how to call it. This description is provided in a language called **WSDL**.

WSDL stands for **Web Services Description Language**. It is an XML format that defines and describes the functionalities of the web service, including the method names, parameter names and types, and returning data types of the web service.

For a Microsoft ASMX web service, you can see the WSDL by adding `?WSDL` to the end of the web service URL, say `http://localhost/MyService/MyService.asmx?WSDL`.

Web service proxy

A client application calls a web service through a proxy. A web service proxy is a stub class between a web service and a client. It is normally autogenerated by a tool such as Visual Studio IDE, according to the WSDL of the web service. It can be reused by any client application. The proxy contains stub methods mimicking all the methods of the web service so that a client application can call each method of the web service through these stub methods. It also contains other necessary information required by the client to call the web service such as custom exceptions, custom data and class types, and so on.

The address of the web service can be embedded within the proxy class, or it can be placed inside a configuration file.

A proxy class of a web service could be generated for a specific language. For example, there could be a proxy class for Java clients, a proxy class for C# clients, and yet another proxy class for COBOL clients. A proxy class could also be generated in a commonly understood way such as in XML format. Different clients written in different languages can reuse this same common proxy class to communicate with the web service.

To call a web service from a client application, the proper proxy class first has to be added to the client project. Then, with an optional configuration file, the address of the web service can be defined. Within the client application, a web service object can be instantiated and its methods can be called just as for any other normal method.

SOAP

There are many standards for web services—SOAP is one of them. **SOAP** was originally an acronym for **Simple Object Access Protocol** and was designed by Microsoft. As this protocol became popular with the spread of web services and its original meaning was misleading, the original acronym was dropped with version 1.2 of the standard. It is now merely a protocol, maintained by W3C.

SOAP, now, is a protocol for exchanging XML-based messages over computer networks. It is widely used by web services and has become its de facto protocol. With SOAP, the client application can send a request in XML format to a server application, and the server application will send back a response in XML format. The transport for SOAP is normally HTTP/HTTPS, and the wide acceptance of HTTP is one of the reasons why SOAP is also widely accepted today.

Web services: standards and specifications

Because SOA is an architectural style and web service is now the de facto standard for building SOA applications, we need to know what standards and specifications there are for web services.

As discussed in previous sections, there are many standards and specifications for web services. Some have been well-developed and widely accepted, some are being developed, and others are just at the proposal stage. These specifications are in varying degrees of maturity, and are maintained or supported by various standards and entities. Specifications may complement, overlap, and compete with each other. As most of these standards committees and specifications are for future web services, not all of them are implemented in current web service frameworks.

Web service standards and specifications are occasionally referred to as "WS-*" although there is not a single managed set of specifications that this consistently refers to, nor a recognized owning body across all of them. The reference term "WS-*" is more of a general nod to the fact that many specifications are named with "WS-" as their prefix.

Besides XML, SOAP, and WSDL, here is a brief list of some other important standards and specifications for web services.

WS-I Profiles

The **Web Services Interoperability Organization (WS-I)** is an industry consortium chartered to promote interoperability across the stack of web services specifications. It publishes web service profiles, sample applications, and test tools to help determine profile conformance. One of the popular profiles it has published is the WS-I Basic Profile. WS-I is governed by a Board of Directors, and Microsoft is one of the board members. The web address for the WS-I organization is `http://www.ws-i.org`.

WS-Addressing

WS-Addressing is a mechanism that allows web services to communicate addressing information. With traditional web services, addressing information is carried by the transport layer, and the web service message itself knows nothing about its destination. With this new standard, addressing information will be included in the XML message itself. A SOAP header can be added to the message for this purpose. The network-level transport is now responsible only for delivering that message to a dispatcher capable of reading the metadata.

WS-Security

WS-Security describes how to handle security issues within SOAP messages. It attaches signature and encryption information as well as security tokens to SOAP messages. In addition to the traditional HTTP/HTTPS authentications, it incorporates extra security features in the header of the SOAP message, working in the application layer. Also, it ensures end-to-end security.

There are several specifications associated with WS-Security, such as WS-SecureConversation, WS-Federation, WS-Authorization, WS-Policy, WS-Trust, and WS-Privacy.

WS-ReliableMessaging

WS-ReliableMessaging describes a protocol that allows SOAP messages to be delivered reliably between distributed applications.

The WS-ReliableMessaging model enforces reliability between the message source and destination. If a message cannot be delivered to the destination, the model must raise an exception or indicate to the source that the message can't be delivered.

There are several Delivery Assurance options for WS-ReliableMessaging, including AtLeastOnce, AtMostOnce, Exactly Once, and InOrder.

WS-Coordination and WS-Transaction

WS-Coordination describes an extensible framework for providing protocols that coordinate the actions of distributed applications. The framework enables existing transaction processing, workflow, and other systems for coordination, to hide their proprietary protocols and to operate in a heterogeneous environment. Additionally, this specification provides a definition for the structure of the context and the requirements for propagating context between cooperating services.

WS-Transaction describes coordination types that are used with the extensible coordination framework described in the WS-Coordination specification. It defines two coordination types: **Atomic Transaction (AT)** for individual operations and **Business Activity (BA)** for long-running transactions.

WS-AtomicTransaction provides the definition of the atomic transaction coordination type that is used with the extensible coordination framework described in the WS-Coordination specification. This protocol can be used to build applications that require consistent agreement on the outcome of short-lived distributed activities that have all-or-nothing semantics.

WS-BusinessActivity provides the definition of the business activity coordination type that is used with the extensible coordination framework described in the WS-Coordination specification. This protocol can be used to build applications that require consistent agreement on the outcome of long-running distributed activities.

WCF: Windows Communication Foundation

WCF is the latest technology from Microsoft for building services, including web services. In this section, we will explain what WCF is and what it is composed of. We will also explain various .NET runtimes, .NET Frameworks, Visual Studio versions, the relationships between them, and what is needed to develop or deploy WCF services. You will see some code snippets that will help you to further understand WCF concepts although they are not in a completed WCF project. Once we have grasped the basic concepts of WCF, we will develop a complete WCF service and create a client application to consume it, in the next chapter.

What is WCF?

WCF is the acronym for **Windows Communication Foundation**. It is Microsoft's latest technology that enables applications in a distributed environment to communicate with each other.

WCF is Microsoft's unified programming model for building service-oriented applications. It enables developers to build secure, reliable, transacted solutions that integrate across platforms and interoperate with existing investments. WCF is built on the Microsoft .NET Framework and simplifies the development of connected systems. It unifies a broad array of distributed systems capabilities in a composable, extensible architecture that supports multiple transports, messaging patterns, encodings, network topologies, and hosting models. It is the next generation version of several existing products—ASP.NET's web methods (ASMX) and Microsoft **Web Services Enhancements** (**WSE**) for Microsoft .NET, .NET Remoting, Enterprise Services, and System.Messaging.

The purpose of WCF is to provide a single programming model, that can be used to create services on the .NET platform, for organizations.

Why is WCF used for SOA?

As we have seen in the previous section, WCF is an umbrella technology that covers ASMX web services, .NET remoting, WSE, Enterprise Service, and System. Messaging. It is designed to offer a manageable approach to distributed computing, broad interoperability, and direct support for service orientation. WCF supports many styles of distributed application development by providing a layered architecture. At its base, the WCF channel architecture provides asynchronous, untyped message-passing primitives. Built on top of this base are protocol facilities for secure, reliable, transacted data exchange, and a broad choice of transport and encoding options.

Let us take an example to see why WCF is a good approach for SOA. Suppose a company is designing a service to get loan information. This service could be used by the internal call center application, an Internet web application, and a third-party Java J2EE application such as a banking system. For interactions with the call center client application, performance is important. For communication with the J2EE-based application, however, interoperability becomes the highest goal. The security requirements are also quite different between the local Windows-based application and the J2EE-based application running on another operating system. Even transactional requirements might vary with only the internal application being allowed to make transactional requests.

With these complex requirements, it is not easy to build the desired service with any single existing technology. For example, ASMX technology may serve well for the interoperability, but its performance may not be ideal. .NET remoting is a good choice from the performance perspective, but it is not good at interoperability. Enterprise Services could be used for managing object lifetimes and defining distributed transactions, but Enterprise Services supports only a limited set of communication options.

Now with WCF, it is much easier to implement this service. As WCF has unified a broad array of distributed systems capabilities, the **get loan** service can be built with WCF for all of its application-to-application communication. The following shows how WCF addresses each of these requirements:

- Because WCF can communicate using web service standards, interoperability with other platforms that also support SOAP, such as the leading J2EE-based application servers, is straightforward.

- You can also configure and extend WCF to communicate with web services using messages not based on SOAP, for example, simple XML formats such as RSS.

- Performance is of paramount concern for most businesses. WCF was developed with the goal of being one of the fastest-distributed application platforms developed by Microsoft.

- To allow for optimal performance when both parties in a communication are built on WCF, the wire encoding used in this case is an optimized binary version of an XML Information Set. Using this option makes sense for communication with the call center client application because it is also built on WCF and performance is an important concern.

- Managing object lifetimes, defining distributed transactions, and other aspects of Enterprise Services are now provided by WCF. They are available to any WCF-based application, which means that the get loan service can use them with any of the other applications that it communicates with.

- Because it supports a large set of the WS-* specifications, WCF helps to provide reliability, security, and transactions, when communicating with any platform that supports these specifications.

- The WCF option for queued messaging, built on **Message Queuing**, allows applications to use persistent queuing without using another set of application programming interfaces.

The result of this unification is greater functionality and significantly reduced complexity.

WCF architecture

The following diagram illustrates the principal layers of the Windows Communication Foundation (WCF) architecture. This diagram is taken from the Microsoft website (http://msdn.microsoft.com/en-us/library/ms733128.aspx):

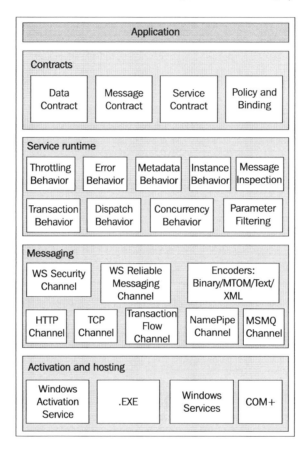

- The **Contracts** layer defines various aspects of the message system. For example, the **Data Contract** describes every parameter that makes up every message that a service can create or consume.

- The **Service runtime** layer contains the behaviors that occur only during the actual operation of the service, that is, the runtime behaviors of the service.

- The **Messaging** layer is composed of channels. A channel is a component that processes a message in some way, for example, in authenticating a message.

- In its final form, a service is a program. Like other programs, a service must be run in an executable format. This is known as the **hosting** application.

In the next section, we will explain these concepts in detail.

Basic WCF concepts—WCF ABCs

There are many terms and concepts surrounding WCF such as address, binding, contract, endpoint, behavior, hosting, and channels. Understanding these terms is very helpful when using WCF.

Address

The WCF **Address** is a specific location for a service. It is the specific place to which a message will be sent. All WCF services are deployed at a specific address, listening at that address for incoming requests.

A WCF Address is normally specified as a URL, with the first part specifying the transport mechanism, and the hierarchical parts specifying the unique location of the service. For example, `http://www.myweb.com/myWCFServices/SampleService` is an address for a WCF service. This WCF service uses HTTP as its transport protocol, and it is located on the server `www.myweb.com`, with a unique service path of `myWCFServices/SampleService`. The following diagram illustrates the three parts of a WCF service address.

Binding

Bindings are used to specify the transport, encoding, and protocol details required for clients and services to communicate with each other. Bindings are what WCF uses to generate the underlying wire representation of the endpoint. So, most of the details of the binding must be agreed upon by the parties that are communicating. The easiest way to achieve this is for clients of a service to use the same binding that the service uses.

A binding is made up of a collection of binding elements. Each element describes some aspect of how the service communicates with clients. A binding must include at least one transport binding element, at least one message encoding binding element (which can be provided by the transport binding element by default), and any number of other protocol binding elements. The process that builds a runtime out of this description allows each binding element to contribute code to that runtime.

WCF provides bindings that contain common selections of binding elements. These can either be used with their default settings or the default values can be modified according to user requirements. These system-provided bindings have properties that allow direct control over the binding elements and their settings.

The following are some examples of system-provided bindings:

BasicHttpBinding, WSHttpBinding, WSDualHttpBinding, WSFederationHttpBinding, NetTcpBinding, NetNamedPipeBinding, NetMsmqBinding, NetPeerTcpBinding, and **MsmqIntegrationBinding**.

Each one of these built-in bindings has predefined required elements for a common task, and is ready to be used in your project. For instance, the BasicHttpBinding uses HTTP as the transport for sending SOAP 1.1 messages, and it has attributes and elements such as `receiveTimeout`, `sendTimeout`, `maxMessageSize`, and `maxBufferSize`. You can use the default settings of its attributes and elements, or overwrite them as needed.

Contract

A WCF contract is a set of specifications that define the interfaces of a WCF service. A WCF service communicates with other applications according to its contracts. There are several types of WCF contracts such as Service Contract, Operation Contract, Data Contract, Message Contract, and Fault Contract.

Service contract

A **service contract** is the interface of the WCF service. Basically, it tells others what the service can do. It may include service-level settings such as the name of the service, the namespace of the service, and the corresponding callback contracts of the service. Inside the interface, it can define a bunch of methods, or service operations, for specific tasks. Normally, a WCF service has at least one service contract.

Operation contract

An **operation contract** is defined within a service contract. It defines the parameters and return type of an operation. An operation can take data of a primitive (native) data type such as an integer as a parameter, or it can take a message, which should be defined as a message contract type. Just as a service contract is an interface, an operation contract is a definition of an operation. It has to be implemented in order for the service to function as a WCF service. An operation contract also defines operation-level settings such as the transaction flow of the operation, the directions of the operation (one-way, two-way, or both ways), and the fault contract of the operation.

The following is an example of an operation contract:

```
[FaultContract(typeof(ProductFault))]
GetProductResponse GetProduct(GetProductRequest request);
```

In this example, the operation contract's name is `GetProduct` and it takes one input parameter, which is of the type `GetProductRequest` (a message contract) and has one return value, which is of the type `GetProductResponse` (another message contract). It may return a fault message, which is of the type `ProductFault` (a fault contract), to the client applications. We will cover **message contract** and **fault contract** in the following sections.

Message contract

If an operation contract needs to pass a message as a parameter or return a message, the type of these messages will be defined as message contracts. A message contract defines the elements of the message as well as any message-related settings such as the level of message security, and also whether an element should go to the header or to the body.

The following is a message contract example:

```
namespace MyWCF.EasyNorthwind.MessageContracts
{
  /// <summary>
  /// Service Contract Class - GetProductResponse
  /// </summary>
  [WCF::MessageContract(IsWrapped = false)]
  public partial class GetProductResponse
  {
    private MyWCF.EasyNorthwind.DataContracts.Product product;
    [WCF::MessageBodyMember(Name = "Product")]
    public MyWCF.EasyNorthwind.DataContracts.Product Product
    {
```

```
      get { return product; }
      set { product = value; }
    }
  }
}
```

In this example, the namespace of the message contract is `MyWCF.EasyNorthwind.MessageContracts`, and the message contract's name is `GetProductResponse`. This message contract has one member, which is of the type `Product`.

Data contract

Data contracts are data types of the WCF service. All data types used by the WCF service must be described in metadata to enable other applications to interoperate with the service. A data contract can be used by an operation contract as a parameter or return type, or it can be used by a message contract to define elements. If a WCF service uses only primitive (native) data types, it is not necessary to define any data contract.

The following is an example of data contract:

```
namespace MyWCF.EasyNorthwind.DataContracts
{
  /// <summary>
  /// Data Contract Class - Product
  /// </summary>
  [WcfSerialization::DataContract(Namespace = "http://MyCompany.com/
             ProductService/EasyWCF/2008/05", Name = "Product")]
  public partial class Product
  {
    private int productID;
    private string productName;
    [WcfSerialization::DataMember(Name = "ProductID",
                      IsRequired = false, Order = 0)]
    public int ProductID
    {
      get { return productID; }
      set { productID = value; }
    }
    [WcfSerialization::DataMember(Name =
                    "ProductName", IsRequired = false, Order = 1)]
    public string ProductName
    {
      get { return productName; }
      set { productName = value; }
```

```
        }
      }
    }
```

In this example, the namespace of the data contract is `MyWCF.EasyNorthwind.DataContracts`, the name of the data contract is `Product`, and this data contract has two members (`ProductID` and `ProductName`).

Fault contract

In any WCF service operation contract, if an error is returned to the caller, the caller should be warned of that error. These error types are defined as fault contracts. An operation can have zero or more fault contracts associated with it.

The following is a fault contract example:

```
namespace MyWCF.EasyNorthwind.FaultContracts
{
  /// <summary>
  /// Data Contract Class - ProductFault
  /// </summary>
  [WcfSerialization::DataContract(Namespace = "http://MyCompany.com/
           ProductService/EasyWCF/2008/05", Name = "ProductFault")]
  public partial class ProductFault
  {
    private string faultMessage;
    [WcfSerialization::DataMember(Name =
                       "FaultMessage", IsRequired = false, Order = 0)]
    public string FaultMessage
    {
      get { return faultMessage; }
      set { faultMessage = value; }
    }
  }
}
```

In this example, the namespace of the fault contract is `MyWCF.EasyNorthwind.FaultContracts`, the name of the fault contract is `ProductFault`, and the fault contract has only one member (`FaultMessage`).

Endpoint

Messages are sent between **endpoints**. Endpoints are places where messages are sent or received (or both), and they define all of the information required for the message exchange. A service exposes one or more application endpoints (as well as zero or more infrastructure endpoints). A service can expose this information as the metadata that clients process to generate the appropriate WCF clients and communication stacks. When needed, the client generates an endpoint that is compatible with one of the service's endpoints.

A WCF service endpoint has an address, a binding, and a service contract (WCF ABC).

The endpoint's address is a network address where the endpoint resides. It describes, in a standard-based way, where messages should be sent. Each endpoint normally has one unique address, but sometimes two or more endpoints can share the same address.

The endpoint's binding specifies how the endpoint communicates with the world, including things such as transport protocol (TCP, HTTP), encoding (text, binary), and security requirements (SSL, SOAP message security).

The endpoint's contract specifies what the endpoint communicates, and is essentially a collection of messages organized in the operations that have basic **Message Exchange Patterns** (**MEPs**) such as one-way, duplex, or request/reply.

The following diagram shows the components of a **WCF service endpoint**.

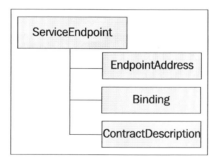

Behavior

A WCF **behavior** is a type or settings to extend the functionality of the original type. There are many types of behaviors in WCF such as service behavior, binding behavior, contract behavior, security behavior, and channel behavior. For example, a new service behavior can be defined to specify the transaction timeout of the service, the maximum concurrent instances of the service, and whether the service publishes metadata. Behaviors are configured in the WCF service configuration file. We will configure several specific behaviors in the chapters that follow.

Hosting

A WCF service is a component that can be called by other applications. It must be hosted in an environment in order to be discovered and used by others. The WCF **host** is an application that controls the lifetime of the service. With .NET 3.0 and beyond, there are several ways to host the service.

Self hosting

A WCF service can be **self-hosted**, which means that the service runs as a standalone application and controls its own lifetime. This is the most flexible and easiest way of hosting a WCF service, but its availability and features are limited.

Windows services hosting

A WCF service can also be hosted as a Windows service. A **Windows service** is a process managed by the operating system and it is automatically started when Windows is started (if it is configured to do so). However, it lacks some critical features (such as versioning) for WCF services.

IIS hosting

A better way to host a WCF service is to use **IIS**. This is the traditional way of hosting a web service. IIS, by its nature, has many useful features such as process recycling, idle shutdown, process health monitoring, message-based activation, high availability, easy manageability, versioning, and deployment scenarios. All of these features are required for enterprise-level WCF services.

Windows Activation Services hosting

The IIS hosting method, however, comes with several limitations in the service-orientation world, the dependency on HTTP being the main culprit. With IIS hosting, many of WCF's flexible options can't be utilized. This is the reason why Microsoft specifically developed a new method called **Windows Process Activation Services (WAS)** to host WCF services.

WAS is the new process activation mechanism for Windows Server 2008 that is also available on Windows Vista and Windows 7. It retains the familiar IIS 6.0 process model application pools and message-based process activation and hosting features (such as rapid failure protection, health monitoring, and recycling), but it removes the dependency on HTTP from the activation architecture. IIS 7.0 uses WAS to accomplish message-based activation over HTTP. Additional WCF components also plug into WAS to provide message-based activation over the other protocols that WCF supports, such as TCP, MSMQ, and named pipes. This allows applications that use the non-HTTP communication protocols to use the IIS features such as process recycling, rapid fail protection, and the common configuration systems that were only previously available to HTTP-based applications.

This hosting option requires WAS to be properly configured, but it does not require you to write any hosting code as part of the application. (Microsoft MSN, *Hosting Services*, retrieved on 3/6/2008 from `http://msdn2.microsoft.com/enus/ library/ms730158.aspx`.)

Channels

As we have seen in the previous sections, a WCF service has to be hosted in an application on the server side. On the client side, the client applications have to specify the bindings to connect to the WCF services. The binding elements are interfaces, and they have to be implemented in concrete classes. The concrete implementation of a binding element is called a **channel**. The binding represents the configuration and the channel is the implementation associated with that configuration. Therefore, there is a channel associated with each binding element. Channels stack on top of one another to create the concrete implementation of the binding—the channel stack.

The **WCF channel stack** is a layered communication stack with one or more channels that process messages. At the bottom of the stack is a transport channel that is responsible for adapting the channel stack to the underlying transport (for example, TCP, HTTP, SMTP, and other types of transport). Channels provide a low-level programming model for sending and receiving messages. This programming model relies on several interfaces and other types collectively known as the WCF channel model. The following diagram shows a simple channel stack:

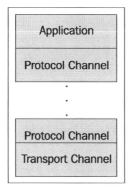

Metadata

The **metadata** of a service describes the characteristics of the service that an external entity needs to understand in order to communicate with the service. Metadata can be consumed by the ServiceModel Metadata Utility Tool (svcutil.exe) to generate a WCF client and the accompanying configuration that a client application can use to interact with the service.

The metadata exposed by the service includes XML schema documents, which define the data contract of the service, and WSDL documents, which describe the methods of the service.

Though WCF services always have metadata, it is possible to hide the metadata from outsiders. If you do so, you have to pass the metadata to the client side by other means. This practice is not common but it gives your services an extra layer of security. When enabled through the configuration settings through metadata behavior, metadata for the service can be retrieved by inspecting the service and its endpoints. The following configuration setting in a WCF service configuration file will enable metadata publishing for HTTP transport protocol:

```
<serviceMetadata httpGetEnabled="true" />
```

WCF production and development environments

WCF was first introduced in Microsoft's .NET **Common Language Runtime (CLR)** version 2.0. The corresponding framework is .NET 3.0. To develop and run WCF services, Microsoft .NET Framework 3.0 or above is required.

Visual Studio is the preferred IDE for developing WCF service applications. Both Visual Studio 2008 and Visual Studio 2010 support WCF service application development. Visual Studio 2008 also supports application development for .NET Framework 2.0, 3.0, and 3.5 (this is called multi-targeting), and Visual Studio 2010 supports application development for .NET Framework 2.0, 3.0, 3.5, and 4.0.

The following table shows all of the different versions of the .NET runtimes, .NET Frameworks, and Visual Studios, along with their relationships:

CLR	.NET Framework	Components						Visual Studio
CLR 4.0	.NET 4.0	Parallel Computing						2010
	.NET 3.5 SP1	ASP.NET MVC	Entity Framework	LINQ to Entities		Cloud Computing		2008,2010
CLR 2.0	.NET 3.5	LINQ LINQ to SQL	LINQ to XML	LINQ to Objects	ASP .NET AJAX	REST	RSS	2008,2010
	.NET 3.0	WCF		WPF	WF	CardSpace		
	.NET 2.0	Winforms		ASP.NET		ADO.NET		2005,2008,2010
CLR 1.0	.NET 1.1	Winforms		ASP.NET		ADO.NET		2003
	.NET 1.0							2002

Summary

In this chapter, we have learned and clarified many concepts related to SOA, web services, and WCF. The key points in this chapter are:

- SOA is an architectural design pattern
- Web services are the most popular and practical way of realizing SOA today
- There are many standards and specifications for web services, including (but not limited to) WSDL, SOAP, WS-I Profiles, and various WS-* standards
- WCF is a better technology for developing SOA services
- A WCF service has at least one service endpoint
- A WCF service endpoint has an address, a binding, and a service contract
- A WCF service can be self-hosted or can be hosted in a managed or an unmanaged application

- A WCF service can publish metadata and communicates with client applications through channels
- .NET Framework 3.0 or above is required to develop and run WCF service applications
- Visual Studio 2008 and 2010 are the preferred IDEs for WCF service application development

2
Implementing a Basic HelloWorld WCF Service

In the previous chapter, we learned several WCF concepts and looked at a few code snippets.

In this chapter, we will implement a basic WCF service from scratch. We will build a `HelloWorld` WCF service by carrying out the following steps:

- Create the solution and project
- Create the WCF service contract interface
- Implement the WCF service
- Host the WCF service in the ASP.NET Development Server
- Create a client application to consume this WCF service

Creating the HelloWorld solution and project

Before we can build the WCF service, we need to create a solution for our service project. We also need a directory in which we will save all the files. Throughout this book, we will save our project source codes in the `C:\SOAWithWCFandLINQ\Projects` directory. We will have a subfolder for each solution we create, and under this solution folder, we will have one subfolder for each project.

For this `HelloWorld` solution, the final directory structure is shown in the following image:

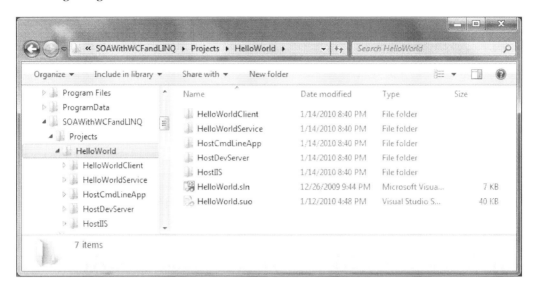

 You don't need to manually create these directories with Windows Explorer; Visual Studio will create them automatically when you create the solutions and projects.

Now follow these steps to create our first solution and the `HelloWorld` project:

1. Start Visual Studio 2010. If the **Open Project** dialog box pops up, click on **Cancel** to close it.

2. Go to menu **File | New | Project**. The **New Project** dialog window will appear.

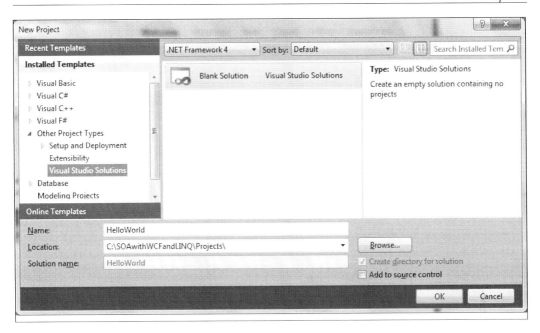

3. From the left-hand side of the window (**Installed Templates**), expand **Other Project Types** and then select **Visual Studio Solutions** as the template. From the middle section of the window, select **Blank Solution**.

4. At the bottom of the window, type **HelloWorld** as the **Name** and **C:\SOAWithWCFandLINQ\Projects** as the **Location**. Note that you should not enter HelloWorld within the location because Visual Studio will automatically create a folder for a new solution.

5. Click on the **OK** button to close this window and your screen should look like the following image with an empty solution.

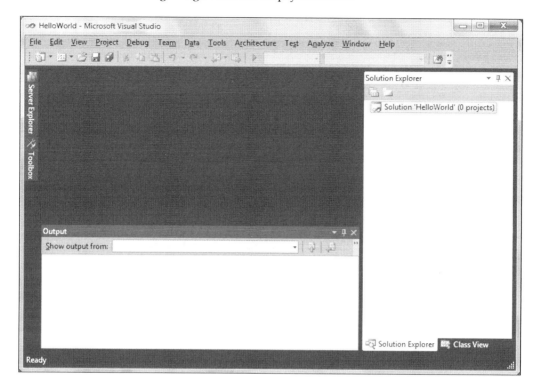

6. Depending on your settings, the layout may be different. But you should still have an empty solution in your **Solution Explorer**. If you don't see **Solution Explorer**, go to menu **View | Solution Explorer** or press *Ctrl + Alt + L* to bring it up.

7. In **Solution Explorer**, right-click on the solution and select **Add | New Project...** from the context menu. You can also go to menu **File | Add | New Project...** to get the same result. The following image shows the context menu for adding a new project.

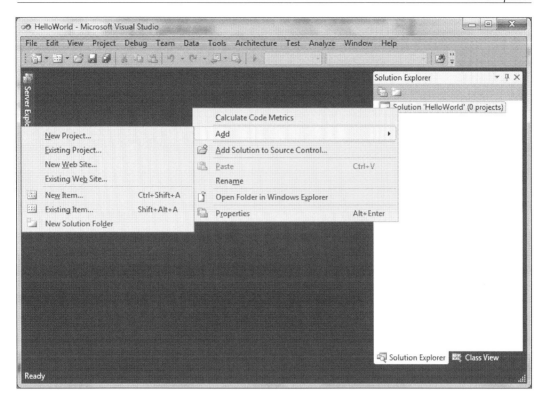

8. The **Add | New Project** window should now appear on your screen. In the left-hand side of this window (**Installed Templates**), select **Visual C#** as the template, and in the middle section of the window, select **Class Library**.

9. At the bottom of the window, type **HelloWorldService** as the **Name**. Write **C:\SOAWithWCFandLINQ\Projects\HelloWorld** as the **Location**. Again, don't add `HelloWorldService` to the location, as Visual Studio will create a subfolder for this new project (Visual Studio will use the solution folder as the default base folder for all the new projects added to the solution).

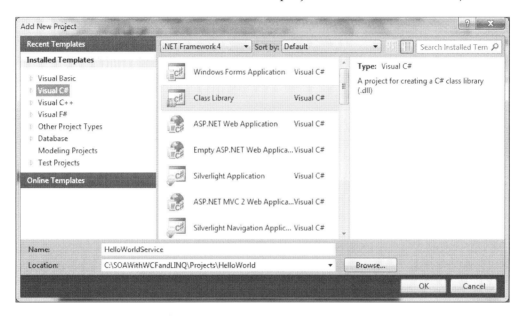

You may have noticed that there is already a template for **WCF Service Application** in Visual Studio 2010. For this very first example, we will not use this template. Instead, we will create everything by ourselves to understand the purpose of each template. This is an excellent way for you to understand and master this new technology. In the next chapter, we will use this template to create the project, so we don't need to manually type a lot of code.

10. Now you can click on the **OK** button to close this window.

Once you click on the **OK** button, Visual Studio will create several files for you. The first file is the project file. This is an XML file under the project directory, and it is called `HelloWorldService.csproj`.

Visual Studio also creates an empty class file called `Class1.cs`. Later, we will change this default name to a more meaningful one and change its namespace to our own one.

Three directories are created automatically under the project folder—one to hold the binary files, another to hold the object files, and a third one for the properties files of the project.

The window on your screen should now look like the following image:

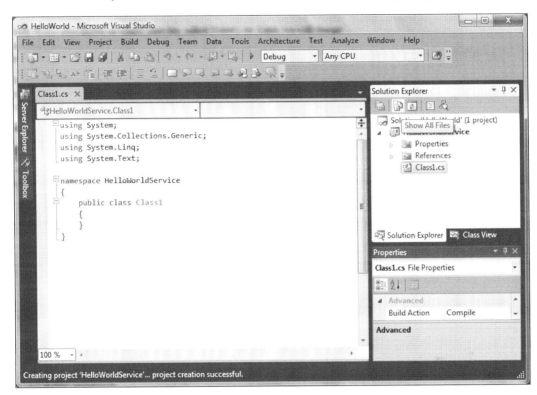

We have now created a new solution and project. Next, we will develop and build this service. But before we go any further, we need to do two things to this project:

1. Click on the **Show All Files** button on the **Solution Explorer** toolbar. It is the second button from the left, just above the word **Solution** inside the **Solution Explorer**. If you allow your mouse to hover above this button, you will see the hint, **Show All Files**, as shown in above screenshot. Clicking on this button will show all files and directories in your hard disk under the project folder, even those items that are not included in the project. Make sure that you don't have the solution item selected. Otherwise you can't see the **Show All Files** button.

2. Change the default namespace of the project. From **Solution Explorer**, right-click on the **HelloWorldService** project, select **Properties** from the context menu or go to menu item **Project | HelloWorldService Properties...**. You will see the project properties dialog window. On the **Application** tab, change the **Default namespace** to **MyWCFServices**.

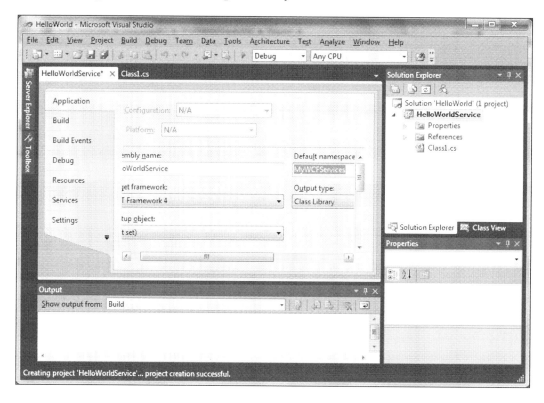

Lastly, in order to develop a WCF service, we need to add a reference to the System.ServiceModel namespace.

1. On the **Solution Explorer** window, right-click on the **HelloWorldService** project, and select **Add Reference...** from the context menu. You can also go to menu item **Project | Add Reference...** to do this. The **Add Reference** dialog window should appear on your screen.

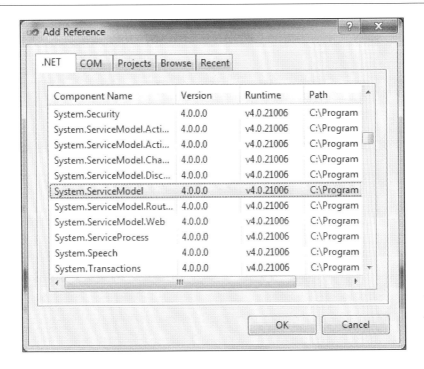

2. Select **System.ServiceModel** from the **.NET** tab and click on **OK**.

Now, on **Solution Explorer**, if you expand the references of the HelloWorldService project, you will see that System.ServiceModel has been added. Also, note that System.Xml.Linq is added by default. We will use this later when we query a database.

Creating the HelloWorldService service contract interface

In the previous section, we created the solution and the project for the HelloWorld WCF service. From this section on, we will start building the HelloWorld WCF service. First, we need to create the service contract interface.

1. In **Solution Explorer**, right-click on the **HelloWorldService** project, and
    select **Add | New Item...** from the context menu. The following **Add New
    Item - HelloWorldService** dialog window should appear on your screen.

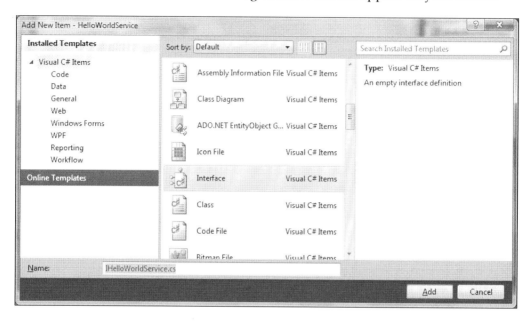

2. On the left-hand side of the window (**Installed Templates**), select
    Visual C# Items as the template, and from the middle section of the
    window, select **Interface**.

3. At the bottom of the window, change **Name** from **Interface1.cs** to
    IHelloWorldService.cs.

4. Click on the **Add** button.

Now an empty service interface file has been added to the project. Follow the steps
below to customize it.

1. Add a `using` statement:

    ```
    using System.ServiceModel;
    ```

2. Add a `ServiceContract` attribute to the interface. This will designate the
    interface as a WCF service contract interface.

    ```
    [ServiceContract]
    ```

3. Add a `GetMessage` method to the interface. This method will take a string as the input and return another string as the result. It also has an attribute, `OperationContract`.

```
[OperationContract]
String GetMessage(String name);
```

4. Change the interface to public.

The final content of the file, `IHelloWorldService.cs`, should look like the following:

```csharp
using System;
using System.Collections.Generic;
using System.Linq;
using System.Text;
using System.ServiceModel;
namespace MyWCFServices
{
    [ServiceContract]
    public interface IHelloWorldService
    {
        [OperationContract]
        String GetMessage(String name);
    }
}
```

Implementing the HelloWorldService service contract

Now that we have defined a service contract interface, we need to implement it. For this purpose we will reuse the empty class file that Visual Studio created for us earlier, and modify this to make it the implementation class of our service.

Before we modify this file, we need to rename it. In the **Solution Explorer** window, right-click on the file, **Class1.cs**, select **rename** from the context menu, and rename it `HelloWorldService.cs`.

 Visual Studio is smart enough to change all the related files which are references to use this new name. You can also select the file and change its name from the **Properties** window.

Next, follow the steps below to customize this class file.

1. Change its namespace from `HelloWorldService` to `MyWCFServices`. This is because this file was added before we changed the default namespace of the project.

2. Make it inherit from the interface, `IHelloWorldService`.

   ```
   public class HelloWorldService: IHelloWorldService
   ```

3. Add a `GetMessage` method to the class. This is an ordinary C# method that returns a string.

   ```
   public String GetMessage(String name)
   {
     return "Hello world from " + name + "!";
   }
   ```

The final content of the file, `HelloWorldService.cs`, should look like the following:

```
using System;
using System.Collections.Generic;
using System.Linq;
using System.Text;
namespace MyWCFServices
{
    public class HelloWorldService: IHelloWorldService
    {
        public String GetMessage(String name)
        {
            return "Hello world from " + name + "!";
        }
    }
}
```

Now, build the project. If there is no build error, it means that you have successfully created your first WCF service. If you see a compilation error, such as **'ServiceModel' does not exist in the namespace 'System'**, this is probably because you didn't add the `System.ServiceModel` namespace reference correctly. Revisit the previous section to add this reference, and you are all set.

Next, we will host this WCF service in an environment and create a client application to consume it.

Hosting the WCF service in ASP.NET Development Server

`HelloWorldService` is a class library. It has to be hosted in an environment so that client applications may access it. In this section, we will explain how to host it using ASP.NET Development Server. Later, in the next chapter, we will discuss more hosting options for a WCF service.

Creating the host application

There are several built-in host applications for WCF services within Visual Studio 2010. However, in this section, we will manually create the host application so that you can have a better understanding of what a hosting application is really like under the hood. In subsequent chapters, we will explain and use the built-in hosting application.

To host the library using ASP.NET Development Server, we need to add a new website to the solution. Follow these steps to create this website:

1. In **Solution Explorer**, right-click on the **Solution** file and select **Add | New Web Site...** from the context menu. The **Add New Web Site** dialog window should pop up.

2. Select **Visual C# | Empty Web Site** as the template, and leave the **Web location** as **File System**. Change the website name from **WebSite1** to **C:\SOAWithWCFandLINQ\Projects\HelloWorld\HostDevServer** and click on **OK**.

3. Now in **Solution Explorer**, you have one more item (HostDevServer) within the solution. It will look like the following:

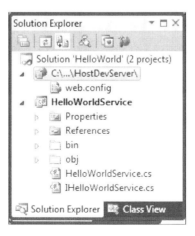

4. Next, we need to set the website as the startup project. In **Solution Explorer**, right-click on the website, **C:\...\HostDevServer**, select **Set as StartUp Project** from the context menu (or you can first select the website from **Solution Explorer**, and then select menu item **Website | Set as StartUp Project**). The website, **C:\...\HostDevServer**, should be highlighted in **Solution Explorer** indicating that it is now the startup project.

5. Because we will host HelloWorldService from this website, we need to add a HelloWorldService reference to the website. In **Solution Explorer**, right-click on the website, **C:\...\HostDevServer**, and select **Add Reference...** from the context menu. The following **Add Reference** dialog box should appear:

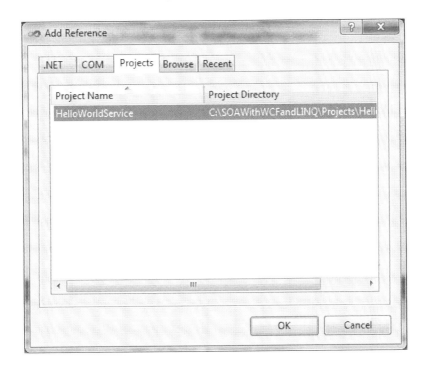

6. In the **Add Reference** dialog box, click on the **Projects** tab, select the **HelloWorldService** project, and then click on **OK**. You will see that a new directory (bin) has been created under the HostDevServer website and two files from the HelloWorldService project have been copied to this new directory. Later on, when this website is accessed, the web server (either ASP.NET Development Server or IIS) will look for executable code in this bin directory.

Testing the host application

Now we can run the website inside ASP.NET Development Server. If you start the website, `HostDevServer`, by pressing *Ctrl + F5* or by selecting **Debug | Start Without Debugging...** in the menu, you will see an empty website in your browser. Because we have set this website as the startup project, but haven't set any start page, it lists all of the files and directories inside the `HostDevServer` directory (Directory Browsing is always enabled for a website within ASP.NET Development Server).

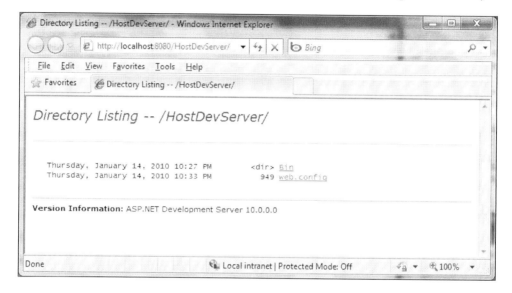

If you pressed *F5* (or selected **Debug | Start Debugging** from the menu), you may see a dialog saying, **Debugging Not Enabled** (as shown below). Choose the option, **Run without debugging** (equivalent to *Ctrl + F5*) and click on the **OK** button to continue. We will explore the debugging options of a WCF service later. Until then we will continue to use *Ctrl + F5* to start the website without debugging.

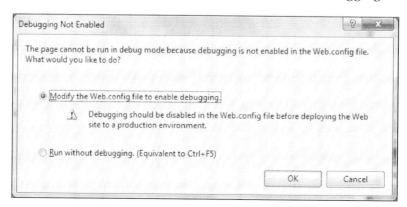

ASP.NET Development Server

At this point, you should have the `HostDevServer` site up and running. This site is actually running inside the built-in ASP.NET Development Server. It is a new feature that was introduced in Visual Studio 2005. This web server is intended to be used by developers only and has functionality similar to that of the **Internet Information Services (IIS)** server. It also has some limitations, for example, you can only run ASP. NET applications locally. You can't use it as a real IIS server to publish a website.

By default, ASP.NET Development Server uses a dynamic port for the web server each time it is started. You can change it to use a static port using the **Properties** page of the website. Just change the **Use dynamic ports** setting to `false`, and specify a static port, such as 8080, from the **Properties** window of the `HostDevServer` website. You can't set the port to 80 because IIS is already using this port. However, if you stop your local IIS, you can set your ASP.NET Development Server to use port 80.

 Even if you set its port to 80, it is still a local web server. It can't be accessed from outside your local PC.

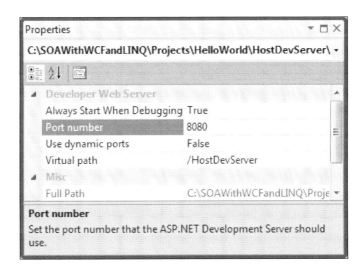

It is recommended that you use a static port so that client applications know in advance where to connect to the service. From now on, we will always use port 8080 in all of our examples.

ASP.NET Development Server is normally started from within Visual Studio when you need to debug or unit test a web project. If you really need to start it from outside Visual Studio, you can use a command line statement in the following format:

```
start /B WebDev.WebServer [/port:<port number>] /path:<physical path> [/
vpath:<virtual path>]
```

For our website, the statement should be like this:

```
start /B webdev.webserver.exe /port:8080 /path:"C:\SOAWithWCFandLINQ\
Projects\HelloWorld\HostDevServer" /vpath:/HostDevServer
```

`webdev.webserver.exe` is located under your .NET framework installation
directory (`C:\WINDOWS\Microsoft.NET\Framework\v2.0.50727` or `C:\Program
Files\Common Files\Microsoft Shared\DevServer`), and it may be called with
a different name such as `webdev.webserver20.exe` or `webdev.webserver40.exe`.

Adding an SVC file to the host application

Although we can start the website now, it is only an empty site. Currently it does not
host our `HelloWorldService`. This is because we haven't specified which service this
website should host or an entry point for this website. Just as an `asmx` file is the entry
point for a non-WCF web service, a `.svc` file is the entry point for a WCF service, if it
is hosted on a web server. We will now add such a file to our website.

From **Solution Explorer**, right-click on the website `C:\...\HostDevServer` and
select **Add New Item...** from the context menu. The **Add New Item** dialog window
should appear, as shown below. Select **Text File** as the template and change **Name**
from **TextFile.txt** to **HelloWorldService.svc** in this dialog window.

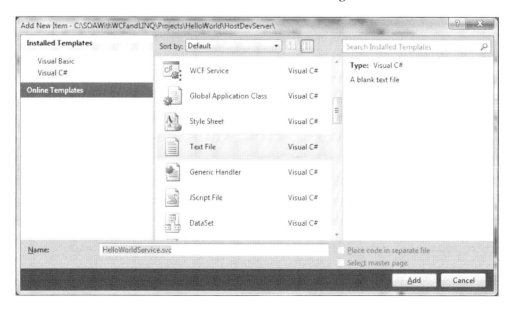

You may have noticed that there is a template, **WCF Service**, in the list. We won't use it now as it will create a new WCF service within this website for you (we will use this template later).

After you click on the **Add** button in the **Add New Item** dialog box, an empty svc file will be created and added to the website. Now enter the following line in this file:

```
<%@ServiceHost Service="MyWCFServices.HelloWorldService"%>
```

Modifying the web.config file

The final step is to modify the web.config file of the website. Open the web.config file of the website and change it to be like this:

```
<?xml version="1.0"?>

<configuration>

    <system.web>
        <compilation debug="false" targetFramework="4.0" />
    </system.web>
    <system.webServer>
      <modules runAllManagedModulesForAllRequests="true"/>
    </system.webServer>
  <system.serviceModel>
    <behaviors>
      <serviceBehaviors>
        <behavior name="MyServiceTypeBehaviors">
          <serviceMetadata httpGetEnabled="true" />
          <serviceDebug includeExceptionDetailInFaults="false" />
        </behavior>
      </serviceBehaviors>
    </behaviors>
    <services>
      <service name="MyWCFServices.HelloWorldService"
        behaviorConfiguration="MyServiceTypeBehaviors">
        <endpoint address="" binding="wsHttpBinding"
          contract="MyWCFServices.IHelloWorldService"/>
        <endpoint contract="IMetadataExchange"
          binding="mexHttpBinding" address="mex"/>
      </service>
    </services>
  </system.serviceModel>

</configuration>
```

The behavior, `httpGetEnabled`, is essential because we want other applications to be able to locate the metadata of this service. Without the metadata, client applications can't generate the proxy and thus won't be able to use the service.

We use `WSHttpBinding` for this hosting, which means that it is secure (messages are encrypted while being transmitted) and transaction-aware (we will discuss this in a later chapter). However, because this is a WS-* standard, some existing applications (for example, a QA tool) may not be able to consume this service. In this case, you can change the service to use `basicHttpBinding`, which uses plain unencrypted texts when transmitting messages, and is backward compatible with traditional ASP.NET web services (`asmx` web services).

The following is a brief explanation of the other elements in this configuration file:

- `Configuration` is the root node of the file.
- `system.serviceModel` is the top node for all WCF service-specific settings.
- Within the `services` node, you can specify WCF services that are hosted on this website. In our example, we have only one WCF service—`HelloWorldService`—hosted in this website.
- Each `service` element defines one WCF service, including its name, behavior, and endpoint.
- Two endpoints have been defined for `HelloWorldService`: one for the service itself (an application endpoint) and another for the metadata exchange (an infrastructure endpoint).
- Within the `serviceBehaviors` node, you can define specific behaviors for a service. In our example, we have specified one behavior, which enables the service metadata exchange for the service.

Starting the host application

Now, if you start the website by pressing *Ctrl + F5* (don't use *F5* or menu option **Debug | Start Debugging** until we discuss these later), you will now find the file, `HelloWorldService.svc`, listed on the web page. Clicking on this file will give the description of this service, that is, how to get the `wsdl` file of this service and how to create a client to consume this service. You should see a page similar to the following one. You can also set this file as the start page file so that every time you start this website, you will go to this page directly. You can do this by right-clicking on this file in **Solution Explorer** and selecting **Set as Start Page** from the context menu.

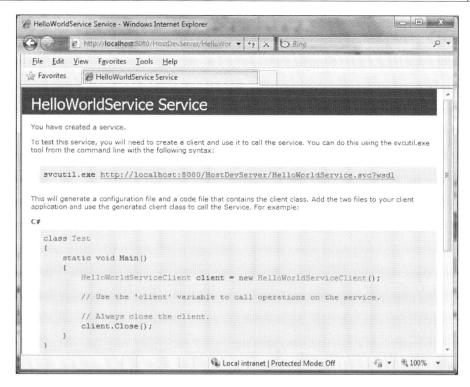

Now, click on the `wsdl` link on this page and you will get the `wsdl xml` file for this service. The `wsdl` file gives all of the contract information for this service. In the next section, we will use this `wsdl` to generate a proxy for our client application.

Close the browser. Then, from the Windows system tray (`systray`), find the little icon labeled **ASP.NET Development Server – Port 8080** (it is on the lower-right of your screen, just next to the clock), right-click on it, and select **Stop** to stop the service.

Creating a client to consume the WCF service

Now that we have successfully created and hosted a WCF service, we need a client to consume the service. We will create a C# client application to consume `HelloWorldService`.

In this section, we will create a Windows console application to call the WCF service.

Creating the client application project

First, we need to create a console application project and add it to the solution. Follow these steps to create the console application:

1. In **Solution Explorer**, right-click on the solution, HelloWorld, and select **Add | New Project...** from the context menu. The **Add New Project** dialog window should appear, as shown below.

2. Select **Visual C# | Console Application** as the template, change the project name from the defaulted value of **ConsoleApplication1** to **HelloWorldClient**, and leave the **Location** as C:\SOAWithWCFandLINQ\ **Projects\HelloWorld**. Click on the **OK** button. The new client project has now been created and added to the solution.

Generating the proxy and configuration files

In order to consume a WCF service, a client application must first obtain or generate a proxy class.

We also need a configuration file to specify things such as the binding of the service, the address of the service, and the contract.

To generate these two files, we can use the `svcutil.exe` tool from the command line. You can follow these steps to generate the two files:

1. Start the service by pressing *Ctrl + F5* or by selecting menu option **Debug | Start Without Debugging** (at this point your startup project should still be `HostDevServer`; if not, you need to set this to be the startup project). Now you should see the introduction window for the `HelloWorldService` service, as we saw in the previous section.

2. After the service has been started, run the command line `svcutil.exe` tool with the following syntax (`SvcUtil.exe` may be in a different directory in your machine, for example in Windows 7, it is under `v7.0A` directory):

    ```
    C:\SOAWithWCFandLINQ\Projects\HelloWorld\HelloWorldClient>

    "C:\Program Files\Microsoft SDKs\Windows\v6.0\Bin\SvcUtil.exe"
    http://localhost:8080/HostDevServer/HelloWorldService.svc?wsdl
    /out:HelloWorldServiceRef.cs /config:app.config
    ```

You will see an output similar to that shown in the following screenshot:

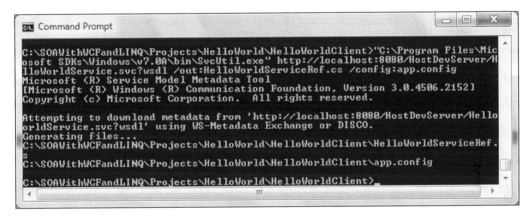

Here, two files have been generated: one for the proxy (`HelloWorldServiceRef.cs`) and the other for the configuration (`app.config`).

If you open the proxy file, you will see that the interface of the service (`IHelloWorldService`) is mimicked inside the proxy class and a client class (`HelloWorldServiceClient`) is created to implement this interface. Inside this client class, the implementation of the service operation (`GetMessage`) is only a wrapper that delegates the call to the actual service implementation of the operation.

Inside the configuration file, you will see the definitions of `HelloWorldService` such as the endpoint address, binding, timeout settings, and security behaviors of the service.

Customizing the client application

Before we can run the client application, we still have some more work to do. Follow these steps to finish the customization:

1. Add the two generated files to the project. In **Solution Explorer**, click **Show All Files** to show all the files under the HelloWorldClient folder and you will see these two files. However, they are not included in the project. Right-click on each of them and select **Include In Project** to include both of them in the client project. You can also use menu **Project | Add Existing Item ...** (or the context menu **Add | Existing Item ...**) to add them to the project.

2. Add a reference to the System.ServiceModel namespace. Just as we did for the project, HelloWorldService, we also need to add a reference to the WCF .NET System.ServiceModel assembly. From **Solution Explorer**, just right-click on the **HelloWorldClient** project, select **Add Reference...** and choose **.NET System.ServiceModel**. Then click on the **OK** button to add the reference to the project.

3. Modify program.cs to call the service. In program.cs, add the following line to initialize the service client object:

```
HelloWorldServiceClient client = new HelloWorldServiceClient();
```

Then we can call its method just as we would do for any other object:

```
Console.WriteLine(client.GetMessage("Mike Liu"));
```

Pass your name as the parameter to the GetMessage method so that it prints out a message for you.

Running the client application

We are now ready to run this client program.

First, make sure HelloWorldService has been started. If you previously stopped it, start it now (you need to set HostDevServer as the startup project, and press *Ctrl + F5* to start it in non-debugging mode).

Then, from **Solution Explorer**, right-click on the project, **HelloWorldClient**, select **Set as StartUp Project**, and then press *Ctrl + F5* to run it.

You will see output as shown in the following image:

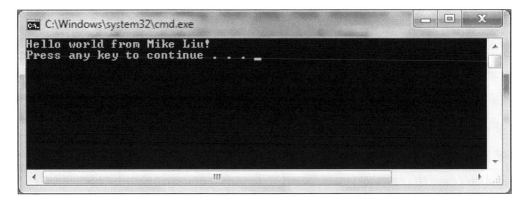

Setting the service application to AutoStart

Because we know we have to start the service before we run the client program, we can make some changes to the solution to automate this task, that is, to automatically start the service immediately before we run the client program.

To do this, in **Solution Explorer**, right-click on **Solution**, select **Properties** from the context menu, and you will see the **Solution 'HelloWorld' Property Pages** dialog box.

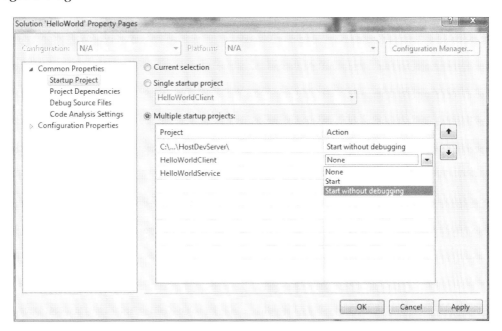

On this page, first select the option button, **Multiple startup projects**. Then change the action of C:\...\HostDevServer\ to **Start without debugging**. Change **HelloWorldClient** to the same action.

 HostDevServer must be above **HelloWorldClient**. If it is not, use the arrows to move it to the top.

To test it, first stop the service, and then press *Ctrl + F5*. You will notice that HostDevServer is started first, and then the client program runs without errors.

Note that this will only work inside Visual Studio IDE. If you start the client program from Windows Explorer (C:\SOAWithWCFandLINQ\Projects\HelloWorld\ HelloWorldClient\bin\Debug\HelloWorldClient.exe) without first starting the service, the service won't get started automatically and you will get an error message saying **'Could not connect to http://localhost:8080/HostDevServer/ HelloWorldService.svc'**.

Summary

In this chapter, we have implemented a basic WCF service, hosted it within ASP.NET Development Server, and created a command line program to reference and consume this basic WCF service. At this point, you should have a thorough understanding as to what a WCF is under the hood. You will benefit from this when you develop WCF services using Visual Studio WCF templates or automation guidance packages. The key points covered in this chapter are:

- A WCF service is a class library, which defines one or more WCF service interface contracts
- The System.ServiceModel assembly is referenced by all of the WCF service projects
- The implementations of a WCF service are just regular C# classes
- A WCF service must be hosted in a hosting application
- Visual Studio 2010 has a built-in hosting application for WCF services, which is called ASP.NET Development Server
- A client application uses a proxy to communicate with WCF services
- A configuration file can be used to specify settings for WCF services

3
Hosting and Debugging the HelloWorld WCF Service

In the previous chapter, we built a basic `HelloWorld` WCF service and hosted it with ASP.NET Development Server. In this chapter, we will explore more hosting options for WCF services including hosting WCF services in a managed application, in a Windows Service, in IIS, and in other advanced WCF hosting applications.

We will also explain how to debug WCF services including debugging from the client application, debugging only the WCF service, attaching to the WCF service process, and the Just-In-Time debugger.

In this chapter, we will discuss:

- Hosting the service in a console application
- Hosting the service in a Windows Service application
- Hosting the service in IIS
- Testing the service
- Debugging the service from the client application
- Debugging the service only
- Attaching to the service process
- Just-In-Time debugger

Hosting the HelloWorld WCF service

In the previous chapter, we hosted our `HelloWorldService` in ASP.NET Development Server. In addition to this we have several other options for hosting a WCF service. In this section, we will explore them one by one.

Hosting the service in a managed application

We can create a .NET managed application and host a WCF service inside the application. The hosting application can be a command-line application, a Windows Forms application, or a web application. This hosting method gives you full control over the lifetime of the WCF service. It is very easy to debug and deploy, and supports all bindings and transports. The drawback of this hosting method is that you have to start the hosting application manually and it has only limited support for high availability, easy manageability, robustness, recoverability, versioning, and deployment scenarios.

Hosting the service in a console application

Following are the steps to host `HelloWorldService` in a command-line application. Note that these steps are very similar to the steps in the previous section where we hosted a WCF service in ASP.NET Development Server. However, we must remember that we don't need a `.svc` file and that the configuration file is called `app.config` and not `web.config`. Refer to the previous section for diagrams. If you want to host a WCF service in a Windows Forms application or a web application, you can follow the same steps we have listed here simply by creating the project using an appropriate project template.

1. Add a console application project to the solution:

   In Solution Explorer, right-click on the `solution` file and select **Add | New Project...** from the context menu. The **Add New Project** dialog box should appear. Select **Visual C# | Console Application** as the template. Then change the name from **ConsoleApplication1** to **HostCmdLineApp** and click on the **OK** button. A new project is added to the solution.

2. Set the project, `HostCmdLineApp`, as the startup project:

   In Solution Explorer, right-click on the project, `HostCmdLineApp`, and select **Set as StartUp Project** from the context menu. You can also select the project in Solution Explorer and click on menu item **Project | Set as StartUp Project** to do this.

3. Add a reference to the `HelloWorldService` project:

   In Solution Explorer, right-click on the project, `HostCmdLineApp`, and select **Add Reference...** from the shortcut menu. The **Add Reference** dialog box will appear. Click on the **Projects** tab, select the `HelloWorldService` project, and then click on **OK**. Now, `HelloWorldService` is under the **References** folder of this project. You will also notice that two files from the `HelloWorldService` project have been copied to the `bin` directory under this project. If you can't see the bin directory, press *F4* or click on the **Show All Files** icon in Solution Explorer.

4. Add a reference to `System.ServiceModel`:

   This reference is required as we will manually create a service host application and start and stop it in the steps that follow. In the Solution Explorer window, right-click on the `HostCmdLineApp` project and select **Add Reference…** from the context menu. You can also select menu item **Project | Add Reference…** to do this. Select `System.ServiceModel` from the .NET tab and click on **OK**.

5. Add a reference to `System.Configuration`:

   This reference is required as we will set the base address of the service in a configuration file and read this base address from the configuration file at runtime.

6. Add a configuration file to define the endpoints of the service:

   The configuration file will be very similar to the configuration file we created for the `HostDevServer` project. In Windows Explorer, copy the `web.config` file from the project folder of `HostDevServer` to the project folder of `HostCmdLineApp` and change its name to `app.config`, then from Solution Explorer, include this file in the project, `HostCmdLineApp`, (if you can't see `app.config` file under this project, click on the **Show All Files** button in Solution Explorer or click on the **Refresh** button to refresh the screen).

7. Open this configuration file and add a new section, `appSetting`, for the **HTTPBaseAddress** and set its value to **http://localhost:8080/HostCmdLineApp/HelloWorldService/**. This means we will host `HelloWorldService` using HTTP, at port 8080, and under the `HostCmdLineApp` virtual directory.

8. The following is the full content of the `app.config` file:

```
<?xml version="1.0"?>
<configuration>
  <appSettings>
    <add key="HTTPBaseAddress" value="http://localhost:8080/
HostCmdLineApp/HelloWorldService/"/>
  </appSettings>
  <system.web>
      <compilation debug="false" targetFramework="4.0" />
    </system.web>
    <system.webServer>
      <modules runAllManagedModulesForAllRequests="true"/>
    </system.webServer>
  <system.serviceModel>
```

```xml
      <behaviors>
        <serviceBehaviors>
          <behavior name="MyServiceTypeBehaviors">
            <serviceMetadata httpGetEnabled="true" />
            <serviceDebug includeExceptionDetailInFaults="false" />
          </behavior>
        </serviceBehaviors>
      </behaviors>
      <services>
        <service name="MyWCFServices.HelloWorldService" behaviorConf
  iguration="MyServiceTypeBehaviors">
          <endpoint address="" binding="wsHttpBinding"
  contract="MyWCFServices.IHelloWorldService"/>
          <endpoint contract="IMetadataExchange"
  binding="mexHttpBinding" address="mex"/>
        </service>
      </services>
    </system.serviceModel>

</configuration>
```

9. Now we need to modify the `Program.cs` file to write some code to start and stop the WCF service inside `Program.cs`.

10. First, add two `using` statements as follows:

```csharp
using System.ServiceModel;
using System.Configuration;
```

11. Then add the following lines of code within the static `Main` method:

```csharp
Type serviceType=typeof(MyWCFServices.HelloWorldService);
string httpBaseAddress =
      ConfigurationManager.AppSettings["HTTPBaseAddress"];
Uri[] baseAddress = new Uri[] {new Uri(httpBaseAddress)};
ServiceHost host = new ServiceHost(serviceType, baseAddress);
host.Open();
Console.WriteLine("HelloWorldService is now running. ");
Console.WriteLine("Press any key to stop it ...");
Console.ReadKey();
host.Close();
```

12. As you can see we get the type of `HelloWorldService`, construct a base address for the WCF service, create a service host passing the type and base address, and call the `Open` method of the host to start the service. To stop the service, we just call the `Close` method of the service host.

13. Below is the full content of the `Program.cs` file.

```
using System;
using System.Collections.Generic;
using System.Linq;
using System.Text;
using System.ServiceModel;
using System.Configuration;

namespace HostCmdLineApp
{
    class Program
    {
        static void Main(string[] args)
        {
         Type serviceType=typeof(MyWCFServices.HelloWorldService);

         string httpBaseAddress =
             ConfigurationManager.AppSettings["HTTPBaseAddress"];
         Uri[] baseAddress = new Uri[] {new Uri(httpBaseAddress)};

         ServiceHost host = new ServiceHost(serviceType,
                         baseAddress);
         host.Open();
         Console.WriteLine("HelloWorldService is now running. ");
         Console.WriteLine("Press any key to stop it ...");
         Console.ReadKey();
         host.Close();
        }
    }
}
```

14. After the project has been successfully built, you can press *Ctrl + F5* to start the service. You will see a command-line window indicating that `HelloWorldService` is available and is waiting for requests.

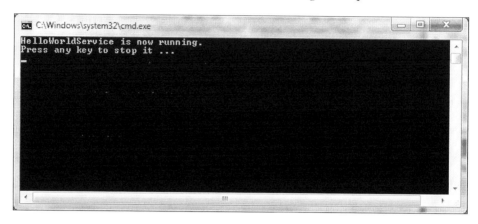

Under Windows Vista and Windows 7, you may get an error message of **System. ServiceModel.AddressAccessDeniedException** saying, **Your process does not have access rights to this namespace**. This is because Visual Studio has to register the namespace for our `HelloWorld` service and, by default, Windows runs applications in a limited-rights user account even when you are logged on to the computer as an administrator. You can run Visual Studio as an administrator to solve this issue. Just right-click on the Visual Studio 2010 executable file, `devenv.exe`, and select **Run as administrator**, or change the property **Privilege Level** to **Run this program as an administrator**, so you can always run Visual Studio as an administrator.

Alternatively, if you don't want to run as administrator, you can manually register the namespace using tools like `HttpSysConfig`. You can Google **Your process does not have access rights to this namespace** to see various options for this issue. However, it seems to me no matter which option is taken, the process to manually register a namespace for .NET is a little bit complex, so I would simply run Visual Studio as administrator.

If you get the **Access is denied** error message under Windows XP, make sure you are logged on as an administrator.

Consuming the service hosted in a console application

To consume the service hosted in the previous console application you can follow the same steps described in the section, *Creating a client to consume the WCF service (Chapter 2)*, except that you pass `http://localhost:8080/HostCmdLineApp/HelloWorldService/?wsdl` and not `http://localhost:8080/HostDevServer/HelloWorldService.svc?wsdl` to the `SvcUtil.exe` when you generate the proxy class and the configuration file.

In fact you can reuse the same client project, but inside the `app.config` file, change the following line:

```
<endpoint address=
   "http://localhost:8080/HostDevServer/HelloWorldService.svc"
```

to this line:

```
<endpoint address=
   "http://localhost:8080/HostCmdLineApp/HelloWorldService/"
```

Now, when you run this client program, it will use the WCF service hosted in our newly created command-line application and not the previously-created `HostDevServer` application. You will get the same result as before when ASP.NET Development Server was used to host the WCF service.

Hosting the service in a Windows service

If you don't want to manually start the WCF service, you can host it in a Windows service. In addition to the automatic start, Windows service hosting gives you some other features such as recovery ability when failures occur, security identity under which the service is run, and some degree of manageability. Just like the self-hosting method, this hosting method also supports all bindings and transports. However, it has some limitations. For example, you have to deploy it with an installer and it doesn't fully support high availability, easy manageability, versioning, or deployment scenarios.

The steps to create such a hosting application are very similar to what we did to host a WCF service in a command-line application, except that you have to create an installer to install the Windows service in the Service Control Manager (or you can use the .NET Framework `Installutil.exe` utility).

Hosting the service in Internet Information Server

It is a better option to host a WCF service within Internet Information Services Server (IIS) because IIS provides a robust, efficient, and secure host for the WCF services. IIS also has better thread and process execution boundaries handling (in addition to many other features) compared to a regular managed application. Actually, web service development on IIS has long been the domain of ASP.NET. When ASP.NET 1.0 was released, a web service framework was part of it. Microsoft leveraged the ASP.NET HTTP pipeline to make web services a reality on the Windows platform.

The main drawback of hosting the service within IIS prior to version 7.0 is the tight coupling between ASP.NET and web services, which limits the transport protocol to HTTP/HTTPs. But with IIS 7.0, in addition to HTTP, you can now host a WCF service with TCP, Named pipe, or MSMQ. You are no longer limited to HTTP.

Another thing you need to pay particular attention to when hosting WCF in IIS is that the process and/or application domain may be recycled if certain conditions are met. By default the WCF service session state is saved in memory so that each recycle will lose all such information. This will be a big problem if you run a website in a load-balanced or web-farm (web-garden) environment. In this case, you might want to turn on the ASP.NET compatibility mode (add the attribute, `AspNetCompatibilityRequirements`, to your WCF service) so that the session state can be persisted in a SQL Server database or in the ASP.NET State Server.

Now we will explain how to host `HelloWorldService` within IIS. We will still host it with HTTP protocol in this example but you should choose an appropriate protocol for your service according to your needs.

Preparing the folders and files

First, we need to prepare the folders and files for the host application. Follow these steps to create the folders and copy the required files:

1. Create the folders:

   In Windows Explorer, create a new folder called `HostIIS` under `c:\SOAwithWCFandLINQ\Projects\HelloWorld` and a new subfolder called `bin` under this `HostIIS` folder. You should now have the following new folders:

   ```
   C:\SOAwithWCFandLINQ\Projects\HelloWorld\HostIIS
   C:\SOAwithWCFandLINQ\Projects\HelloWorld\HostIIS\bin
   ```

2. Copy the files:

Now copy the files `HelloWorldService.dll` and `HelloWorldService.pdb` from the `HelloWorldService` project folder `C:\SOAwithWCFandLINQ\Projects\HelloWorld\HelloWorldService\bin\Debug` to the new folder we created, `C:\SOAwithWCFandLINQ\Projects\HelloWorld\HostIIS\bin`.

3. Copy the files, `HelloWorldService.svc`, and `Web.config`, from the `HostDevServer` project folder, `C:\SOAwithWCFandLINQ\Projects\HelloWorld\HostDevServer`, to the new folder, `C:\SOAwithWCFandLINQ\Projects\HelloWorld\HostIIS`.

The files under the two new directories should now be like the following:

Parent Folder: `C:\SOAwithWCFandLINQ\Projects\HelloWorld\`

Folder	HostIIS	HostIIS\bin
Files	`HelloWorldService.svc`	`HelloWorldService.dll`
	`Web.config`	`HelloWorldService.pdb`

4. Create Visual Studio Solution Folder:

To make it easier to view and manage from Visual Studio Solution Explorer, you can add a new solution folder, `HostIIS`, to the solution and add the files, `web.config`, and `HelloWorldService.svc`, to this folder. Add another new solution folder, `bin`, under `HostIIS`, and add the files, `HelloWorldService.dll`, and `HelloWorldService.pdb` under this `bin` folder. Your Solution Explorer should be like following image.

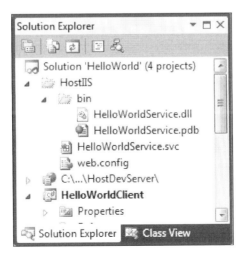

Turn on Internet Information Services

By default, Internet Information Services is not turned on in Windows 7. You can follow these steps to turn it on:

1. Go to **Control Panel | Programs | Turn Windows features on or off**.

2. From the **Windows Features** dialog box, check **Internet Information Services**.

3. Click on **OK**.

Internet Information Services is now turned on but since Visual Studio 2010 was installed before IIS was turned on, at this point IIS does not have any ASP.NET features enabled. This means if you create an ASP.NET website within IIS now, when you try to access it, you will get an error.

There are two ways to enable WCF support from IIS. The first one is to run `aspnet_regiis.exe` to enable `aspnet_isapi` as a web sevice extension, then run `ServiceModelReg.exe` to register the required script maps in IIS, and manually create Application Extension Mapping and Managed Handlers for SVC files inside IIS.

The second and the easier way is to reinstall .NET Framework 4.0. After you have turned on IIS features, as we just did previously in this section, uninstall and then reinstall .NET Framework 4.0. ASP.NET 4.0 will be supported by IIS, once .NET 4.0 is reinstalled. I used this method as it is much easier.

Creating the IIS application

Next, we need to create an IIS application named `HelloWorldService`. Follow these steps to create this application in IIS 7.0.

1. Open the IIS manager through menu option **Control Panel | Administrative Tools** (or just type **start inetmgr** in a command prompt).

2. Expand the nodes of the tree in the left-hand pane until the node named **Default Web Site** becomes visible.

3. Right-click on that node and choose **New | Add Application...** from the context menu.

4. In the **Add Application** window, enter **HelloWorldService** as the **Alias**.

5. Choose or enter **C:\SOAWithWCFandLINQ\Projects\HelloWorld\ HostIIS** as the **Physical path**.

6. Leave **DefaultAppPool** as the **Application pool**. You can click on the
    Select... button to verify this application pool is a .NET 4.0 application
    pool. If it is not, you need to enable IIS to support .NET 4.0, as described
    in previous section.

7. Click on the **OK** button.

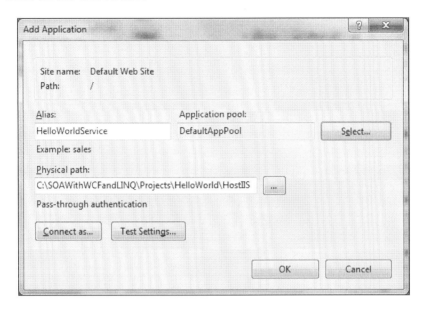

 If you are under Windows XP (IIS 6.0), you can create a new **Virtual Directory** for HostIIS. Just make sure you choose .Net 4.0.21006 as the ASP.NET version for your new virtual directory.

Starting the WCF service in IIS

Once you have the files copied to the HostIIS folder and have the virtual directory
created, the WCF service is ready to be called by the clients. When a WCF service is
hosted within IIS, we don't need to explicitly start the service. As with other normal
web applications, IIS will control the lifetime of the service. As long as the IIS website
is started, client programs can access it.

Testing the WCF service hosted in IIS

To test the WCF service, open an Internet browser and enter the following URL in the address bar of the browser. You will get an almost identical screen to the one you got previously:

```
http://localhost/HelloWorldService/HelloWorldService.svc
```

You don't need to add a port after the host because it is now hosted in IIS with the default HTTP port 80. This also means that you can access it using your real computer (host) name and even outside of your network if you are connected to the Internet. Two example URLs are as follows:

```
http://[your_pc_name]/HelloWorldService/HelloWorldService.svc
```

```
http://[your_pc_name].[your_company_domain].com/
    HelloWorldService/HelloWorldService.svc
```

We can reuse the client program we created earlier to consume this WCF service hosted within IIS. Just change the endpoint address line from this:

```
<endpoint address=
    "http://localhost:8080/HostCmdLineAPP/HelloWorldService/"
```

to this:

```
<endpoint address=
    "http://localhost/HelloWorldService/HelloWorldService.svc"
```

Now, when you run this client program, it will use the WCF service hosted within IIS and not the previously-created `HostCmdLineApp` application. You will get the same result as before, when it was hosted in our own host application.

Other WCF service hosting options

From previous sections, we know that a WCF service can be hosted in ASP.NET Development Server, in a website, in a Windows Service application, in a command-line application, or in IIS. Besides these options, there are some other ways to host a WCF service.

In Visual Studio 2010, there is a built-in, general-purpose WCF Service Host (`WcfSvcHost.exe`), which makes the WCF host and development test much easier. This host will be used by default if you create a WCF service using a WCF Service Library template. We will cover this new feature in the next chapter.

Another option is to create a WCF service using a WCF Service Application template, in which case the WCF service project itself is a website and is ready to run within its own project folder. We will also cover this new feature in the next chapter.

If you want to learn more about hosting a WCF service, you can go to the Microsoft MSDN site and search for WCF hosting. Here is one of those pages on the MSDN site for WCF hosting, though at the time of writing, this page was still not updated to .NET 4.0: `http://msdn.microsoft.com/en-us/library/ms733766.aspx`.

Debugging the HelloWorld WCF service

Now that we have a fully working WCF service, let us have a look at the debugging options of this service.

Debugging from the client application

The first and most common scenario is to debug from the client program. This means that you start a client program in debug mode and then step into your WCF service.

Starting the debugging process

Follow these steps to start the debugging process from the client application:

1. Change the client program's web configuration file to call `HelloWorldService` hosted within ASP.NET Development Server. Open the file, **app.config**, inside the **HelloWorldClient** project and set the address of the endpoint to this:

   `http://localhost:8080/HostDevServer/HelloWorldService.svc`

2. In Solution Explorer, right-click on the **HelloWorldClient** project and select **Set as Startup Project** from the context menu.

3. Open the `Program.cs` file inside the `HelloWorldClient` project and set a breakpoint at the following line:

```
HelloWorldServiceClient client = new HelloWorldServiceClient();
```

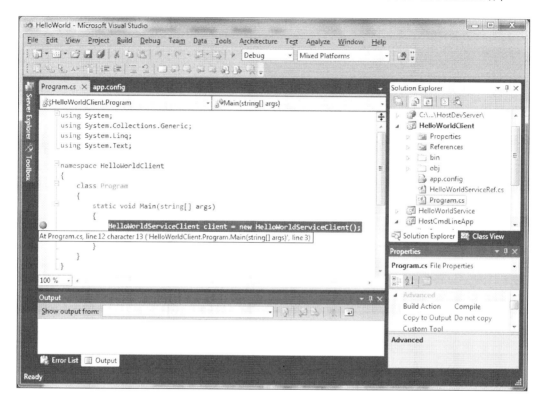

4. You can set a breakpoint by clicking on the gray strip to the left of the code (the little ball in the diagram above), pressing *F9* while the cursor is on the line, or selecting the menu item **Debug | Toggle Breakpoint**. You should ensure that the breakpoint line is highlighted, and if you hover your mouse over the red breakpoint dot, an information line will pop up.

5. Now press *F5* or select menu option **Debug | Start Debugging** to start the debugging process.

As soon as you press *F5*, you will notice a little window pop up in the lower-right corner of the screen, as shown in the following image:

This is because the client program, `HelloWorldClient`, is referencing `HelloWorldService`, which is hosted in ASP.NET Development Server (`HostDevServer`), and you have the project property **Always Start When Debugging** set to `True`.

Note that this setting is for the WCF hosting project, not for the client or WCF service project. This is very useful when debugging because you don't need to start it explicitly. However, sometimes it might be annoying, especially when you have several hosting projects within the same solution. In this case, you can turn it off by setting it to `False`. However, you then have to start the service prior to debugging the client application. Otherwise you will get an exception. We will discuss more about this later in this chapter.

Debugging on the client application

The cursor should have stopped on the breakpoint line, as you can see in the following **HelloWorld (Debugging)** screenshot. The active line is highlighted and you can examine the variables just as you do for any other C# applications.

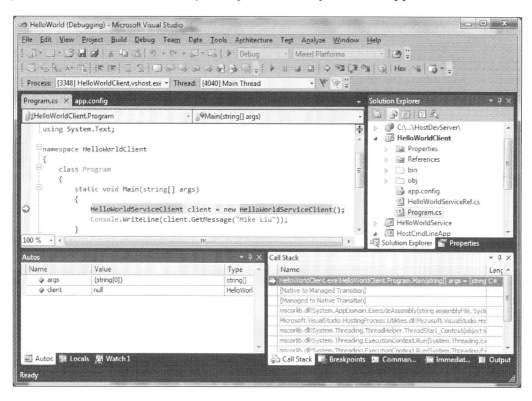

At this point, the channel between the client and the hosting server (`HostDevServer`) hasn't been created. Press *F10* or select menu option **Debug | Step Over** to skip over this line. If you don't have the menu option **Debug | Step Over**, you may have to reset your development environment settings through menu option **Tools | Import and Export Settings...** (select **General Development Settings** from the **Import and Export Settings Wizard** and check all of the available options).

Now, the following line of source code should be active and highlighted. At this point, we have a valid client object which contains all of the information related to the WCF service such as the channel, the endpoint, the members, and the security credentials. The following **Autos** image shows the details of the **Endpoint** local variable.

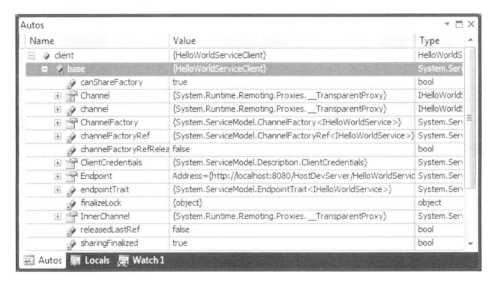

Attaching to ASP.NET Development Server

Press *F11* to step into the WCF service. But instead of stepping in, we will step over the whole line. The cursor will stop at the end of program source code. This is because now the Visual Studio 2010 debugger hasn't been attached to ASP.NET Development Server (Visual Studio 2008 or prior will attach to ASP.NET Development Server automatically).

Let's follow these steps to attach to ASP.NET Development Server:

1. Stop the current debugging process.
2. Start a new debugging process by pressing *F5*.
3. ASP.NET Development Server at port 8080 should be started automatically.

4. While the cursor is stopped on the first line within the **Main** method of HelloWorldClient's Program.cs file, select menu **Debug | Attach to Process…**.

5. In the **Attach to Process** window, select **WebDev.WebServer40.EXE** and click on the **Attach** button.

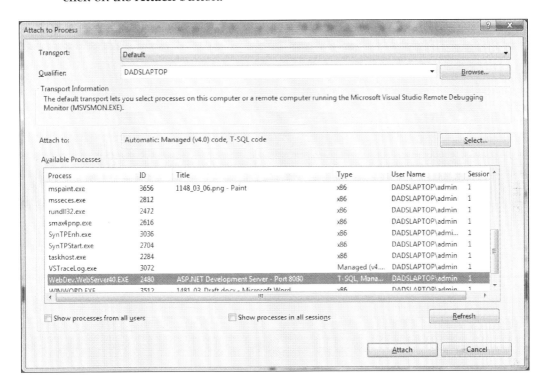

Now ASP.NET Development Server is attached to Visual Studio 2010. We will continue our debugging in the next section.

Before you can step into the service code from the client code, we need to set a breakpoint on the service code. Open the file, HelloWorldService.cs, inside the HelloWorldService project and set a breakpoint on the GetMessage method. Now we are ready to continue the debugging process.

Stepping into the WCF service

Now press *F10* to skip the first line, and then press *F11* to step into the service code. The cursor now resides on the opening bracket of the GetMessage method of HelloWorldService. You can now examine the variables inside HelloWorldService just as you would for any other program. Keep pressing *F10* and you should eventually come back to the client program.

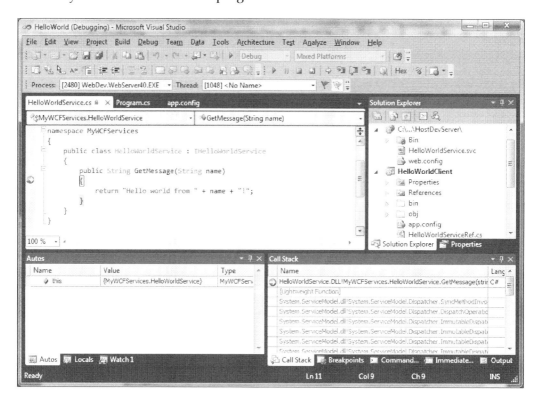

However, if you stay inside HelloWorldService for too long, when you come back to HelloWorldClient you will get an exception window saying that it has timed out. This is because, by default, HelloWorldClient will call HelloWorldService and wait for a response for a maximum time of one minute. You can change this to a longer value in the configuration file, app.config, depending on your own needs.

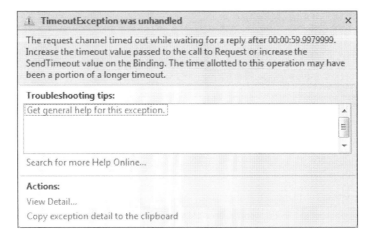

You may also have noticed that you don't see the output window of
`HelloWorldClient`. This is because, in debug mode, once a console application finishes,
the console window is closed. You can add one line to the end of `Program.cs` to wait
for a keystroke so that you can look at the output before it closes. You can do this by
adding the following line of code:

```
Console.ReadKey();
```

Debugging only the WCF service

In the previous section, we started debugging from the client program and then
stepped into the service program. Sometimes we may not want to run the client
application in debug mode. For example, if the client application is a third-party
product we won't have the source code or the client application may be a BPM
product that runs on a different machine. In this case, if we need to, we can run
the service in debugging mode and debug only the service.

Starting the WCF Service in debugging mode

To start `HelloWorldService` in debug mode, first set `HostDevServer` as the startup project (if the **Set as Startup Project** is disabled, it means Visual Studio is still attached to ASP.NET Development Server; just detach it or stop the debugging process). Then open `HelloWorldService.cs` from the `HelloWorldService` project and set a breakpoint at the line inside the `GetMessage` method, as shown in the following:

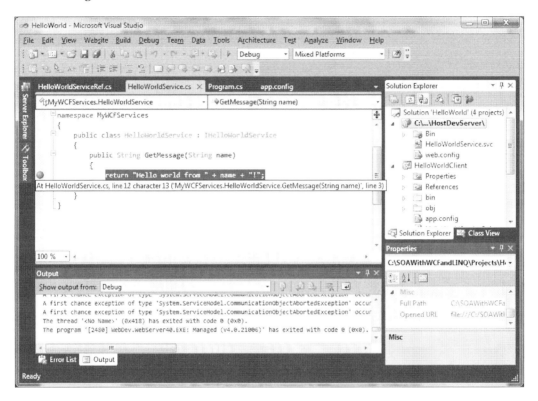

Now press *F5* to start the service in debugging mode. A dialog window will pop up warning **Debugging Not Enabled**. Select **Modify the Web.config file to enable debugging** and click on the **OK** button to continue. This will modify the debug value from false to true in the `web.config` file.

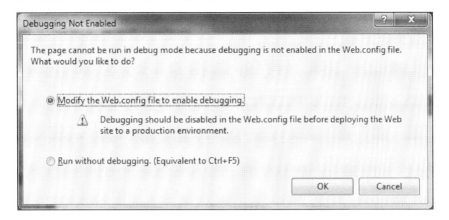

Now the WCF service will be running in debugging mode, waiting for requests. A browser will open displaying all of the files under the `HostDevServer` folder. If you go back to Visual Studio IDE, you may find that a new solution folder, **Script Documents**, has been added to the solution. This folder is the actual content of the web page being displayed in the browser. Because its content is dynamically generated, this folder will only be included in the solution when `HostDevServer` is being debugged. Whenever you stop the debugging session, this folder will go away automatically.

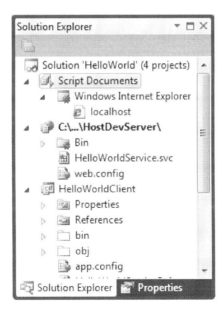

After you press *F5* to start a WCF service in debugging mode, you might see an error message warning you that script debugging is disabled. For this dialog box, you can do as instructed: clear the checkbox from Internet Explorer under **Tools | Internet Options | Advanced | Browsing | Disable Script Debugging**, or just click the **Yes** button to continue debugging without enabling script debugging for Internet Explorer. We will not debug any script from Internet Explorer (our application is not a web application).

Once you have clicked on the **Yes** button (or you may never see this message box because you have the correct settings), the service will be started in debugging mode.

Starting the client application in non-debugging mode

Now that we have the WCF service running in debugging mode, we need to start the client application in non-debugging mode so that the debugging process can start from the WCF service side and not from the client side.

For this example, you can't start the `HelloWorldClient` program from the same Visual Studio IDE instance. The reason for this is that, once you have started `HelloWorldService` in debugging mode, the solution is in running status. You can't start another project from the same solution inside the same Visual Studio instance while the `HelloWorldService` project is running. Actually, the **Set as Startup Project** menu option is disabled, making it impossible to set any other project as the startup project. Also, a bunch of other menu options are disabled, meaning that you can't change them while in debugging mode.

There are two ways to start the `HelloWorldClient` program in non-debugging mode. The first one is to start it in another instance of Visual Studio. While leaving the previous instance of Visual Studio running for `HelloWorldService` in debugging mode, start a new Visual Studio instance and open the `HelloWorld` solution. Set `HelloWorldClient` as the startup project and then press *Ctrl + F5* to start it in non-debugging mode. As soon as you press *Ctrl + F5*, you will see that the previous Visual Studio is active and the cursor has stopped on the breakpoint line. You can now examine all of the variables inside `HelloWorldService` as you would do for any other program. Press *F10* once and you will be taken to the end of the `GetMessage` method; press *F10* again and you will be taken outside of the `HelloWorldService` project. Because `HelloWorldClient` is now not running in debugging mode, you will see the output window immediately.

Another way to start `HelloWorldClient` is to start it from Windows Explorer. Go to the `C:\SOAwithWCFandLINQ\Projects\HelloWorld\HelloWorldClient\bin\Debug` directory and double-click on the **HelloWorldClient.exe** file. You will then get the same result as you did when you started it from inside a new Visual Studio instance.

Starting the WCF service and client applications in debugging mode

What if you start `HelloWorldClient` in debugging mode while `HelloWorldService` is also running in debugging mode? Suppose you have started `HelloWorldService` in debugging mode and have set a breakpoint inside the `GetMessage` method. Now, if you start another Visual Studio instance, open the solution, set `HelloWorldClient` as the startup project, and press *F5* to start `HelloWorldClient` also in debugging mode, you will be able to step inside the service from the client. This is actually the same as when you start the client application in debugging mode first and then attach another Visual Studio instance to ASP.NET Development Server, as we did in the previous section.

Attaching to a WCF service process

Another common scenario for debugging is when attaching to a running WCF service. Suppose that `HelloWorldService` is hosted and running outside Visual Studio, either in IIS or a managed application such as `HostCmdLineApp`. The client application is also running outside of Visual Studio. At a certain point, you may want to start debugging the running WCF service. In this case, we can attach to the WCF service process and start debugging from the middle of a process.

Running the WCF service and client applications in non-debugging mode

To test this scenario, change the `app.config` file to use the IIS hosting `HelloWorldService`. This means that we use the following address for the endpoint in the `app.config` file for the `HelloWorldClient` project:

```
http://localhost/HelloWorldService/HelloWorldService.svc
```

Build the solution and set a breakpoint inside the `GetMessage` method of the `HelloWorldService` project. Then run `HelloWorldClient` in non-debugging mode by pressing *Ctrl + F5*. You will see there is no way to hit the breakpoint we had previously set inside `HelloWorldService`. This is because the service is now hosted by IIS, and it is not under debugging by any debugger.

Debugging the WCF service hosted in IIS

To debug the service hosted by IIS, we can attach it to the IIS process. But before we can debug it, we have to enable debugging for the web application. Just open the `web.config` file under the `HostIIS` folder and change the debug value to `True`.

Now start Visual Studio and select menu option **Debug | Attach to Process...**. The **Attach to Process** window should now appear. If you can't see the **Debug** menu from Visual Studio, just open any project or create an empty new project.

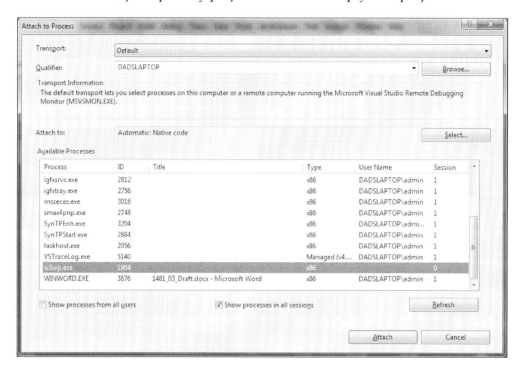

Select the process, `w3wp.exe` (`aspnet_wp.exe` if you are using Windows XP), from the list of available processes and click on the **Attach** button. Note that you need to check **Show processes in all sessions** in order to see **w3wp.exe** in the available processes list. If it still is not there, run `HelloWorldClient` once and hit the **Refresh** button. **w3wp.exe** will appear in the list.

Now you will find the IIS worker process attached to the debugger. Open the `HelloWorldService.cs` file and set a breakpoint if you haven't done so already. Now run the `HelloWorldClient` program in non-debugging mode (use *Ctrl + F5*) from another Visual Studio instance or from Windows Explorer, and you will see that the breakpoint is now hit.

If you are not able to set a breakpoint inside the `HelloWorldService.cs` file (or the breakpoint is disabled after you attach to the `w3wp.exe` process), make sure you have enabled debugging for the HostIIS application (as we did at the beginning of this section), and the folder, `HostIIS\bin`, contains the latest binary files from the `HelloWorldService` folder.

If you didn't start Visual Studio as an administrator, you will get a dialog window asking you to restart Visual Studio in a different credential. Select **Restart under different credentials** and you will be able to continue.

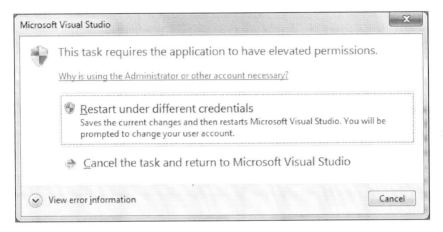

When you have finished debugging `HelloWorldService` using this method, you can select menu option **Debug | Detach All** or **Debug | Stop Debugging** to exit debugging mode.

You may also have noticed that when you attach to `w3wp.exe` (or `aspnet_wp.exe`), ASP.NET Development Server is also started, even though we will not use it at all at this time. This is again because the **Always Start When Debugging** property of `HostDevServer` is set to `True` and, as we did earlier, you can turn it off if you feel it is annoying.

Just-In-Time debugger

As you can see, we have to start HelloWorldService before we can run the client program. The actual step to start HelloWorldService varies depending on the hosting method that you are using. For example, if you are hosting HelloWorldService in a managed application as we did for HostCmdLineApp, you have to start the application manually. If you are hosting HelloWorldService in ASP.NET Development Server, you can manually start it from Visual Studio or set **Always Start When Debugging** to True. If you are hosting HelloWorldService in IIS, you don't need to do anything (except to make sure that the IIS web application has been started). Lastly, if you host HelloWorldService in a Windows service, you should set its startup type to automatic or you will have to manually start it.

What happens when you run the client program, the service is not started, and it is not set to automatically start when being referenced? For example, if you have hosted HelloWorldService in IIS and for some reason IIS has been stopped, then what will happen to the client program?

To test this, we need to first stop IIS. Just open Internet Information Services Manager, select **Default Web Site**, and click on **Stop** from the Content View window.

Once IIS has been stopped, HelloWorldService is no longer accessible. If you start the HelloWorldClient program now, you will get an error. Depending on the mode in which you are running HelloWorldClient, you will get two different errors.

First, if you start HelloWorldClient in debugging mode (by pressing *F5*) from Visual Studio, it will stop on the line to call the GetMessage method, showing you an exception. This is because the client program can't connect to the server (the server has actively refused it). As we haven't added any code to handle exceptions, .NET runtime throws an unhandled exception. We will discuss exceptions (WCF Fault Contracts) in one of the following chapters. For now, you have to select menu option **Debug | Stop Debugging** to stop the client program.

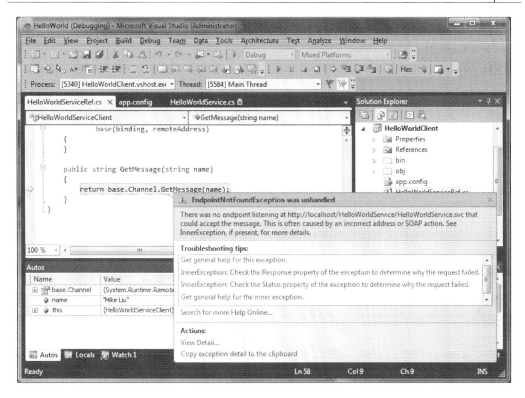

If you start `HelloWorldClient` in non-debugging mode (by pressing *Ctrl + F5* or by double-clicking the `HelloWorldClient.exe` file from Windows Explorer `C:\ SOAwithWCFandLINQ\Projects\HelloWorld\HelloWorldClient\bin\Debug\`), you will see the **Visual Studio Just-In-Time Debugger** screen.

This is a nice feature of the .NET framework because even though we have started the program in non-debugging mode, we can still step into the code if something unexpected happens (however, the executable must be built with debugging information, that is, not a release one). In this case, if you click on the **Yes** button, the Visual Studio window with the HelloWorld solution will be active, and you will see the same image as when you started the debugging process from Visual Studio. So you know it is due to HelloWorldService. This will be very helpful when you are testing a big application, as you don't need to restart your program in debugging mode and repeat what you've done to reach the same problem spot. Instead, you can start the debugging process right on the spot and then fix it quickly if it is only a configuration problem.

In the previous example, if the client program is started from Windows Explorer and the HelloWorld solution is not open in any Visual Studio IDE, it may even offer to start a new instance of Visual Studio for debugging. If you have multiple versions of Visual Studio .NET IDEs installed, it will list all of them for you to pick one.

Summary

In this chapter, we have hosted the HelloWorld WCF service in several different ways and explained different scenarios when debugging a WCF service. The key points in this chapter include:

- A WCF service can be hosted in ASP.NET Development Server, in a managed application, in a Windows service, or in IIS
- IIS is a better WCF hosting option for interacting with legacy applications
- You can start the debugging process for a WCF service from the client application, from the service application, or by attaching to the service process
- The Just-In-Debugger is helpful for determining the reason for the exception when the application is running outside of Visual Studio

4
Implementing a WCF Service in the Real World

In the previous chapter, we created a basic WCF service. The WCF service we created, `HelloWorldService`, has only one method, called `GetMessage`. Because this was just an example, we implemented this WCF service in one layer only. Both the service interface and implementation are within one deployable component.

Note that the service we will create in the next two chapters is only a simplified version of a real-world WCF service. In a real-world situation, there is no doubt that the WCF service would contain more custom scenarios, more business logics, and more data constraints. For learning purposes, here we will just create a WCF service in three layers, with minimum business logic and some basic functionality. After you have acquired the basic skills to create the framework for a layered WCF service, you can customize this solution to your own needs.

Another thing I want to mention here is the design pattern that the next two chapters will talk about is exactly what the Microsoft Service Software Factory is doing. In a previous version of this book, we dedicated two chapters to discussing Service Factory, but since Service Factory for Visual Studio 2010 is still not available (at the time of writing this version), we have to skip it. However, you will have a solid understanding of the layered WCF service structures after you have finished following these two chapters, and at that time you should go to the Microsoft Service Factory website (`http://www.codeplex.com/servicefactory`) to check if Service Factory is available. If it is available, you should consider using Service Factory to create your WCF service structures.

Returning to our example in this book, in this chapter and the next one, we will implement a WCF service, which will be called `RealNorthwindService`, to reflect a real-world solution. In this chapter, we will separate the service interface layer from the business logic layer, and in the next chapter, we will add a data access layer to the service.

In this chapter, we will create and test the WCF service by following these steps:

- Create the project using a WCF Service Library template
- Create the project using a WCF Service Application template
- Create the Service Operation Contracts
- Create the Data Contracts
- Add a Product Entity project
- Add a business logic layer project
- Call the business logic layer from the service interface layer
- Test the service

Why layer a service?

An important aspect of SOA design is that service boundaries should be explicit, which means hiding all the details of the implementation behind the service boundary. This includes revealing or dictating what particular technology was used.

Furthermore, inside the implementation of a service, the code responsible for the data manipulation should be separated from the code responsible for the business logic. So in the real world, it is always good practice to implement a WCF service in three or more layers. The three layers are the service interface layer, the business logic layer, and the data access layer.

- Service interface **layer**: This layer will include the service contracts and operation contracts that are used to define the service interfaces that will be exposed at the service boundary. Data contracts are also defined to pass in and out of the service. If any exception is expected to be thrown outside of the service, then Fault contracts will also be defined at this layer.

- Business logic layer: This layer will apply the actual business logic to the service operations. It will check the preconditions of each operation, perform business activities, and return any necessary results to the caller of the service.

- Data access layer: This layer will take care of all of the tasks needed to access the underlying databases. It will use a specific data adapter to query and update the databases. This layer will handle connections to databases, transaction processing, and concurrency controlling. Neither the service interface layer nor the business logic layer needs to worry about these things.

Layering provides separation of concerns and better factoring of code, which gives you better maintainability and the ability to split out layers into separate physical tiers for scalability. The data access code should be separated into its own layer that focuses on performing translation services between the databases and the application domain. Services should be placed in a separate service layer that focuses on performing translation services between the service-oriented external world and the application domain.

The service interface layer will be compiled into a separate class assembly and hosted in a service host environment. The outside world will only know about and have access to this layer. Whenever a request is received by the service interface layer, the request will be dispatched to the business logic layer, and the business logic layer will get the actual work done. If any database support is needed by the business logic layer, it will always go through the data access layer.

Creating a new solution and project using WCF templates

We need to create a new solution for this example and add a new WCF project to this solution. This time we will use the built-in Visual Studio WCF templates for the new project.

Using the C# WCF service library template

There are a few built-in WCF service templates within Visual Studio 2010; two of them are Visual Studio WCF Service Library and Visual Studio WCF Service Application. In this section, we will use the service library template, and in the next section, we will use the service application template. Later, we will explain the differences between these two templates and choose the template that we are going to use for this chapter.

Follow these steps to create the `RealNorthwind` solution and the project using the service library template:

1. Start Visual Studio 2010, select menu option **File | New | Project...**, and you will see the **New Project** dialog box. Do not open the `HelloWorld` solution from the previous chapter as, from this point onwards, we will create a completely new solution and save it in a different location.

2. In the **New Project** window, specify **Visual C# | WCF | WCF Service Library** as the project template, **RealNorthwindService** as the (project) name, and **RealNorthwind** as the solution name. Make sure that the checkbox **Create directory for solution** is selected.

3. Click on the **OK** button, and the solution is created with a WCF project inside it. The project already has an `IService1.cs` file to define a service interface and `Service1.cs` to implement the service. It also has an `app.config` file, which we will cover shortly.

Using the C# WCF service application template

Instead of using the Visual Studio WCF Service Library template to create our new WCF project, we can use the Visual Studio Service Application template to create the new WCF project.

Because we have created the solution, we will add a new project using the Visual Studio WCF Service Application template.

1. Right-click on the solution item in Solution Explorer, select menu option **Add | New Project...** from the context menu, and you will see the **Add New Project** dialog box.

2. In the **Add New Project** window, specify **Visual C# | WCF Service Application** as the project template, **RealNorthwindService2** as the (project) name, and leave the default location of **C:\ SOAWithWCFandLINQ\Projects\RealNorthwind** unchanged.

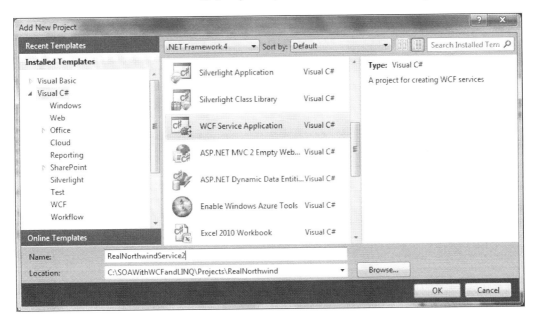

3. Click on the **OK** button and the new project will be added to the solution. The project already has an `IService1.cs` file to define a service interface, and `Service1.svc.cs` to implement the service. It also has a `Service1.svc` file and a `web.config` file, which are used to host the new WCF service. It has also had the necessary references added to the project such as `System. ServiceModel`.

You can follow these steps to test this service:

- Change this new project, **RealNorthwindService2,** to be the startup project (right-click on it from Solution Explorer and select **Set as Startup Project**). Then run it (*Ctrl + F5* or *F5*). You will see that it can now run. You will see that ASP.NET Development Server has been started, and a browser is open listing all of the files under the `RealNorthwindService2` project folder. Clicking on the `Service1.svc` file will open the metadata page of the WCF service in this project. This is the same as we discussed in the previous chapter for the `HostDevServer` project.

- If you have pressed *F5* in the previous step to run this project, you might see a warning message box asking you if you want to enable debugging for the WCF service. As we said earlier, you can choose enable debugging or just run in the non-debugging mode.

You may also have noticed that the WCF Service Host is started together with ASP. NET Development Server. This is actually another way of hosting a WCF service in Visual Studio 2010. It has been started at this point because, within the same solution, there is a WCF service project (`RealNorthwindService`) created using the WCF Service Library template. We will cover more of this host in a later section.

So far we have used two different Visual Studio WCF templates to create two projects. The first project, using the C# WCF Service Library template, is a more sophisticated one because this project is actually an application containing a WCF service, a hosting application (`WcfSvcHost`), and a WCF Test Client. This means that we don't need to write any other code to host it, and as soon as we have implemented a service, we can use the built-in WCF Test Client to invoke it. This makes it very convenient for WCF development.

The second project, using the C# WCF Service Application template, is actually a website. This is the hosting application of the WCF service so you don't have to create a separate hosting application for the WCF service. This is like a combination of the `HelloWorldService` and the `HostDevServer` applications we created in the previous chapter. As we have already covered them and you now have a solid understanding of these styles, we will not discuss them further. But keep in mind that you have this option, although in most cases it is better to keep the WCF service as clean as possible, without any hosting functionalities attached to it.

To focus on the WCF service using the WCF Service Library template, we now need to remove the project `RealNorthwindService2` from the solution.

In Solution Explorer, right-click on the **RealNorthwindService2** project item and select **Remove** from the context menu. Then you will see a warning message box. Click on the **OK** button in this message box and the RealNorthwindService2 project will be removed from the solution. Note that all the files of this project are still on your hard drive. You will need to delete them using Windows Explorer.

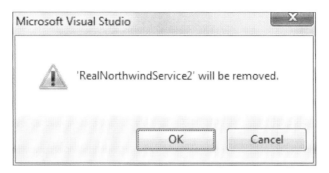

Creating the service interface layer

In the previous section, we created a WCF project using the WCF Service Library template. In this section, we will create the service interface layer contracts.

Because two sample files have already been created for us, we will try to reuse them as much as possible. Then we will start customizing these two files to create the service contracts.

Creating the service interfaces

To create the service interfaces, we need to open the IService1.cs file and do the following:

1. Change its namespace from RealNorthwindService to:

   MyWCFServices.RealNorthwindService

2. Change the interface name from **IService1** to **IProductService**. Don't be worried if you see the warning message before the interface definition line, as we will change the web.config file in one of the following steps.

3. Change the first operation contract definition from this line:

   ```
   string GetData(int value);
   ```

   to this line:

   ```
   Product GetProduct(int id);
   ```

4. Change the second operation contract definition from this line:

```
CompositeType GetDataUsingDataContract(CompositeType composite);
```

to this line:

```
bool UpdateProduct(Product product);
```

5. Change the filename from **IService1.cs** to **IProductService.cs**.

With these changes, we have defined two service contracts. The first one can be used to get the product details for a specific product ID, while the second one can be used to update a specific product. The product type, which we used to define these service contracts, is still not defined. We will define it right after this section.

The content of the service interface for `RealNorthwindService.ProductService` should look like this now:

```
using System;
using System.Collections.Generic;
using System.Linq;
using System.Runtime.Serialization;
using System.ServiceModel;
using System.Text;

namespace MyWCFServices.RealNorthwindService
{
    [ServiceContract]
    public interface IProductService
    {
        [OperationContract]
        Product GetProduct(int id);

        [OperationContract]
        bool UpdateProduct(Product product);

        // TODO: Add your service operations here
    }
}
```

This is not the whole content of the `IProductService.cs` file. The bottom part of this file should still have the class, `CompositeType`, which we will change to our `Product` type in the next section.

Creating the data contracts

Another important aspect of SOA design is that you shouldn't assume that the consuming application supports a complex object model. One part of the service boundary definition is the data contract definition for the complex types that will be passed as operation parameters or return values.

For maximum interoperability and alignment with SOA principles, you should not pass any .NET-specific types such as `DataSet` or `Exceptions` across the service boundary. You should stick to fairly simple data structure objects such as classes with properties and backing member fields. You can pass objects that have nested complex types such as 'Customer with an Order collection'. However, you shouldn't make any assumption about the consumer being able to support object-oriented constructs such as inheritance or base-classes for interoperable web services.

In our example, we will create a complex data type to represent a product object. This data contract will have five properties: `ProductID`, `ProductName`, `QuantityPerUnit`, `UnitPrice`, and `Discontinued`. These will be used to communicate with client applications. For example, a supplier may call the web service to update the price of a particular product or to mark a product for discontinuation.

It is preferable to put data contracts in separate files within a separate assembly but, to simplify our example, we will put `DataContract` in the same file as the service contract. We will modify the file, `IProductService.cs`, as follows:

1. Change the `DataContract` name from `CompositeType` to `Product`.

2. Change the fields from the following lines:

```
bool boolValue = true;
string stringValue = "Hello ";
```

   to these seven lines:

```
int productID;
string productName;
string quantityPerUnit;
decimal unitPrice;
bool discontinued;
```

3. Delete the old `boolValue` and `StringValue` `DataMember` properties. Then, for each of the above fields, add a `DataMember` property. For example, for `productID`, we will have this `DataMember` property:

```
[DataMember]
public int ProductID
{
    get { return productID; }
```

```
        set { productID = value; }
    }
```

A better way is to take advantage of the automatic property feature of C#, and add the following `ProductID DataMember` without defining the `productID` field:

```
    [DataMember]
    public int ProductID { get; set; }
```

To save some space, we will use the latter format. So, we need to delete all of those field definitions and add an automatic property for each field, with the first letter capitalized.

The data contract part of the finished service contract file, `IProductService.cs`, should now look like this:

```
[DataContract]
public class Product
{
        [DataMember]
        public int ProductID { get; set; }
        [DataMember]
        public string ProductName { get; set; }
        [DataMember]
        public string QuantityPerUnit { get; set; }
        [DataMember]
        public decimal UnitPrice { get; set; }
        [DataMember]
        public bool Discontinued { get; set; }
}
```

Implementing the service contracts

To implement the two service interfaces that we defined in the previous section, open the `Service1.cs` file and do the following:

1. Change its namespace from `RealNorthwindService` to `MyWCFServices.RealNorthwindService`.

2. Change the class name from `Service1` to `ProductService`. Make it inherit from the `IProductService` interface, instead of `IService1`. The class definition line should be like this:

    ```
    public class ProductService : IProductService
    ```

3. Delete the `GetData` and `GetDataUsingDataContract` methods.

4. Add the following method, to get a product:

```
public Product GetProduct(int id)
{
    // TODO: call business logic layer to retrieve product
    Product product = new Product();
    product.ProductID = id;
    product.ProductName = "fake product name from service layer";
    product.UnitPrice = (decimal)10.0;
    return product;
}
```

 In this method, we created a fake product and returned it to the client. Later, we will remove the hard-coded product from this method and call the business logic to get the real product.

5. Add the following method to update a product:

```
public bool UpdateProduct(Product product)
{
    // TODO: call business logic layer to update product
    if (product.UnitPrice <= 0)
        return false;
    else
        return true;
}
```

Also, in this method, we don't update anything. Instead, we always return `true` if a valid price is passed in. In one of the following sections, we will implement the business logic to update the product and apply some business logic to the update.

6. Change the filename from `Service1.cs` to `ProductService.cs`. The content of the `ProductService.cs` file should be like this:

```
using System;
using System.Collections.Generic;
using System.Linq;
using System.Runtime.Serialization;
using System.ServiceModel;
using System.Text;

namespace MyWCFServices.RealNorthwindService
{
```

```
public class ProductService : IProductService
{
    public Product GetProduct(int id)
    {
        // TODO: call business logic layer to retrieve product
        Product product = new Product();
        product.ProductID = id;
        product.ProductName = "fake product name
        from service layer";
        product.UnitPrice = (decimal)10;
        return product;
    }
    public bool UpdateProduct(Product product)
    {
        // TODO: call business logic layer to update product
        if (product.UnitPrice <= 0)
            return false;
        else
            return true;
    }
}
```

Modifying the app.config file

Because we have changed the service name, we have to make the appropriate changes to the configuration file. Note that when you rename the service, if you have used the refactor feature of Visual Studio, some of the following tasks may have been done by Visual Studio.

Follow these steps to change the configuration file:

1. Open the `app.config` file from Solution Explorer.

2. Change all instances of the `RealNorthwindService` string except the one in `baseAddress` to `MyWCFServices.RealNorthwindService`. This is for the namespace change.

3. Change the `RealNorthwindService` string in `baseAddress` to `MyWCFServices/RealNorthwindService`.

4. Change all instances of the `Service1` string to `ProductService`. This is for the actual service name change.

5. Change the service address port from 8731 to 8080. This is to prepare for the client application, which we will create soon.

6. You can also change Design_Time_Addresses to whatever address you want, or delete the baseAddress part from the service. This can be used to test your service locally. We will leave it unchanged for our example.

The content of the app.config file should now look like this:

```
<?xml version="1.0" encoding="utf-8" ?>
<configuration>
  <system.web>
    <compilation debug="true" />
  </system.web>
  <!-- When deploying the service library project, the content of the
       config file must be added to the host's app.config file.
  System.Configuration does not support config files for libraries. -->
  <system.serviceModel>
    <services>
      <service name="MyWCFServices.RealNorthwindService.
                      ProductService">
        <endpoint address="" binding="wsHttpBinding"
                            contract="MyWCFServices.
                            RealNorthwindService.IProductService">
          <identity>
            <dns value="localhost" />
          </identity>
        </endpoint>
        <endpoint address="mex" binding="mexHttpBinding"
                            contract="IMetadataExchange" />
        <host>
          <baseAddresses>
            <add baseAddress="http://localhost:8080/Design_Time_
                            Addresses/MyWCFServices/
                            RealNorthwindService/ProductService/" />
          </baseAddresses>
        </host>
      </service>
    </services>
    <behaviors>
      <serviceBehaviors>
        <behavior>
          <!-- To avoid disclosing metadata information,
          set the value below to false and remove the metadata
          endpoint above before deployment -->
          <serviceMetadata httpGetEnabled="True"/>
```

```
        <!-- To receive exception details in faults for debugging
        purposes, set the value below to true.  Set to false before
        deployment
        to avoid disclosing exception information -->
        <serviceDebug includeExceptionDetailInFaults="False" />
      </behavior>
    </serviceBehaviors>
  </behaviors>
  </system.serviceModel>
</configuration>
```

Testing the service using WCF Test Client

Because we are using the WCF Service Library template in this example, we are now ready to test this web service. As we pointed out when creating this project, this service will be hosted in the Visual Studio 2010 WCF Service Host environment.

To start the service, press *F5* or *Ctrl + F5*. WcfSvcHost will be started and WCF Test Client is also started. This is a Visual Studio 2010 built-in test client for WCF Service Library projects.

In order to run the WCF Test Client you have to log into your machine as a local administrator. You also have to start Visual Studio as an administrator because we have changed the service port from 8732 to 8080 (port 8732 is pre-registered but 8080 is not).

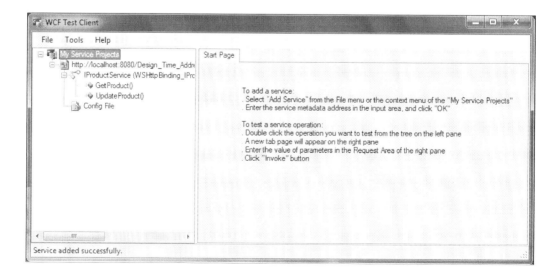

Again, if you get an **Access is denied** error, make sure you run Visual Studio as an administrator (under Windows XP you need to log on as an administrator).

Now from this WCF Test Client we can double-click on an operation to test it. First, let us test the GetProduct operation.

1. In the left panel of the client double-click on the **GetProduct()** operation; **GetProduct Request** will be shown on the right-side panel.

2. In this **Request** panel specify an integer for the product ID and click on the **Invoke** button to let the client call the service. You may get a dialog box to warn you about the security of sending information over the network. Click on the **OK** button to acknowledge this warning (you can check the **In the future, do not show this message** option so that it won't be displayed again).

Now the message **Invoking Service...** will be displayed in the status bar as the client is trying to connect to the server. It may take a while for this initial connection to be made as several things need to be done in the background. Once the connection has been established, a channel will be created and the client will call the service to perform the requested operation. Once the operation has been completed on the server side, the response package will be sent back to the client, and the WCF Test Client will display this response in the bottom panel.

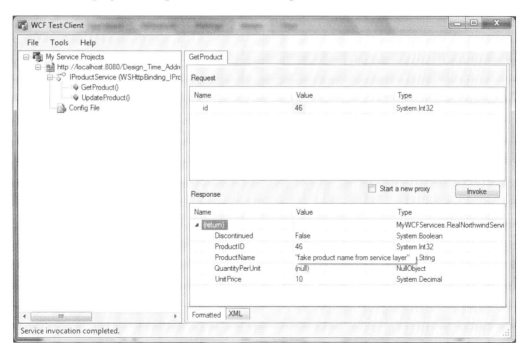

If you started the test client in debugging mode (by pressing *F5*), you can set a breakpoint at a line inside the `GetProduct` method in the `RealNorthwindService.cs` file, and when the **Invoke** button is clicked, the breakpoint will be hit so that you can debug the service as we explained earlier. However, unlike in previous chapters where you had to attach to ASP.NET Development Server, here you don't need to attach to the WCF Service Host.

Note that the response is always the same, no matter what product ID you use to retrieve the product. Specifically, the product name is hard-coded, as shown in the diagram. Moreover, from the client response panel, we can see that several properties of the `Product` object have been assigned default values.

Also, because the product ID is an integer value from the WCF Test Client, you can only enter an integer for it. If a non-integer value is entered, when you click on the **Invoke** button, you will get an error message box to warn you that you have entered a value with the wrong type.

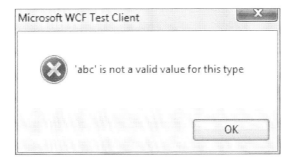

Now let's test the operation, `UpdateProduct`.

- Double-click on the **UpdateProduct()** operation in the left panel, and **UpdateProduct()** will be shown in the right-side panel in a new tab.

- Enter a decimal value for the `UnitPrice` parameter and then click on the **Invoke** button to test it. Depending on the value you entered in the `UnitPrice` column, you will get a `True` or `False` response package back.

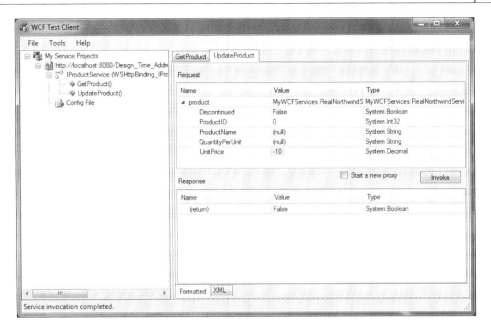

The **Request/Response** packages are displayed in grids by default but you have the option of displaying them in XML format. Just select the **XML** tab at the bottom of the right-side panel, and you will see the XML-formatted **Request/Response** packages. From these XML strings, you can see that they are SOAP messages.

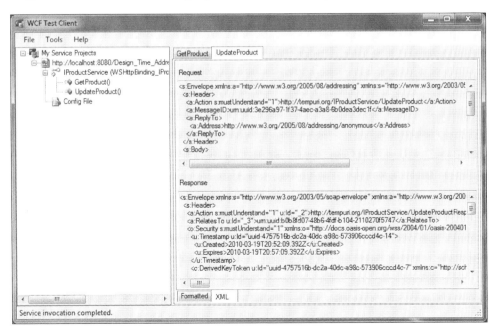

Besides testing operations, you can also look at the configuration settings of the web service. Just double-click on **Config File** from the left-side panel and the configuration file will be displayed in the right-side panel. This will show you the bindings for the service, the addresses of the service, and the contract for the service.

 What you see here for the configuration file is not an exact image of the actual configuration file. It hides some information such as debugging mode and service behavior, and includes some additional information on reliable sessions and compression mode.

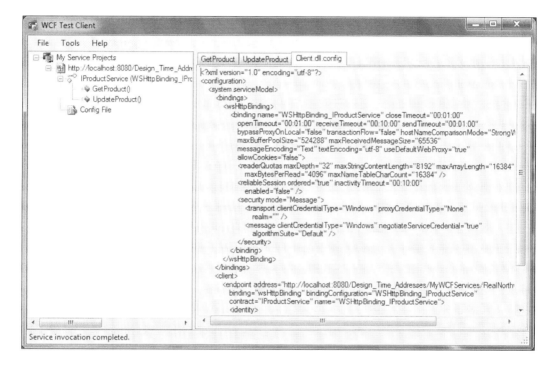

If you are satisfied with the test results, just close the WCF Test Client, and you will go back to Visual Studio IDE. Note that as soon as you close the client, the WCF Service Host is stopped. This is different from hosting a service inside ASP.NET Development Server, where ASP.NET Development Server still stays active even after you close the client.

Testing the service using our own client

It is very convenient to test a WCF service using the built-in WCF Test Client, but sometimes it is desirable to test a WCF service using your own test client. The built-in WCF Test Client is limited to only simple WCF services. For complex WCF services, we have to create our own test client. For this purpose, we can use the methods we learned earlier to host the WCF service in IIS, ASP.NET Development Server, or a managed .NET application, and create a test client to test the service.

In addition to the previous methods we learned, we can also use the built-in WCF Service Host to host the WCF service. So we don't need to create a host application but just need to create a client. In this section, we will use this hosting method to save us some time.

First, let us find a way to get the metadata for the service. From the Visual Studio 2010 built-in WCF Test Client, you can't examine the WSDL of the service, although the client itself must have used the WSDL to communicate with the service. To see the WSDL outside of the WCF Service Test Client, just copy the address of the service from the configuration file and paste it into a web browser. In our example, the address of the service is: `http://localhost:8080/Design_Time_Addresses/MyWCFServices/RealNorthwindService/ProductService/`. So copy and paste this address to a web browser, and we will see the WSDL languages of the service, just as we have seen many times before.

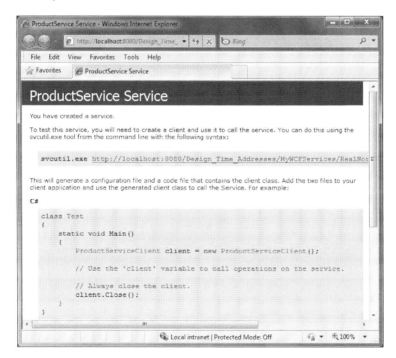

To get the metadata for the service, the service host application must run. The easiest way to start `RealNorthwindService` in the WCF Service Host is to start the WCF Test Client and leave it running.

Now that we know how to get the metadata for our service, we can start building the test client. We can leave the host application running, and manually generate the proxy classes using the same method that we used earlier. But this time we will let Visual Studio do it for us, So you can close the WCF Test Client for now.

Follow these steps to build your own client to test the WCF service:

1. Add a new **Console Application** project to the `RealNorthwind` solution. Let's call it `RealNorthwindClient`.

2. Add a reference to the WCF service. In Visual Studio Solution Explorer, right-click on the **RealNorthwindClient** project, select **Add Service Reference...** from the context menu, and you will see the **Add Service Reference** dialog box.

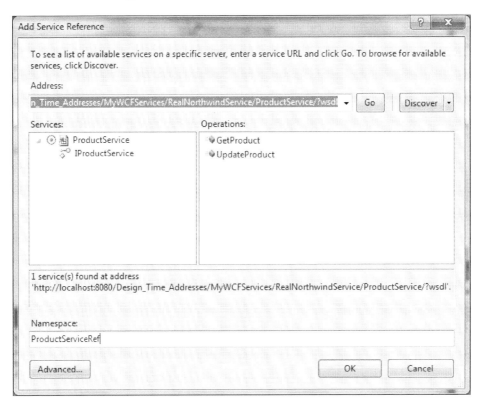

3. In the **Add Service Reference** dialog box, type the following address into the **Address** box, and then click on the **Go** button to connect to the service:

```
http://localhost:8080/Design_Time_Addresses/MyWCFServices/
RealNorthwindService/ProductService/
```

You can also simply click on the **Discover** button (or click on the little arrow next to the **Discover** button, and select **Services in Solution**) to find this service.

In order to connect to or discover a service in the same solution you don't have to start the host application for the service. The WCF Service Host will be automatically started for this purpose. However, if it is not started in advance, it may take a while for the **Add Service Reference** window to download the required metadata information for the service.

`ProductService` should now be listed on the left-hand side of the window. You can expand it and select the service contract to view its details.

4. Next, let's change the namespace of this service from `ServiceReference1` to `ProductServiceRef`. This will make the reference meaningful in the code.

5. If you want to make this client run under .NET 2.0, click on the **Advanced...** button in the **Add Service Reference** window, and in the **Service Reference Settings** pop-up dialog box, click on the **Add Web Reference...** button. This will cause the proxy code to be generated based on .NET 2.0 web service standards.

In this example, we won't do this, So click on the **Cancel** button to discard these changes.

6. Now click on the **OK** button in the **Add Service Reference** dialog box to add the service reference. You will see that a new folder named **ProductServiceRef** is created under **Service References** in **Solution Explorer** for the **RealNorthwindClient** project. This folder contains lots of files including the WSDL file, the service map, and the actual proxy code. If you can't see them, click on **Show All Files** in Solution Explorer.

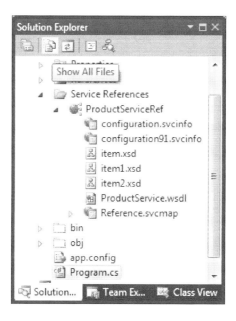

A new file, App.config, is also added to the project as well as several WCF-related references such as System.ServiceModel and System.Runtime.Serialization.

At this point, the proxy code to connect to the WCF service and the required configuration file have both been created and added to the project for us without us having to enter a single line of code. What we need to do next is to write just a few lines of code to call this service.

Just as we did earlier, we will modify `Program.cs` to call the WCF service.

1. First open the `Program.cs` file, and add the following `using` line to the file:

   ```
   using RealNorthwindClient.ProductServiceRef;
   ```

2. Then inside the `Main` method add the following line of code to create a client object:

   ```
   ProductServiceClient client = new ProductServiceClient();
   ```

3. Finally add the following lines to the file to call the WCF service to get and update a product:

   ```
   Product product = client.GetProduct(23);
   product.UnitPrice = (decimal)20.0;
   bool result = client.UpdateProduct(product);
   ```

The content of the `Program.cs` file is:

```
using System;
using System.Collections.Generic;
using System.Linq;
using System.Text;
using RealNorthwindClient.ProductServiceRef;

namespace RealNorthwindClient
{
    class Program
    {
        static void Main(string[] args)
        {
            ProductServiceClient client = new ProductServiceClient();

            Product product = client.GetProduct(23);
            Console.WriteLine("product name is " +
                        product.ProductName);
            Console.WriteLine("product price is " +
                    product.UnitPrice.ToString());

            product.UnitPrice = (decimal)20.0;
            bool result = client.UpdateProduct(product);
            Console.WriteLine("Update result is " +
                        result.ToString());
        }
    }
}
```

Now you can run the client application to test the service. Remember that you need to run Visual Studio as an administrator.

- If you want to start it in debugging mode (*F5*), you need to add a `Console.ReadLine();` statement to the end of the program so that you can see the output of the program. Also remember to set the `RealNorthwindClient` application as the startup project. The WCF Service Host application will be started automatically before the client is started (but the WCF Test Client won't be started).

- If you want to start the client application in non-debugging mode (*Ctrl + F5*), you need to start the WCF Service Host application (and the WCF Test Client application) in advance. You can start the WCF Service Host application (and the WCF Test Client) from another Visual Studio IDE instance, or you can set `RealNorthwindService` as the startup project, start it in non-debugging mode (*Ctrl + F5*), leave it running, and then change `RealNorthwindClient` to be the startup project, and start it in non-debugging mode. Also, you can set the solution to start with multiple projects with `RealNorthwindService` as the first project to be run and `RealNorthwindClient` as the second project to be run. In my environment, I set the solution to start with multiple projects, so I am sure that the WCF service is always started before the client application, no matter whether it is in debugging mode or not.

The output of this client program is as shown in the following figure:

```
C:\Windows\system32\cmd.exe

product name is fake product name from service layer
product price is 10
Update result is True
Press any key to continue . . .
```

Adding a business logic layer

Until now the web service has contained only one layer. In this section, we will add a business logic layer and define some business rules in this layer.

Adding the product entity project

Before we add the business logic layer, we need to add a project for business entities. The business entities project will hold all business entity object definitions such as products, customers, and orders. These entities will be used across the business logic layer, the data access layer, and the service layer. They will be very similar to the data contracts we defined in the previous section, but will not be seen outside of the service. The Product entity will have the same properties as the product contract data, plus some extra properties such as `UnitsInStock` and `ReorderLevel`. These properties will be used internally and shared by all layers of the service. For example, when an order is placed, `UnitsInStock` should be updated as well. Also, if the updated `UnitsInStock` is less than `ReorderLevel`, an event should be raised to trigger the reordering process.

The business entities by themselves do not act as a layer. They are just pure C# classes representing internal data within the service implementations. There is no logic inside these entities. Also, in our example, these entities are very similar to the data contracts (with only two extra fields in the entity class). In reality, the entity classes could be very different from the data contracts, from property names and property types to data structures.

As with the data contracts, the business entities' classes should be in their own assembly. So we first need to create a project for them. Just add a new C# class library, `RealNorthwindEntities`, to the Solution. Then rename `Class1.cs` to `ProductEntity.cs`, and modify it as follows:

1. Change its namespace from `RealNorthwindEntities` to `MyWCFServices.RealNorthwindEntities`.

2. Change the class name from `Class1` to `ProductEntity`.

3. Add the following properties to this class:

   `ProductID`, `ProductName`, `QuantityPerUnit`, `UnitPrice`, `Discontinued`, `UnitsInStock`, `UnitsOnOrder`, and `ReorderLevel`.

Five of the above properties are also in the Product service data contract. The last three properties are for use inside the service implementations. We will use UnitsOnOrder to trigger business logic when updating a product, and update UnitsInStock and ReorderLevel to trigger business logic when saving an order (in this book we will not create a service for saving an order but we assume that this is a required operation and will be implemented later).

The following is the code list of the ProductEntity class:

```csharp
using System;
using System.Collections.Generic;
using System.Linq;
using System.Text;

namespace MyWCFServices.RealNorthwindEntities
{
    public class ProductEntity
    {
            public int ProductID { get; set; }
            public string ProductName { get; set; }
            public string QuantityPerUnit { get; set; }
            public decimal UnitPrice { get; set; }
            public int UnitsInStock { get; set; }
            public int ReorderLevel { get; set; }
            public int UnitsOnOrder { get; set; }
            public bool Discontinued { get; set; }
    }
}
```

Adding the business logic project

Next, let us create the business logic layer project. Again, we just need to add a new C# class library project, RealNorthwindLogic, to the solution. So rename Class1.cs to ProductLogic.cs, and modify it as follows:

1. Change its namespace from RealNorthwindLogic to MyWCFServices. RealNorthwindLogic.

2. Change the class name from Class1 to ProductLogic.

3. Add a reference to the project, `RealNorthwindEntities`, as shown in the following **Add Reference** image:

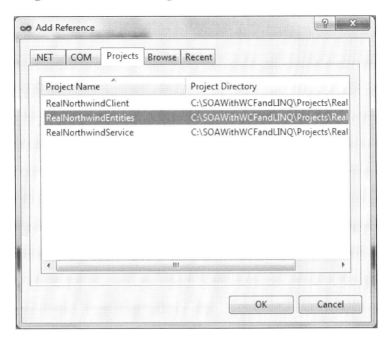

Now we need to add some code to the `ProductLogic` class.

1. Add the following `using` line:

    ```
    using MyWCFServices.RealNorthwindEntities;
    ```

2. Add the method, `GetProduct`. It should look like this:

    ```
    public ProductEntity GetProduct(int id)
    {
        // TODO: call data access layer to retrieve product
        ProductEntity p = new ProductEntity();
        p.ProductID = id;
        p.ProductName = "fake product name from business logic layer";
        p.UnitPrice = (decimal)20.00;
        return p;
    }
    ```

    In this method we create a `ProductEntity` object, assign values to some of its properties, and return it to the caller. Everything is still hardcoded so far.

We hardcode the product name as 'fake product name from business logic layer' so that we know this is a different product from the one returned directly from the service layer.

3. Add the method, `UpdateProduct`, as follows:

```
public bool UpdateProduct (ProductEntity product)
{
    // TODO: call data access layer to update product
    // first check to see if it is a valid price
    if (product.UnitPrice <= 0)
        return false;
    // ProductName can't be empty
    else if (product.ProductName == null
|| product.ProductName. Length == 0)
        return false;
    // QuantityPerUnit can't be empty
    else if (product.QuantityPerUnit == null
  || product. QuantityPerUnit.Length == 0)
        return false;
    // then validate other properties
    else
    {
        ProductEntity productInDB = GetProduct (product.ProductID);
        // invalid product to update
        if (productInDB == null)
            return false;
        // a product can't be discontinued if there are
         //        non-fulfilled orders
        if (product.Discontinued == true
&& productInDB. UnitsOnOrder > 0)
            return false;
        else
            return true;
    }
}
```

4. Add test logic to the `GetProduct` method.

   We still haven't updated anything in a database but this time we have added several pieces of logic to the `UpdateProduct` method. First, we checked the validity of the `UnitPrice` property and returned `false` if it was not valid. We then checked the product name and quantity per unit properties to make sure they were not empty. We then tried to retrieve the product to see if it was a valid product to update. We also added a check to make sure that a supplier can't discontinue a product if there are unfulfilled orders for this product. However, at this stage, we can't truly enforce this logic because when we check the `UnitsOnOrder` property of a product it is always `0` as we didn't assign a value to it in the `GetProduct` method. For test purposes, we can change the `GetProduct` method to include the following line of code:

   ```
   if(id > 50) p.UnitsOnOrder = 30;
   ```

   Now, when we test the service, we can select a product with an ID that is greater than 50, and try to update its `Discontinued` property to see what result we will get.

After you put all of this together the content of the `ProductLogic.cs` file should be as follows:

```
using System;
using System.Collections.Generic;
using System.Linq;
using System.Text;
using MyWCFServices.RealNorthwindEntities;

namespace MyWCFServices.RealNorthwindLogic
{
    public class ProductLogic
    {
        public ProductEntity GetProduct(int id)
        {
            // TODO: call data access layer to retrieve product
            ProductEntity p = new ProductEntity();
            p.ProductID = id;
            p.ProductName =
                        "fake product name from business logic layer";
            p.UnitPrice = (decimal)20.0;
            if(id > 50) p.UnitsOnOrder = 30;
            return p;
        }

        public bool UpdateProduct(ProductEntity product)
        {
```

```
// TODO: call data access layer to update product
// first check to see if it is a valid price
if (product.UnitPrice <= 0)
    return false;
// ProductName can't be empty
else if (product.ProductName == null || product.
                   ProductName.Length == 0)
    return false;
// QuantityPerUnit can't be empty
else if (product.QuantityPerUnit == null || product.
                   QuantityPerUnit.Length == 0)
    return false;
// then validate other properties
else
{
    ProductEntity productInDB =
                          GetProduct(product.ProductID);
    // invalid product to update
    if (productInDB == null)
        return false;
    // a product can't be discontinued if there are
    //   non-fulfilled orders
    else if (product.Discontinued == true && productInDB.
       UnitsOnOrder > 0)
        return false;
    else
        return true;
}
        }
    }
}
```

Calling the business logic layer from the service interface layer

We now have the business logic layer ready and can modify the service contracts to call this layer so that we can enforce some business logic.

First, we want to make it very clear that we are going to change the service implementations and not the interfaces. So we will only change the `ProductService.cs` file.

We will not touch the file, `IProductService.cs`. All of the existing clients (if there are any) that are referencing our service will not notice that we are changing the implementation.

Follow these steps to customize the service interface layer:

1. Add a reference to the business logic layer.

   In order to call a method inside the business logic layer we need to add a reference to the assembly that the business logic is included in. We will also use the `ProductEntity` class. So we need a reference to the `RealNorthwind-Entities` as well.

   To add the references from Solution Explorer right-click on the project, **RealNorthwindService**, select **Add Reference…** from the context menu, and select **RealNorthwindLogic** from the **Projects** tab. Also, select `RealNorthwindEntities`, as we will need a reference to `ProductEntity` inside it. Just hold down the *Ctrl* key if you want to select multiple projects. Click on the **OK** button to add references to the selected projects.

2. Now we have added two references. We can add the following two `using` statements to the `ProductService.cs` file so that we don't need to type the full names for their classes.

   ```
   using MyWCFServices.RealNorthwindEntities;
   using MyWCFServices.RealNorthwindLogic;
   ```

3. Now, inside the `GetProduct` method, we can use the following statements to get the product from our business logic layer:

   ```
   ProductLogic productLogic = new ProductLogic();
   ProductEntity product = productLogic.GetProduct(id);
   ```

4. However, we cannot return this product back to the caller because this product is of the type, `ProductEntity`, which is not the type that the caller is expecting. The caller is expecting a return value of the type, `Product`, which is a data contract defined within the service interface. We need to translate this `ProductEntity` object to a `Product` object. To do this, we add the following new method to the `ProductService` class:

   ```
           private void TranslateProductEntityToProductContractData(
               ProductEntity productEntity,
               Product product)
           {
               product.ProductID = productEntity.ProductID;
               product.ProductName = productEntity.ProductName;
               product.QuantityPerUnit = productEntity.
   QuantityPerUnit;
   ```

```
        product.UnitPrice = productEntity.UnitPrice;
        product.Discontinued = productEntity.Discontinued;
    }
```

Inside this translation method we copy all of the properties from the
`ProductEntity` object to the service contract data object, but not the last
three properties—`UnitsInStock`, `UnitsOnOrder`, and `ReorderLevel`. These
three properties are used only inside the service implementations. Outside
callers cannot see them at all.

The `GetProduct` method should now look like this:

```
public Product GetProduct(int id)
{
    ProductLogic productLogic = new ProductLogic();
    ProductEntity productEntity = productLogic.GetProduct(id);
    Product product = new Product();
    TranslateProductEntityToProductContractData
                        (productEntity, product);
    return product;
}
```

We can modify the `UpdateProduct` method in the same way, making it
like this:

```
public bool UpdateProduct(Product product)
{
    ProductLogic productLogic = new ProductLogic();
    ProductEntity productEntity = new ProductEntity();
    TranslateProductContractDataToProductEntity(
                        product, productEntity);

    return productLogic.UpdateProduct(productEntity);
}
```

5. Note that we have to create a new method to translate a product contract
    data object to a `ProductEntity` object. In translation we leave the three
    extra properties unassigned in the `ProductEntity` object because we
    know a supplier won't update these properties. Also, we have to create
    a `ProductLogic` variable in both the methods so that we can make it a
    class member:

```
ProductLogic productLogic = new ProductLogic();
```

The final content of the `ProductService.cs` file is as follows:

```
using System;
using System.Collections.Generic;
using System.Linq;
using System.Runtime.Serialization;
using System.ServiceModel;
using System.Text;
using MyWCFServices.RealNorthwindEntities;
using MyWCFServices.RealNorthwindLogic;

namespace MyWCFServices.RealNorthwindService
{
    // NOTE: If you change the class name "Service1" here, you must
        also update the reference to "Service1" in App.config.
    public class ProductService : IProductService
    {
        ProductLogic productLogic = new ProductLogic();

        public Product GetProduct(int id)
        {
            /*
            // TODO: call business logic layer to retrieve product
            Product product = new Product();
            product.ProductID = id;
            product.ProductName =
                            "fake product name from service layer";
            product.UnitPrice = (decimal)10.0;
            */
            ProductEntity productEntity = productLogic.GetProduct(id);
            Product product = new Product();
            TranslateProductEntityToProductContractData(
                            productEntity, product);

            return product;
        }
        public bool UpdateProduct(Product product)
        {
            /*
            // TODO: call business logic layer to update product
            if (product.UnitPrice <= 0)
                return false;
            else
                return true;
            */

            ProductEntity productEntity = new ProductEntity();
```

```
            TranslateProductContractDataToProductEntity(
                            product, productEntity);

            return productLogic.UpdateProduct(productEntity);
        }

        private void TranslateProductEntityToProductContractData(
            ProductEntity productEntity,
            Product product)
        {

            product.ProductID = productEntity.ProductID;
            product.ProductName = productEntity.ProductName;
            product.QuantityPerUnit = productEntity.QuantityPerUnit;
            product.UnitPrice = productEntity.UnitPrice;
            product.Discontinued = productEntity.Discontinued;
        }

        private void TranslateProductContractDataToProductEntity(
            Product product,
            ProductEntity productEntity)
        {

            productEntity.ProductID = product.ProductID;
            productEntity.ProductName = product.ProductName;
            productEntity.QuantityPerUnit = product.QuantityPerUnit;
            productEntity.UnitPrice = product.UnitPrice;
            productEntity.Discontinued = product.Discontinued;
        }
    }
}
```

Testing the WCF service with a business logic layer

We can now compile and test the new service with a business logic layer.
We will use the WCF Test Client to simplify the process.

1. Make the project, `RealNorthwindService`, the startup project.

2. Start the WCF Service Host application and WCF Service Test Client
    by pressing *F5* or *Ctrl + F5*.

3. In the WCF Service Test Client, double-click on the `GetProduct`
    operation to bring up the `GetProduct` test screen.

4. Enter a value of **56** for the ID field and then click on the **Invoke** button.

You will see that this time the product is returned from the business logic layer, instead of the service layer. Also note that the UnitsOnOrder property is not displayed as it is not part of the service contract data type. However, we know that a product has a property, UnitsOnOrder, and we will use this for our next test.

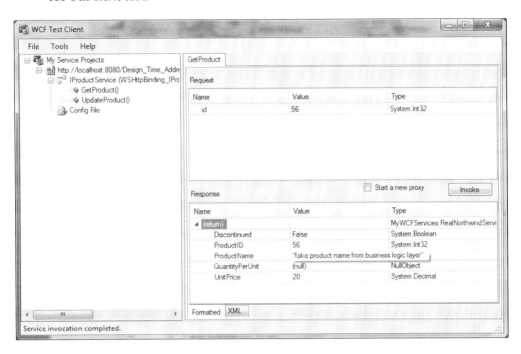

Now let us try to update a product.

1. In the WCF Service Test Client, double-click on the **UpdateProduct()** operation to bring up the **UpdateProduct()** test screen.

2. Enter **-10** as the price and click on the **Invoke** button. You will see that the **Response** result is **False**.

3. Enter a valid price, say **25.60**, a name, and a quantity per unit, and leave the **Discontinued** property set to **False**, and then click on the **Invoke** button. You will see that the **Response** result is now **True**.

4. Change the **Discontinued** value from **False** to **True** and click on the **Invoke** button again. The **Response** result is still **True**. This is because we didn't change the product ID and it has defaulted to 0. This is because in our business logic layer GetProduct operation, for a product with id <= 50, we didn't set the property, UnitsOnOrder, thus it defaults to 0, and in our business logic UpdateProduct operation, it is okay to set the **Discontinued** property to be **True**, if UnitsOnOrder is < 0.

5. Change the product ID to **51**, leave the **Discontinued** value as **True** and the product price as **25.60**, and click on the **Invoke** button again. This time you will see that the **Response** result is **False**. This is because the business logic layer has checked the `UnitsOnOrder` and `Discontinued` properties and didn't allow us to make the update.

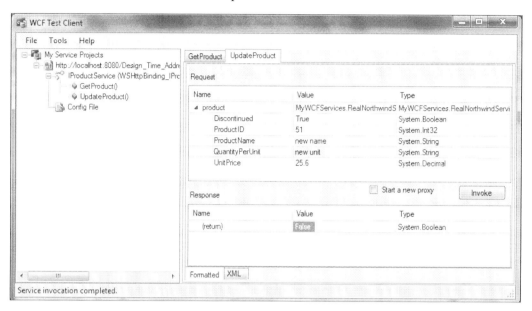

Summary

In this chapter, we have created a real world WCF service that has a service contract layer and a business logic layer. The key points in this chapter include:

- WCF services should have explicit boundaries
- The WCF Service Application template can be used to create WCF services with a hosting website created within the project
- The WCF Service Library template can be used to create WCF services that are hosted by the WCF Service Host, and these can be tested using the WCF service Test Client
- The service interface layer should contain only the service contracts such as the operation contracts and data contracts
- The business logic layer should contain the implementation of the service
- The business entities represent the internal data of the service shared by all of the layers of the service and they should not be exposed to the clients

5

Adding Database Support and Exception Handling to the RealNorthwind WCF Service

In the previous chapter, we created a WCF service with two layers. We didn't add the third layer, that is, the data access layer. Therefore, all of the service operations just returned a fake result from the business logic layer.

In this chapter, we will add the third layer to the WCF service. We will also introduce message contracts for service message exchange and fault contracts for service error handling.

We will accomplish the following tasks in this chapter:

- Create the data access layer project
- Modify the business logic layer to call the data access layer
- Prepare the Northwind database for the service
- Connect the WCF service to the Northwind database
- Test the service with the data access layer
- Add a fault contract to the service
- Throw a fault contract exception to the client
- Catch the fault contract in the client program
- Test the service fault contract

Adding a data access layer

We have two layers in our solution. We need to add one more layer—the data access layer. We need to query a real database to get the product information and update the database for a given product.

Creating the data access layer project

First we will create the project for the data access layer. As we did for the business logic layer, what we need to do is add a C# class library project named `RealNorthwindDAL`, where **DAL** stands for **Data Access Layer**, to the solution. Then rename the `Class1.cs` to `ProductDAO.cs` and modify it as follows:

- Change its namespace from `RealNorthwindDAL` to `MyWCFServices.RealNorthwindDAL`.

- Change the class name from `Class1` to `ProductDAO`.

- Add a reference to the project, `RealNorthwindEntities`.

Now let's modify `ProductDAO.cs` for our product service:

- Add the following `using` statement:

  ```
  using MyWCFServices.RealNorthwindEntities;
  ```

- Add two new methods to the `ProductDAO` class. The first method is `GetProduct`, which should be as follows:

  ```
  public ProductEntity GetProduct(int id)
  {
      // TODO: connect to DB to retrieve product
      ProductEntity p = new ProductEntity();
      p.ProductID = id;
      p.ProductName = "fake product name from data access
                      layer";
      p.UnitPrice = (decimal)30.00;
      return p;
  }
  ```

  In this method all the product information is still hardcoded, though we have changed the product name to be specific to the data access layer. We will soon modify this method to retrieve the actual product information from a real `Northwind` database.

- The second method is `UpdateProduct` which should be as follows:

```
public bool UpdateProduct(ProductEntity product)
{
    // TODO: connect to DB to update product
    return true;
}
```

Again, we didn't update any database in this method. We will also modify this method soon to update to the real `Northwind` database.

The content of the `ProductDAO.cs` file should now be as follows:

```
using System;
using System.Collections.Generic;
using System.Linq;
using System.Text;
using MyWCFServices.RealNorthwindEntities;

namespace MyWCFServices.RealNorthwindDAL
{
    public class ProductDAO
    {
        public ProductEntity GetProduct(int id)
        {
            // TODO: connect to DB to retrieve product
            ProductEntity p = new ProductEntity();
            p.ProductID = id;
            p.ProductName = "fake product name from data access layer";
            p.UnitPrice = (decimal)30.00;
            return p;
        }

        public bool UpdateProduct(ProductEntity product)
        {
            // TODO: connect to DB to update product
            return true;
        }
    }
}
```

Calling the data access layer from the business logic layer

Before we modify these two methods to interact with a real database, we will first modify the business logic layer to call them so that we know that the three-layer framework is working.

1. Add a reference of this new layer to the business logic layer project. From Solution Explorer, just right-click on the **RealNorthwindLogic** project item, select **Add Reference…** from the context menu, select **RealNorthwindDAL** from the **Projects** tab, and then click on the **OK** button.

2. Open the `ProductLogic.cs` file under the `RealNorthwindLogic` project and add a `using` statement:

    ```
    using MyWCFServices.RealNorthwindDAL;
    ```

3. Add a new class member:

    ```
    ProductDAO productDAO = new ProductDAO();
    ```

4. Modify the method, `GetProduct`, to contain only this line:

    ```
    return productDAO.GetProduct(id);
    ```

We will use the data access layer to retrieve the product information. At this point we will not add any business logic to this method.

*   Modify the last line of the method, `UpdateProduct`, to call the data access layer. The method should look like this:

    ```
    public bool UpdateProduct(ProductEntity product)
    {
        // TODO: call data access layer to update product
        // first check to see if it is a valid price
        if (product.UnitPrice <= 0)
            return false;
        // ProductName can't be empty
        else if (product.ProductName.Length == 0)
            return false;
        // QuantityPerUnit can't be empty
        else if (product.QuantityPerUnit.Length == 0)
            return false;
        // then validate other properties
        else
        {
            ProductEntity productInDB =
    ```

```
                            GetProduct(product.ProductID);
            // invalid product to update
            if (productInDB == null)
                return false;
            // a product can't be discontinued if there are
              non-fulfilled orders
            if (product.Discontinued == true && productInDB.
                                    UnitsOnOrder > 0)
                return false;
            else
                return productDAO.UpdateProduct(product);
        }
    }
```

In this method we have replaced the last `return` statement to call the data access layer method, `UpdateProduct`. This means that all of the business logic is still enclosed in the business logic layer and the data access layer should be used only to update the product in the database.

Here is the full content of the `ProductLogic.cs` file:

```
using System;
using System.Collections.Generic;
using System.Linq;
using System.Text;
using MyWCFServices.RealNorthwindEntities;
using MyWCFServices.RealNorthwindDAL;

namespace MyWCFServices.RealNorthwindLogic
{
    public class ProductLogic
    {
        ProductDAO productDAO = new ProductDAO();

        public ProductEntity GetProduct(int id)
        {
            /*
            // TODO: call data access layer to retrieve product
            ProductEntity p = new ProductEntity();
            p.ProductID = id;
            p.ProductName =
                    "fake product name from business logic layer";
            p.UnitPrice = (decimal)20.0;
            return p;
            */

            return productDAO.GetProduct(id);
```

```
        }
        public bool UpdateProduct(ProductEntity product)
        {
            // TODO: call data access layer to update product
            // first check to see if it is a valid price
            if (product.UnitPrice <= 0)
               return false;
            // ProductName can't be empty
            else if (product.ProductName == null || product.
                                ProductName.Length == 0)
               return false;
            // QuantityPerUnit can't be empty
            else if (product.QuantityPerUnit == null || product.
                                QuantityPerUnit.Length == 0)
               return false;
            // then validate other properties
            else
            {
                ProductEntity productInDB =
                    GetProduct(product.ProductID);
                // invalid product to update
                if (productInDB == null)
                    return false;
                // a product can't be discontinued if there
                                are non-fulfilled orders
                else if (product.Discontinued ==
                            true && productInDB.UnitsOnOrder > 0)
                    return false;
                else
                    return productDAO.UpdateProduct(product);
            }
        }
    }
}
```

If you run the program and test it using the WCF Test Client, you will get exactly the same result as before, although now it is a three-layer application and you will see a different, but obviously still fake, product name.

Preparing the database

As we have the three-layer framework ready we will now implement the data access layer to actually communicate with a real database.

In this book we will use the Microsoft sample database, **Northwind**. This database is not installed by default in SQL Server 2005 or SQL Server 2008.

- Download the database package. Just search for "Northwind Sample Databases download" on the Internet, or go to this page:

  `http://www.microsoft.com/downloads/details.`
  `aspx?FamilyId=06616212-0356-46A0-8DA2-BC53A68034&displaylang=en`

  and download the file, `SQL2000SampleDb.msi`. Note that this sample database was designed for SQL Server 2000 but it can also be used with SQL Server 2005 and SQL Server 2008.

- Install (extract) it to: `C:\SQL Server 2000 Sample Databases`.

- Change the security of both `Northwnd.mdf` and `Northwnd.ldf` to be read/write-able to your SQL Server service account user (or just give everyone full access).

- Open SQL Server 2005/2008 Management Studio.

- Connect to your database engine.

- Right-click on the **Databases** node and select **Attach...** from the context menu, as shown in the SQL Server Management Studio diagram below:

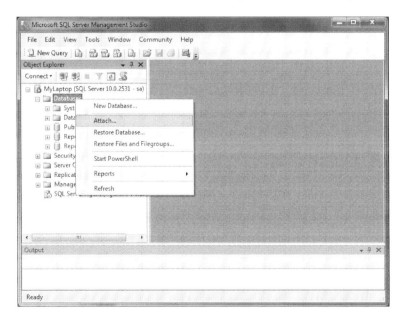

- In the pop up **Attach Databases** dialog box, click on **Add,** browse to the file, **C:\SQL Server 2000 Sample Databases\NORTHWND.MDF,** click on **OK,** and you now have the `Northwind` database attached to your SQL Server 2005 or 2008 engine.

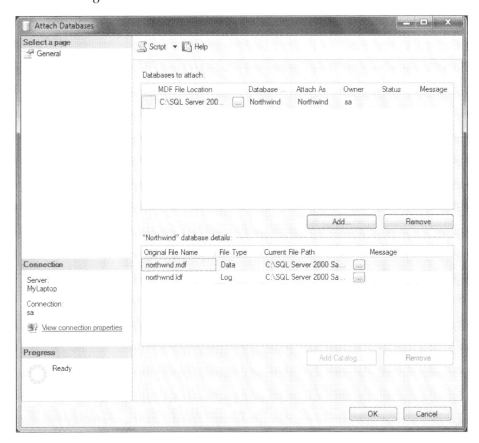

Adding the connection string to the configuration file

Now that we have the `Northwind` database attached, we will modify our data access layer to use this actual database. At this point we will use a raw `SqlClient` adapter to do the database work. We will replace this layer with LINQ to Entities in a later chapter.

Before we start coding we need to finish the following tasks to add a connection string to the configuration file. We don't want to hardcode the connection string in our project. Instead, we will set it in the `App.config` file so that it can be changed on the fly.

- Add a reference to `System.Configuration` to the `RealNorthwindDAL` project. We will store a connection string in the configuration file and we need this assembly to read it.

- Add the following configuration settings to the `App.config` file under the `RealNorthwindService` project (note this connection string is for the SQL login account, other login account types will be explained later in this section).

```
<connectionStrings>
  <add name ="NorthwindConnectionString"
      connectionString="server=your_db_server\your_db_instance;
      uid=your_user_name;pwd=your_password;database=Northwind" />
</connectionStrings>
```

There are a couple of things to note for this new key in the configuration file.

  ○ It should be added to the `App.config` file in the `RealNorthwindService` project, not to the `RealNorthwindDAL` project. Actually, there is no file called `App.config` in the `RealNorthwindDAL` project.

  ○ The node, `connectionStrings`, should be a child node of the root `configuration` node, that is, the highlighted lines should be placed immediately after the line, `<configuration>`. The first few lines of the `App.config` file should be as follows (highlighted lines are new lines to add):

```
<?xml version="1.0" encoding="utf-8" ?>
<configuration>

<connectionStrings>
  <add name ="NorthwindConnectionString"
      connectionString="server=your_db_server\
                             your_db_instance;
      uid=your_user_name; pwd=your_password;
      database=Northwind" />
</connectionStrings>

        <system.web>
          <compilation debug="true" />
        </system.web>
```

- Replace `your_db_server` with your actual database server name. If the database is located on your own machine, you can use `localhost` as the db server name.

- Replace `your_db_instance` with your database's instance name. If you have installed your SQL server with the default instance, don't put anything here.

- Replace `your_user_name` and `your_password` with your actual login and password to the SQL server database. This user must have write access to the `Northwind` database.

- If you use `sa` to log into your database, make sure that, in your database, the `sa` user is enabled for login. Some installations may automatically disable `sa` from logging into the database (inside **SQL Server Management Studio**, right-click on **Security | Logins | sa** and select **Properties**, then click on **Status** to enable `sa`). Also make sure that, in your database, SQL Server authentication mode is turned on (inside **SQL Server Management Studio,** right click on the root node of your Database server/instance, select **Properties**, then click on **Security**, and choose **SQL Server and Windows Authentication mode**).

- If you don't have a SQL Server login or you just want to use Windows authentication, you can use a trusted connection or an SSPI-integrated security connection.

- The connection string for the trusted connection should be:

```
"server=your_db_server\your_db_instance;database=Northwind;
Trusted_Connection=yes"
```

The connection string for the integrated security connection should be:

```
"server=your_db_server\your_db_instance;database=Northwind;
    Integrated Security=SSPI"
```

Or you can use this format for the connection string:

```
    "Data Source=your_db_server\your_db_instance;Initial
    Catalog=Northwind;Integrated Security=True"
```

Querying the database (GetProduct)

Because we have added the connection string as a new key to the configuration file, we need to retrieve this key in the DAO class so that we can use it when we want to connect to the database. Follow these steps to get and use this new key from within the DAO class:

- Open the file, `ProductDAO.cs`, in the `RealNorthwindDAL` project and first add two `using` statements:

```
using System.Data.SqlClient;
using System.Configuration;
```

- Add a new class member to the `ProductDAO` class (note the following code should be in one line in Visual Studio, we break them into three lines just for printing purposes):

```
string connectionString = ConfigurationManager.
ConnectionStrings["NorthwindConnectionString"].
ConnectionString;
```

We will use this connection string to connect to the `Northwind` database for both the `GetProduct` and `UpdateProduct` methods.

- Modify the `GetProduct` method to get the product from the database as follows:

```
public ProductEntity GetProduct(int id)
{
    /*
    // TODO: connect to DB to retrieve product
    ProductEntity p = new ProductEntity();
    p.ProductID = id;
    p.ProductName = "fake product name from data access
                     layer";
    p.UnitPrice = (decimal)30.00;
    if (id > 50) p.UnitsOnOrder = 30;
    return p;
    */

    ProductEntity p = null;
    using (SqlConnection conn =
                    new SqlConnection(connectionString))
    {
        SqlCommand comm = new SqlCommand();
        comm.CommandText =
            "select * from Products where ProductID=" + id;
        comm.Connection = conn;
        conn.Open();
        SqlDataReader reader = comm.ExecuteReader();
        if (reader.HasRows)
        {
            reader.Read();
            p = new ProductEntity();
            p.ProductID = id;
            p.ProductName =
                (string)reader["ProductName"];
            p.QuantityPerUnit =
                (string)reader["QuantityPerUnit"];
            p.UnitPrice =
                (decimal)reader["UnitPrice"];
            p.UnitsInStock =
                (short)reader["UnitsInStock"];
```

```
                  p.UnitsOnOrder =
                      (short)reader["UnitsOnOrder"];
                  p.ReorderLevel =
                      (short)reader["ReorderLevel"];
                  p.Discontinued =
                      (bool)reader["Discontinued"];
              }
          }
          return p;
      }
```

In this method we first create a `SqlConnection` to the `Northwind` database and then issue a SQL query to get product details for the ID.

The following statement is a new feature of C# and an equivalent to the traditional `try...catch...finally...` mechanism to deal with `SqlConnection` matters:

```
using (SqlConnection conn = new SqlConnection(connectionString))
```

Testing the GetProduct method

If you now set `RealNorthwindService` as the startup project and run the application, you can get the actual product information from the database, as seen in the following screenshot:

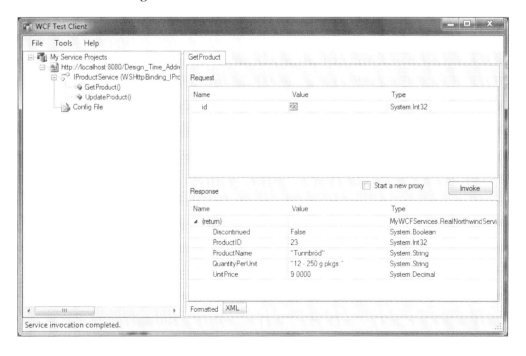

If you get an error screen it is probably because you have set your connection string incorrectly. Double-check the new connection string node in your `App.config` file and try again until you can connect to your database.

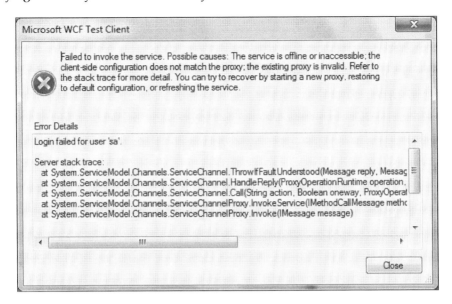

Instead of the connection error message you might see the following error message:

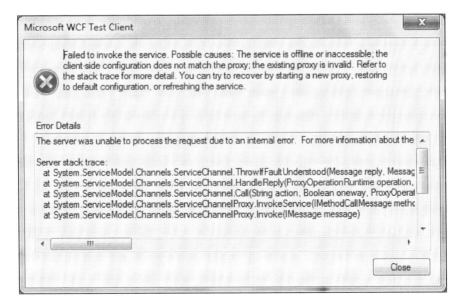

This error will happen when you try to get the product information for a product with a product ID of 0. The error message doesn't give much detail about what went wrong here because we didn't let the server reveal the details of any error. Let's follow the instructions in the error message to change the setting, `IncludeExceptionDetailInFaults`, to `True` in the `App.config` file and run it again. Now you will see that the error detail has changed to **Object reference not set to an instance of an object**.

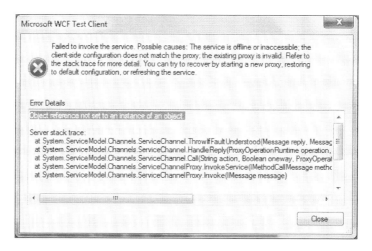

A little investigation will tell us that this is a bug in our `ProductService` class. Inside the `ProductService GetProduct` method, after we call the business logic layer to get the product detail for an ID, we will get a null product if the ID is not a valid product ID in the database. When we pass this null object to the next method (`TranslateProductEntityToProductContractData`) we get the above error message. Actually, this will happen whenever you enter a product ID outside the range of 1 to 77. This is because, in the sample `Northwind` database, there are only 77 products, with product IDs ranging from 1 to 77. To fix this problem we can add the following statement inside the `GetProduct` method right after the call to the business logic layer:

```
if (productEntity == null)
    throw new Exception("No product found with id " + id);
```

In the `ProductService.cs` file, the `GetProduct` method will now be:

```
public Product GetProduct(int id)
{
    ProductLogic productLogic = new ProductLogic();
    ProductEntity productEntity = productLogic.GetProduct(id);
    if (productEntity == null)
      throw new Exception("No product found with id " + id);
```

```
        Product product = new Product();
        TranslateProductEntityToProductContractData(
                    productEntity, product);
        return product;
    }
```

For now, we will raise an exception if an invalid product ID is entered. Later, we will convert this exception to a `FaultContract` so that the caller will know in advance that an error has occurred.

Now run the application again, and if you enter an invalid product ID, say 0, you will get an error message, **No product found with id 0**. This is much clearer than the previous **Object reference not set to an instance of an object** error message.

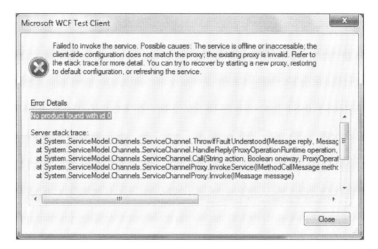

Updating the database (UpdateProduct)

Next, we will modify the `UpdateProduct` method to update the product record in the database. `UpdateProduct` in the `RealNorthwindDAL` project should be modified as follows:

```
public bool UpdateProduct(ProductEntity product)
{
    using (SqlConnection conn = new SqlConnection(connectionString))
    {
        SqlCommand cmd = new SqlCommand("UPDATE products
            SET ProductName=@name,QuantityPerUnit=@unit,UnitPrice=
                                    @price,Discontinued=@discontinued
                                    WHERE ProductID=@id",conn);
        cmd.Parameters.AddWithValue("@name", product.ProductName);
        cmd.Parameters.AddWithValue("@unit",
```

```
                                        product.QuantityPerUnit);
        cmd.Parameters.AddWithValue("@price", product.UnitPrice);
        cmd.Parameters.AddWithValue("@discontinued",
                                        product.Discontinued);
        cmd.Parameters.AddWithValue("@id", product.ProductID);
        conn.Open();
        int numRows = cmd.ExecuteNonQuery();
        if (numRows != 1)
            return false;
    }
    return true;
}
```

Inside this method we have used parameters to specify arguments to the update command. This is a good practice because it will prevent SQL Injection attacks, as the SQL statement is precompiled instead of being dynamically built.

We can follow these steps to test it:

1. Start the WCF Test Client.
2. Double-click on the UpdateProduct() operation.
3. Enter a valid product ID, name, price, and quantity per unit.
4. Click on **Invoke**.

You should get a True response. To prove it, just go to the GetProduct() page, enter the same product ID, click on **Invoke**, and you will see that all of your updates have been saved to the database.

The content of the ProductDAO.cs file is now:

```
using System;
using System.Collections.Generic;
using System.Linq;
using System.Text;
using MyWCFServices.RealNorthwindEntities;
using System.Data.SqlClient;
using System.Configuration;

namespace MyWCFServices.RealNorthwindDAL
{
    public class ProductDAO
    {
                    string connectionString =
                ConfigurationManager.
```

```csharp
            ConnectionStrings["NorthwindConnectionString"].
            ConnectionString;
public ProductEntity GetProduct(int id)
{
    /*
    // TODO: connect to DB to retrieve product
    ProductEntity p = new ProductEntity();
    p.ProductID = id;
    p.ProductName = "fake product name from data access
                    layer";
    p.UnitPrice = (decimal)30.00;
    return p;
    */

    ProductEntity p = null;
    using (SqlConnection conn =
            new SqlConnection(connectionString))
    {
        SqlCommand comm = new SqlCommand();
        comm.CommandText =
            "select * from Products where ProductID=" + id;
        comm.Connection = conn;
        conn.Open();
        SqlDataReader reader = comm.ExecuteReader();
        if (reader.HasRows)
        {
            reader.Read();
            p = new ProductEntity();
            p.ProductID = id;
            p.ProductName =
                (string)reader["ProductName"];
            p.QuantityPerUnit =
                (string)reader["QuantityPerUnit"];
            p.UnitPrice =
                (decimal)reader["UnitPrice"];
            p.UnitsInStock =
                (short)reader["UnitsInStock"];
            p.UnitsOnOrder =
                (short)reader["UnitsOnOrder"];
            p.ReorderLevel =
                (short)reader["ReorderLevel"];
            p.Discontinued =
                (bool)reader["Discontinued"];
        }
    }
```

```
        return p;
    }

    public bool UpdateProduct(ProductEntity product)
    {
        using (SqlConnection conn =
                new SqlConnection(connectionString))
        {
            SqlCommand cmd = new SqlCommand("UPDATE products
            SET ProductName=@name,QuantityPerUnit=@
            unit,UnitPrice=@price,Discontinued=@discontinued
            WHERE ProductID=@id", conn);
            cmd.Parameters.AddWithValue("@name",
                                    product.ProductName);
            cmd.Parameters.AddWithValue("@unit", product.
                                        QuantityPerUnit);
            cmd.Parameters.AddWithValue(
            "@price", product.UnitPrice);
            cmd.Parameters.AddWithValue("@discontinued",
                                    product.Discontinued);
            cmd.Parameters.AddWithValue("@id",
                                    product.ProductID);
            conn.Open();
            int numRows = cmd.ExecuteNonQuery();
            if (numRows != 1)
                return false;
        }

        return true;
    }
  }
}
```

Adding error handling to the service

In the previous sections, when we were trying to retrieve a product but the product ID passed in was not a valid one, we just threw an exception. Exceptions are technology-specific and therefore are not suitable for crossing the service boundary of SOA-compliant services. All exceptions generate a fault on the communication channel, resulting in unhappy proxies, as a recover and retry is not possible. Thus, for WCF services, we should not throw normal exceptions.

What we need are SOAP faults that meet industry standards for seamless interoperability.

In the service interface layer operations that may throw `FaultExceptions` must be decorated with one or more `FaultContract` attributes, defining the exact `FaultException`.

On the other hand, the service consumer should catch specific `FaultExceptions` to be in a position to handle the specified exceptions.

Adding a fault contract

We will now change the exception in the `GetProduct` operation to a `FaultContract`.

Before we implement our first `FaultContract` we need to modify the `App.config` file in the `RealNorthwindService` project. We will change the setting, `includeExceptionDetailInFaults`, back to `False` so that every unhandled, non-Fault exception will be a violation. Client applications won't know the details of those exceptions.

 You can set `includeExceptionDetailInFaults` to `True` when debugging, as this will be very helpful in diagnosing problems during the development stage. In production, it should always be set to `False`.

Open the `App.config` file in the `RealNorthwindService` project, change `includeExceptionDetailInFaults` from `True` to `False`, and save it.

Next, we will define `FaultContract`. For simplicity, we will define only one `FaultContract` and leave it inside the file, `IProductService.cs`, although in a real system you can have as many `FaultContracts` as you want, and they should also normally be in their own files.

`FaultContract` should be as follows:

```
[DataContract]
public class ProductFault
{
    public ProductFault(string msg)
    {
        FaultMessage = msg;
    }
    [DataMember]
    public string FaultMessage;
}
```

We then decorate the service operation, `GetProduct`, with the following attribute:

```
[FaultContract(typeof(ProductFault))]
```

This is to tell the service consumers that this operation may throw a fault of the type, `ProductFault`.

The content of `IProductService.cs` should now be:

```
using System;
using System.Collections.Generic;
using System.Linq;
using System.Runtime.Serialization;
using System.ServiceModel;
using System.Text;
namespace MyWCFServices.RealNorthwindService
{
    [ServiceContract]
    public interface IProductService
    {
        [OperationContract]
        [FaultContract(typeof(ProductFault))]
        Product GetProduct(int id);

        [OperationContract]
        bool UpdateProduct(Product product);

        // TODO: Add your service operations here
    }
    [DataContract]
    public class Product
    {
        [DataMember]
        public int ProductID;

        [DataMember]
        public string ProductName;

        [DataMember]
        public string QuantityPerUnit;

        [DataMember]
        public decimal UnitPrice;

        [DataMember]
        public bool Discontinued;
    }
    [DataContract]
    public class ProductFault
    {
        public ProductFault(string msg)
        {
            FaultMessage = msg;
        }
```

```
        [DataMember]
        public string FaultMessage;
    }
}
```

Throwing a fault exception

Once we have modified the interface we need to modify the implementation. Open the `ProductService.cs` file and change the following lines:

```
    if (productEntity == null)
        throw new Exception("No product found with id " + id);
```

to these lines:

```
    if (productEntity == null)
    {
        //throw new Exception("No product found with id " + id);
        if (id != 999)
            throw new FaultException<ProductFault>(new ProductFault(
                "No product found with id " + id), "Product Fault");
        else
            throw new Exception("Test Exception");
    }
```

This will throw a `ProductFault` exception if an invalid ID is passed to the `GetProduct` operation. However, we will throw a normal C# exception if the passed ID is 999. Later, we will use this special ID to do an extra test.

Now build the `RealNorthwindService` project. After it has been successfully built, we will use the client that we built earlier to test this service. We will examine the channel status after an exception has been thrown. We can't do this with the WCF Service Test Client because in WCF Test Client, each request will create a new channel and we don't have a way to examine the channel state after the service call.

Updating the client program to catch the fault exception

Now let's update the client program so that the fault exception is handled.

1. First we need to update the service reference because we have changed the contracts for the service. From the `RealNorthwindClient` project, expand the **Service References** node and right-click on **ProductServiceRef**. Select **Update Service Reference** from the context menu and the **Updating Service Reference** dialog box will pop up. The WCF Service Host will be started automatically, and the updated metadata information will be downloaded to the client side. Proxy code will be updated with modified and new service contracts.

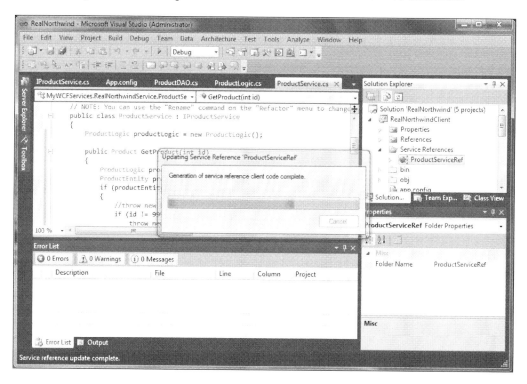

2. Then open `Program.cs` under the `RealNorthwindClient` project and add the following method to the class `Program`:

```
static void TestException(ProductServiceClient client, int
                          id)
{
    Console.WriteLine("\n\nTest {0} Fault Exception for
                      product id {1}...", (id !=
                      999)?"handled":"unhandled", id);
```

```
try
{
    Product product = client.GetProduct(id);
}
catch (TimeoutException ex)
{
    Console.WriteLine("The service operation timed
                      out." + ex.Message);
}
catch (FaultException<ProductFault> ex)
{
    Console.WriteLine("ProductFault: " +
                      ex.ToString());
}
catch (FaultException ex)
{
    Console.WriteLine("Unknown Fault: " +
                      ex.ToString());
}
catch (CommunicationException ex)
{
    Console.WriteLine("There was a communication
                      problem. " + ex.Message +
                      ex.StackTrace);
}
Console.WriteLine("\n\nChannel Status after the
                  exception: " +
                  client.InnerChannel.State.ToString());
Console.WriteLine("Press any key to continue ...");
Console.ReadKey();
}
```

Inside this method we first call GetProduct with a passed-in ID. If the ID is an invalid product ID the service will throw a ProductFault exception. So we have to add the catch statement to catch the ProductFault exception. We examine the channel status after the fault exception. We have also added several other exceptions such as timeout exception, communication exception, and general fault exception, so that we can handle every situation. Note that the order of the catch statements is very important and shouldn't be changed.

If 999 is passed to this method as the ID the service will throw an exception instead of a fault exception. We will also examine the channel status after this unhandled exception.

3. Now add the following statements to the end of the function, `Main`, in this class:

```
TestException(client, 0); // channel is still open after a
                                 FaultException
TestException(client, 999); // channel is Faulted after a
                                 non handled fault exception
Console.WriteLine("\n\nTest Faulted client ...");
product = client.GetProduct(20); // can't use a client with
                                 a Faulted channel
Console.WriteLine("Press any key to continue ...");
Console.ReadLine();
```

So we will first test the `ProductFault` exception, followed by the regular C# exception, and finally we will try to use the faulted channel.

4. You need to add a `using` statement at the beginning of the file:

```
using System.ServiceModel;
```

5. Finally, set the `RealNorthwindClient` project as the startup project.

The full content of `Program.cs` is now as follows:

```
using System;
using System.Collections.Generic;
using System.Linq;
using System.Text;
using RealNorthwindClient.ProductServiceRef;
using System.ServiceModel;

namespace RealNorthwindClient
{
    class Program
    {
        static void Main(string[] args)
        {
            ProductServiceClient client = new ProductServiceClient();

            Product product = client.GetProduct(23);
            Console.WriteLine("product name is " + product.
                                        ProductName);
            Console.WriteLine("product price is " +
                                    product.UnitPrice.ToString());

            product.UnitPrice = (decimal)20.0;
            bool result = client.UpdateProduct(product);
            Console.WriteLine("Update result is " +
                                    result.ToString());
```

```
        TestException(client, 0); // channel is still open after
                                            a FaultException
        TestException(client, 999); // channel is Faulted after a
                                non handled fault exception

        Console.WriteLine("\n\nTest Faulted client ...");
        product = client.GetProduct(20); // can't use a client
                                    with a Faulted channel

        Console.WriteLine("Press any key to continue ...");
        Console.ReadLine();
    }
    static void TestException(
                    ProductServiceClient client, int id)
    {
        Console.WriteLine("\n\nTest {0} Fault Exception for
        product id {1}...", (id != 999)?"handled":"unhandled", id);

        try
        {
            Product product = client.GetProduct(id);
        }
        catch (TimeoutException ex)
        {
            Console.WriteLine("The service operation timed out. "
                                            + ex.Message);
        }
        catch (FaultException<ProductFault> ex)
        {
            Console.WriteLine("ProductFault: " + ex.ToString());
        }
        catch (FaultException ex)
        {
            Console.WriteLine("Unknown Fault: " + ex.ToString());
        }
        catch (CommunicationException ex)
        {
            Console.WriteLine("There was a communication problem.
                        " + ex.Message + ex.StackTrace);
        }
        Console.WriteLine("\n\nChannel Status after the exception:
                    " + client.InnerChannel.State.ToString());
        Console.WriteLine("Press any key to continue ...");
        Console.ReadKey();
    }
}
}
```

Testing the fault exception

Now you can press *F5* to run the client program (remember to set `RealNorthwindClient` to be the startup project). You will get the output shown in the following screenshot:

As you can see from the output, the client channel to the service is still open, after `ProductFault` is handled in the client program. Next, we will use the same client to get the product details for ID 999.

Press *Enter* and more output will be shown, with a `Fault Exception` as shown in the screenshot here:

From the output we know that the channel has now faulted. This means that the client does not now have a valid way to communicate with the service. To prove it press *Enter* to try to connect to the service using the same client object and you will get an unhandled exception **The communication object, System.ServiceModel. Channels.ServiceChannel, cannot be used for communication because it is in the Faulted state**, as shown in the next image. The program will not continue so you have to stop it.

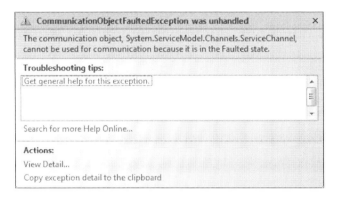

In the source code, if we have to call the service again, we have to abort this client, and create a new one for the communication.

Summary

In this chapter, we have added the third layer—the data access layer—to `RealNorthwindService`. We have also added exception handling to the service. The key points covered in this chapter include:

- Database connection strings should be stored in configuration files, not in C# code

- The data access layer should contain the code to access the underlying databases, it should not contain business logic

- If service contracts have been changed, the client has to update the reference to the service

- You should throw fault contracts instead of exceptions to the client from WCF services

- A handled fault exception won't make a communication channel invalid, but an exception will

6
LINQ—Language Integrated Query

In the previous chapters of this book we created one WCF service with three layers. In the data access layer we used the raw ADO.NET SQL adapters to communicate with the `Northwind` database. In one of the following chapters we will explain how to use LINQ to Entities in our data access layer.

Before using LINQ to Entities in our data access layer we need to understand what LINQ or LINQ to Entities actually mean. Before understanding LINQ, we first need to understand some new C# features related to LINQ. In this chapter we will first explore these new C# features related to LINQ, then we will explore LINQ. In next two chapters we will explore LINQ to Entities, and after that we will apply LINQ to Entities to our WCF service data access layer.

In this chapter we will cover:

- What LINQ is
- New data type `var`
- Automatic properties
- Object initializer and Collection initializer
- Anonymous types
- Extension methods
- Lambda expressions
- Built-in LINQ extension methods and method syntax
- LINQ query syntax and query expression
- Built-in LINQ operators

What is LINQ

Language Integrated Query (LINQ) is a set of extensions to the .NET Framework that encompass language-integrated query, set, and transform operations. It extends C# and Visual Basic with native language syntax for queries and provides class libraries to take advantage of these capabilities.

Let us see an example first. Suppose there is a list of integers like this:

```
List<int> list = new List<int>() { 1, 2, 3, 4, 5, 6, 100 };
```

To find all the even numbers in this list, you might write some code like this:

```
List<int> list1 = new List<int>();
foreach (var num in list)
{
    if (num % 2 == 0)
        list1.Add(num);
}
```

Now with LINQ, you can select all of the even numbers from this list and assign the query result to a variable in just one sentence like this:

```
var list2 = from number in list
            where number % 2 == 0
            select number;
```

In this example `list2` and `list1` are equivalent. `list2` contains the same numbers as `list1` does. As you can see, you don't write a `foreach` loop. Instead you write a SQL statement.

But what do `from`, `where`, and `select` mean here? Where are they defined? How and when can I use them? Let us start the exploration now.

Creating the test solution and project

To show these LINQ-related new features we will need a test project to demonstrate what they are and how to use them. So we first need to create the test solution and the project.

Follow these steps to create the solution and the project.

1. Start Visual Studio 2010.

2. Select menu option **File | New | Project...** to create a new solution.

3. In the **New Project** window, select **Visual C# | Console Application** as the **Template**.

- Enter **TestLINQ** as the **Solution Name** and **TestNewFeaturesApp** as the (project) **Name**.

- Click on **OK** to create the solution and the project.

New data type var

The first new feature that is very important for LINQ is the new data type, var. This is a new keyword that can be used to declare a variable and this variable can be initialized to any valid C# data.

In the C# 3.0 specification such variables are called implicitly-typed local variables.

A var variable must be initialized when it is declared. The compile-time type of the initializer expression must not be of null type but the runtime expression can be null. Once it is initialized its data type is fixed to the type of the initial data.

The following statements are valid uses of the var keyword:

```
// valid var statements
var x = "1";
var n = 0;
string s = "string";
var s2 = s;
s2 = null;
string s3 = null;
var s4 = s3;
```

At compile time, the above var statements are compiled to IL, like this:

```
string x = "1";
int n = 0;
string s2 = s;
string s4 = s3;
```

The var keyword is only meaningful to the Visual Studio compiler. The compiled assembly is actually a valid .NET 2.0 assembly. It doesn't need any special instructions or libraries to support this feature.

The following statements are invalid usages of the var keyword:

```
// invalid var statements
var v;
var nu = null;
var v2 = "12"; v2 = 3;
```

The first one is illegal because it doesn't have an initializer.

The second one initializes variable `nu` to `null`, which is not allowed, although once defined, a `var` type variable can be assigned `null`. If you think that at compile time the compiler needs to create a variable using this type of initializer then you understand why the initializer can't be `null` at compile time.

The third one is illegal because, once defined, an integer can't be converted to a string implicitly (`v2` is of type string).

Automatic properties

In the past, if we wanted to define a class member as a property member, we had to define a private member variable first. For example, for the `Product` class, we can define a property, `ProductName`, as follows:

```
private string productName;
public string ProductName
{
    get { return productName; }
    set { productName = value; }
}
```

This may be useful if we need to add some logic inside the `get` or `set` methods. But if we don't need to the above format gets tedious, especially if there are many members.

Now, with C# 3.0 and above, the previous property can be simplified into one statement:

```
public string ProductName { get; set; }
```

When Visual Studio compiles this statement it will automatically create a private member variable, `productName`, and use the old style's `get` or `set` methods to define the property. This could save lots of typing.

Just as with the new type, `var`, the automatic properties are only meaningful to the Visual Studio compiler. The compiled assembly is actually a valid .NET 2.0 assembly.

Interestingly, later on, if you find you need to add logic to the `get` or `set` methods, you can still convert this automatic property to the old style's property.

Now let us create this class in the test project:

```
public class Product
{
    public int ProductID { get; set; }
    public string ProductName { get; set; }
    public decimal UnitPrice { get; set; }
}
```

We can put this class inside the `Program.cs` file within the namespace, `TestNewFeaturesApp`. We will use this class throughout this chapter to test C# features related to LINQ.

Object initializer

In the past we couldn't initialize an object without using a constructor. For example, we could create and initialize a `Product` object like this if the `Product` class had a constructor with three parameters:

```
Product p = new product(1, "first candy", 100.0);
```

Or we could create the object and then initialize it later, like this:

```
Product p = new Product();
p.ProductID = 1;
p.ProductName = "first candy";
p.UnitPrice=(decimal)100.0;
```

Now with the new **object initializer** feature we can do it as follows:

```
Product product = new Product
{
    ProductID = 1,
    ProductName = "first candy",
    UnitPrice = (decimal)100.0
};
```

At compile time the compiler will automatically insert the necessary property setter code. So again this new feature is a Visual Studio compiler feature. The compiled assembly is actually a valid .NET 2.0 assembly.

We can also define and initialize a variable with an array, like this:

```
var arr = new[] { 1, 10, 20, 30 };
```

This array is called an **implicitly typed array**.

Collection initializer

Similar to the object initializer, we can also initialize a collection when we declare it, like this:

```
List<Product> products = new List<Product> {
    new Product {
        ProductID = 1,
```

```
                    ProductName = "first candy",
                    UnitPrice = (decimal)10.0 },
               new Product {
                    ProductID = 2,
                    ProductName = "second candy",
                    UnitPrice = (decimal)35.0 },
               new Product {
                    ProductID = 3,
                    ProductName = "first vegetable",
                    UnitPrice = (decimal)6.0 },
               new Product {
                    ProductID = 4,
                    ProductName = "second vegetable",
                    UnitPrice = (decimal)15.0 },
               new Product {
                    ProductID = 5,
                    ProductName = "another product",
                    UnitPrice = (decimal)55.0 }
          };
```

Here we created a list and initialized it with five new products. For each new product we used the object initializer to initialize its value.

Just as with the object initializer this new feature, **collection initializer,** is also a Visual Studio compiler feature and the compiled assembly is a valid .NET 2.0 assembly.

Anonymous types

With the new feature of the object initializer and the new `var` data type we can create anonymous data types easily in C# 3.0.

For example, if we define a variable like this:

```
var a = new { Name = "name1", Address = "address1" };
```

at compile time, the compiler will actually create an anonymous type, as follows:

```
class __Anonymous1
{
    private string name;
    private string address;
    public string Name {
        get{
            return name;
        }
```

```
            set {
                name=value
            }
        }
        public string Address {
            get{
                return address;
            }
            set{
                address=value;
            }
        }
    }
```

The name of the anonymous type is automatically generated by the compiler and cannot be referenced in the program text.

If two anonymous types have the same members with the same data types in their initializers, then these two variables have the same types. For example if there is another variable defined like this:

```
    var b = new { Name = "name2", Address = "address2" };
```

then we can assign a to b like this:

```
    b = a;
```

The anonymous type is particularly useful for LINQ when the result of LINQ can be shaped to be whatever you like. We will give more examples of this when we discuss LINQ.

As mentioned earlier, this new feature is again a Visual Studio compiler feature and the compiled assembly is a valid .NET 2.0 assembly.

Extension methods

Extension methods are static methods that can be invoked using the instance method syntax. In effect extension methods make it possible for us to extend existing types and constructed types with additional methods.

For example, we can define an extension method as follows:

```
        public static class MyExtensions
        {
            public static bool IsCandy(this Product p)
            {
```

```
          if (p.ProductName.IndexOf("candy") >= 0)
              return true;
          else
              return false;
      }
  }
```

In this example the static method, `IsCandy`, takes a `this` parameter of `Product` type and searches for the word, `candy`, inside the product name. If it finds a match it assumes this is a `candy` product and returns `true`. Otherwise it returns `false`, meaning this is not a `candy` product.

Because all extension methods must be defined in top-level static classes here to simplify the example, we put this class inside the same namespace as our main test application, `TestNewFeaturesApp`, and made this class on the same level as the `Program` class so that it is a top level class. Now, in the program, we can call this extension method like this:

```
  if (product.IsCandy())
      Console.WriteLine("yes, it is a candy");
  else
      Console.WriteLine("no, it is not a candy");
```

It looks as if `IsCandy` is a real instance method of the `Product` class. Actually it is a real method of the `Product` class but it is not defined inside the `Product` class. Instead it is defined in another static class to extend the functionality of the `Product` class. This is why it is called an extension method.

Not only does it look like a real instance method but this new extension method actually pops up when a dot is typed following the `product` variable. The following image shows the IntelliSense of the `product` variable within Visual Studio.

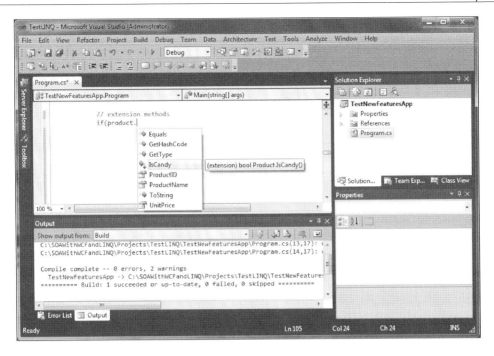

Under the hood in Visual Studio, when a method call on an instance is being compiled, the compiler first checks to see if there is an instance method in the class for this method. If there is no matching instance method it looks for an imported static class or any static class within the same namespace. It also searches for an extension method with the first parameter that is the same as the instance type (or is a super type of the instance type). If it finds a match the compiler will call that extension method. This means that instance methods take precedence over extension methods, and extension methods that are imported in inner namespace declarations take precedence over extension methods that are imported in outer namespaces.

In our example, when `product.IsCandy()` is being compiled the compiler first checks the `Product` class and doesn't find a method named `IsCandy`. It then searches the static class, `MyExtensions`, and finds an extension method with the name, `IsCandy`, and with a first parameter of the type `Product`.

At compile time the compiler actually changes `product.IsCandy()` to this call:

```
MyExtensions.IsCandy(product)
```

Surprisingly, extension methods can be defined for sealed classes. In our example you can change the `Product` class to be sealed and it still runs without any problem. This gives us great flexibility to extend system types because many of the system types are sealed.

On the other hand, extension methods are less discoverable and are harder to maintain, so they should be used with great caution. If your requirements can be achieved with an instance method you should not define an extension method to do the same work.

Not surprisingly, this new feature is again a Visual Studio compiler feature and the compiled assembly is a valid .NET 2.0 assembly.

Extension methods are the bases of LINQ. We will discuss the various extension methods defined by .NET 3.5 in the namespace, `System.Linq`, later.

Now the `Program.cs` file should be like this:

```
using System;
using System.Collections.Generic;
using System.Linq;
using System.Text;

namespace TestNewFeaturesApp
{
    class Program
    {
        static void Main(string[] args)
        {
            // valid var statements
            var x = "1";
            var n = 0;
            string s = "string";
            var s2 = s;
            s2 = null;
            string s3 = null;
            var s4 = s3;
            /*
            string x = "1";
            int n = 0;
            string s2 = s;
            string s4 = s3;
            */

            // invalid var statements
            /*
            var v;
            var nu = null;
            var v2 = "12"; v2 = 3;
            */

            // old way to create and initialize an object
            /*
```

```
Product p = new product(1, "first candy", 100.0);
Product p = new Product();
p.ProductID = 1;
p.ProductName = "first candy";
p.UnitPrice=(decimal)100.0;
*/
//object initializer

Product product = new Product
{
    ProductID = 1,
    ProductName = "first candy",
    UnitPrice = (decimal)100.0
};
var arr = new[] { 1, 10, 20, 30 };

// collection initializer
List<Product> products = new List<Product> {
    new Product {
        ProductID = 1,
        ProductName = "first candy",
        UnitPrice = (decimal)10.0 },
    new Product {
        ProductID = 2,
        ProductName = "second candy",
        UnitPrice = (decimal)35.0 },
    new Product {
        ProductID = 3,
        ProductName = "first vegetable",
        UnitPrice = (decimal)6.0 },
    new Product {
        ProductID = 4,
        ProductName = "second vegetable",
        UnitPrice = (decimal)15.0 },
    new Product {
        ProductID = 5,
        ProductName = "third product",
        UnitPrice = (decimal)55.0 }
};
// anonymous types
var a = new { Name = "name1", Address = "address1" };
var b = new { Name = "name2", Address = "address2" };
b = a;
/*
class __Anonymous1
```

```
        {
            private string name;
            private string address;
            public string Name {
                get{
                    return name;
                }
                set {
                    name=value
                }
            }
            public string Address {
                get{
                    return address;
                }
                set{
                    address=value;
                }
            }
        }
        */

        // extension methods
        if (product.IsCandy()) //if(MyExtensions.IsCandy(product))
            Console.WriteLine("yes, it is a candy");
        else
            Console.WriteLine("no, it is not a candy");
    }
}


public sealed class Product
{
    public int ProductID { get; set; }
    public string ProductName { get; set; }
    public decimal UnitPrice { get; set; }
}
public static class MyExtensions
{
    public static bool IsCandy(this Product p)
    {
        if (p.ProductName.IndexOf("candy") >= 0)
            return true;
        else
            return false;
    }
}
}
```

So far in `Program.cs`, we have

- Defined several `var` type variables
- Defined a sealed class, `Product`
- Created a product with the name of "first candy"
- Created a product list containing five products
- Defined a static class and added a static method, `IsCandy`, with a `this` parameter of the type, `Product`, to it, making this method an extension method
- Called the extension method on the `candy` product and printed out a message according to its name

If you run the program the output will look like this:

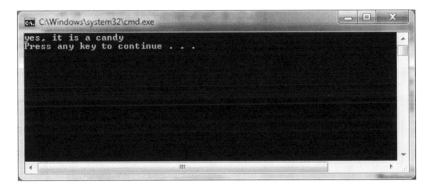

Lambda expressions

With the C# 3.0 new feature extension method and the C# 2.0 new feature anonymous method (or inline method), Visual Studio introduces a new expression called **lambda expression**.

Lambda expression is actually a syntax change for anonymous methods. It is just a new way of writing anonymous methods. Next, let's explain what a lambda expression is, step by step.

First, in C# 3.0, there is a new generic delegate type, `Func<A,R>`, which presents a function taking an argument of type `A` and returns a value of type `R`:

```
delegate R Func<A,R> (A Arg);
```

In fact there are several overloaded versions of `Func` of which `Func<A,R>` is one.

Now we will use this new generic delegate type to define an extension:

```
public static IEnumerable<T> Get<T>(this IEnumerable<T> source,
Func<T, bool> predicate)
{
    foreach (T item in source)
    {
        if (predicate(item))
            yield return item;
    }
}
```

This extension method will apply to an object that extends the `IEnumerable` interface and has one parameter of type, `Func`, which you can think of as a pointer to a function. This parameter function is the predicate to specify the criteria for the selection. This method will return a list of objects that match the predicate criteria.

Now we can create a new function as the predicate:

```
public static bool IsVege(Product p)
{
    return p.ProductName.Contains("vegetable");
}
```

Then we can use the extension method, `Get`, to retrieve all of the vegetable products, like this:

```
var veges1 = products.Get(IsVege);
```

In previous sections we created a products list with five products of which two are vegetables. So `veges1` is actually of the `IEnumerable<Product>` type and should contain two products. We can write the following test statements to print out the results:

```
Console.WriteLine("\nThere are {0} vegetables:", veges1.Count());
foreach (Product p in veges1)
{
    Console.WriteLine("Product ID: {0}  Product name: {1}",
                        p.ProductID, p.ProductName);
}
```

The output will be:

Or we can first create a new variable of type, Func, assign the function pointer of IsVege to this new variable and then pass this new variable to the Get method like this:

```
Func<Product, bool> predicate = IsVege;
var veges2 = products.Get(predicate);
```

The Variable, veges2, will contain the same products as veges1.

Now let us use the C# 2.0 anonymous method to rewrite the above statement which will now become:

```
var veges3 = products.Get(
    delegate (Product p)
    {
        return p.ProductName.Contains("vegetable");
    }
);
```

At this time we put the body of the predicate method, IsVege, inside the extension method call with the keyword, delegate. In order to get the vegetables from the products list we don't have to define a specific predicate method. We can specify the criteria on the spot when we need it.

The lambda expression comes into play right after the above step. In C# 3.0, with lambda expression, we can actually write the following one line statement to retrieve all of the vegetables from the products list:

```
var veges4 = products.Get(p => p.ProductName.Contains("vegetable"));
```

In the above statement the parameter of the method, `Get`, is a lambda expression. The first `p` is the parameter of the lambda expression, just like the parameter `p` in the anonymous method when we get `veges3`. This parameter is implicitly typed and, in this case, is of the type, `Product`, because this expression is applied to a `Products` object which contains a list of `Product` objects. This parameter can also be explicitly typed like this:

```
var veges5 = products.Get((Product p) => p.ProductName.
Contains("vegetable"));
```

The parameter is followed by the `=>` token and then followed by an expression or a statement block which will be the predicate.

So now we can easily write the following statement to get all of the `candy` products:

```
var candies = products.Get(p => p.ProductName.Contains("candy"));
```

At compile time all lambda expressions are translated into anonymous methods according to the lambda expression conversion rules. So again this feature is only a Visual Studio feature. We don't need any special .NET runtime library or instructions to run an assembly containing lambda expressions.

In short, lambda expressions are just another way of writing anonymous methods in a more concise, functional syntax.

Built-in LINQ extension methods and method syntax

.NET framework 3.5 defines lots of extension methods in the namespace, `System.Linq`, including `Where`, `Select`, `SelectMany`, `OrderBy`, `OrderByDescending`, `ThenBy`, `ThenByDescending`, `GroupBy`, `Join`, and `GroupJoin`.

We can use these extension methods just as we would use our own extension methods. For example, we can use the `Where` extension method to get all vegetables from the `Products` list, like this:

```
var veges6 = products.Where(p => p.ProductName.Contains("vegetable"));
```

This will give us the same result as `veges1` through `veges5`.

As a matter of fact the definition of the built-in LINQ extension method, `Where`, is just like our extension method, `Get`, but in a different namespace:

```
namespace System.Linq
{
```

```
public static class Enumerable
{
    public static IEnumerable<T> Where<T>(this IEnumerable<T>
                          source, Func<T, bool> predicate)
    {
        foreach (T item in source)
        {
            if (predicate(item))
                yield return item;
        }
    }
}
```

The statements that use LINQ extension methods are called using the LINQ method syntax.

Unlike the other C# 3.0 new features that we have talked about in previous sections, these LINQ-specific extension methods are defined in .NET framework 3.5. So, to run an assembly containing any of these methods you need .NET framework 3.5 or above installed.

LINQ query syntax and query expression

With built-in LINQ extension methods and lambda expressions, Visual Studio allows us to write SQL-like statements in C# when invoking these methods. The syntax of these statements is called **LINQ query syntax** and the expression in query syntax is called a **query expression**.

For example we can change this statement:

```
var veges6 = products.Where(p => p.ProductName.Contains("vegetable"));
```

to the following query statement by using the new LINQ query syntax:

```
var veges7 = from p in products
             where p.ProductName.Contains("vegetable")
             select p;
```

In the above C# statement we can directly use the SQL keywords, `select`, `from`, and `where`, to "query" an in-memory collection list. In addition to the in-memory collection lists we can use the same syntax to manipulate data in XML files, in the dataset, and in the database. In the following chapters we will see how to query a database using LINQ to Entities.

Combined with the anonymous data type, we can shape the result of the query in the following statement:

```
var candyOrVeges = from p in products
                where p.ProductName.Contains("candy")
                    || p.ProductName.Contains("vegetable")
                orderby p.UnitPrice descending, p.ProductID
                select new { p.ProductName, p.UnitPrice };
```

As you have seen, query syntax is a very convenient, declarative shorthand for expressing queries using the standard LINQ query operators. It offers a syntax that increases the readability and clarity of expressing queries in code and can be easy to read and write correctly.

Not only is query syntax easy to read and write, Visual Studio actually provides complete IntelliSense and compile-time checking support for query syntax. For example, when typing in p and the following dot, we get all of the Product members listed in the IntelliSense list, as shown in the following screenshot:

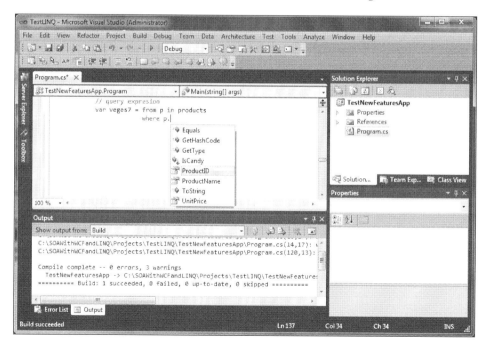

If there is a typo in the syntax (as is the case in this statement: `where p.productName.Contains("vegetable")`, the compiler will tell you exactly where the mistake is and why it is wrong. There won't be any run-time error such as "invalid SQL statement". The following screenshot shows the error message when there is a typo in the statement:

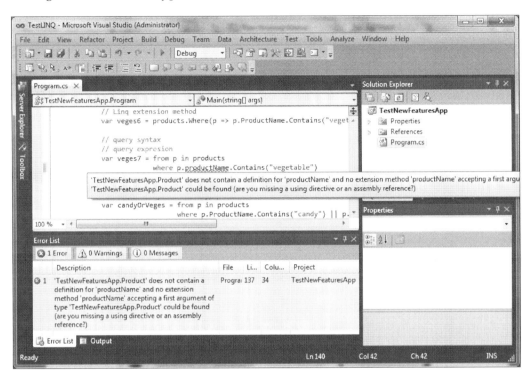

As you can see, you can write a LINQ statement in the query syntax, much like when you are working with a database in Query Analyzer. However, the .NET **Common Language Runtime (CLR)** has no notion itself of the query syntax. Therefore, at compile time, query expressions are translated to something that the CLR does understand: **method calls**. Under the covers, the compiler takes the query syntax expressions and translates them into explicit method-invocation code that utilizes the new LINQ Extension Method and lambda expression language features in C# 3.0.

For example, the `candyOrVeges` query expression will be translated to this method invocation call:

```
products.Where(p => p.ProductName.Contains("candy") || p.ProductName.
Contains("vegetable")).OrderByDescending(p => p.UnitPrice).
ThenBy(p=>p.ProductID).Select(p=>new { p.ProductName, p.UnitPrice })
```

You can print out and compare the results for using query syntax and method syntax to make sure they are equivalent. The following statements will print out the product name and unit price for the products in the query result using query syntax:

```
foreach (var p in candyOrVeges)
{
    Console.WriteLine("{0} {1}", p.ProductName, p.UnitPrice);
}
```

Do the same for the results using method syntax and you will get a printout like this:

In general query syntax is recommended over method syntax because it is usually simpler and more readable. However, there is no semantic difference between method syntax and query syntax.

Built-in LINQ operators

As we have seen in previous sections, there are no semantic differences between method syntax and query syntax. In addition, some queries such as those that retrieve the number of elements matching a specified condition or those that retrieve the element that has the maximum value in a source sequence, can be expressed only as method calls. These kinds of methods are sometimes referred to as **.NET Standard Query Operators** and include `Take`, `ToList`, `FirstOrDefault`, and `Max` and `Min`.

In addition to those methods that can only be expressed as method calls, all the extension methods that can be used in either query syntax or method syntax are also defined as standard query operators such as `select`, `where`, and `from`. So the .NET Standard Query Operators contains all of the LINQ-related methods.

A complete list of these operators can be found at the Microsoft MSDN library for the class, `System.Linq.Enumerable`.

To have a quick look at all those operators, open the `program.cs` file in Visual Studio and type in **System.Linq.Enumerable**. Then type in a dot after **Enumerable**. You will see the whole list of operators in the IntelliSense menu.

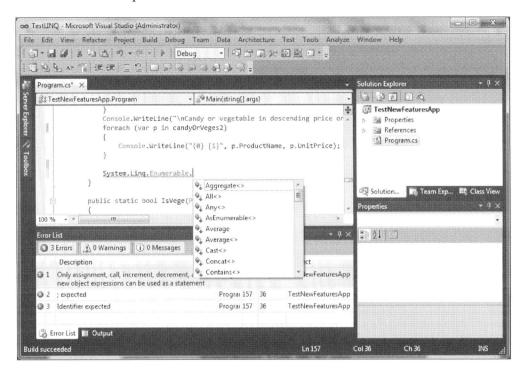

The methods in this static class provide an implementation of the standard query operators for querying data sources that implement IEnumerable<(Of <(T>)>). The standard query operators are general-purpose methods that follow the LINQ pattern and enable you to express traversal, filter, and projection operations over data in any .NET-based programming language.

The majority of the methods in this class are defined as extension methods that extend IEnumerable<(Of <(T>)>). This means that they can be called like an instance method on any object that implements IEnumerable<(Of <(T>)>).

Summary

In this chapter, we have learned new features related to LINQ including the new data type, `var`, object and collection initializers, extension methods, lambda expressions, LINQ syntax, and query expressions. Now that we have the required knowledge for LINQ, we are ready to try LINQ to Entities, which will be discussed in the next chapters.

The key points covered in this chapter include:

- The new data type, `var`, gives extra flexibility when defining new variables
- The Automatic Property feature can be used to define simple properties
- Initial values can be assigned to a new object and collection variables by using Object initializer and Collection initializer
- Actual types will be created for anonymous types at compile time
- Extension methods can be used to extend the public contract of an existing CLR type without having to subclass or recompile the original type
- Lambda expression is just another way of writing anonymous methods in a more concise and functional syntax
- Many LINQ-specific extension methods have been pre-defined in .NET framework 3.5
- All .NET Standard LINQ Query Operators are defined in the static class, `System.Linq.Enumerable`
- LINQ query syntax can be used to make expressions in method syntax but there is no semantic difference between the method syntax and the query syntax
- Some LINQ queries can only be expressed in method calls

7
LINQ to Entities: Basic Concepts and Features

In the previous chapter, we learned new features of C# 3.0 including LINQ. In this chapter and the next, we will explain how to use LINQ to query a database, or in other words, how to use LINQ to Entities in C#. After reading these two chapters we will have a good understanding of LINQ to Entities so that we can rewrite the data access layer of our WCF service with LINQ to Entities, to securely and reliably communicate with the underlying database.

In this chapter, we will cover the basic concepts and features of LINQ to Entities, which include:

- What ORM is
- What LINQ to Entities is
- What LINQ to SQL is
- Comparing LINQ to Entities with LINQ to Objects and LINQ to SQL
- Modeling the `Northwind` database with LINQ to Entities
- Querying and updating a database with a table
- Deferred execution
- Lazy loading and eager loading
- Joining two tables
- Querying with a view

In the next chapter, we will cover the advanced concepts and features of LINQ to Entities such as stored procedure support, inheritance, simultaneous updating, and transaction processing.

ORM—Object-Relational Mapping

LINQ to Entities is considered to be one of Microsoft's new ORM products. So before we start explaining LINQ to Entities let us first understand what ORM is.

ORM stands for **Object-Relational Mapping**. Sometimes it is called O/RM or O/R mapping. It is a programming technique that contains a set of classes that map relational database entities to objects in a specific programming language.

Initially applications could call specified, native database APIs to communicate with a database. For example, `Oracle Pro*C` is a set of APIs supplied by Oracle to query, insert, update, or delete records in an Oracle database from C applications. The `Pro*C` pre-compiler translates embedded SQL into calls to the Oracle runtime library (SQLLIB).

Then **ODBC (Open Database Connectivity)** was developed to unify all of the communication protocols for various RDBMS. ODBC was designed to be independent of programming languages, database systems, and operating systems. So with ODBC, one application can communicate with different RDBMS by using the same code simply by replacing the underlying ODBC drivers.

No matter which method is used to connect to a database the data returned from a database has to be presented in some format in the application. For example, if an `Order` record is returned from the database, there has to be a variable to hold the `Order` number and a set of variables to hold the `Order` details. Alternatively the application may create a class for `Orders` and another class for `Order` details. When another application is developed the same set of classes may have to be created again, or, if it is designed well, they can be put into a library and reused by various applications.

This is exactly where ORM fits in. With ORM, each database is represented by an ORM context object in the specific programming language and database entities such as tables are represented by classes with relationships between these classes. For example, ORM may create an `Order` class to represent the `Order` table and an `OrderDetail` class to represent the `Order Details` table. The `Order` class will contain a collection member to hold all of its details. ORM is responsible for the mappings and the connections between these classes and the database. So, to the application, the database is now fully represented by these classes. The application only needs to deal with these classes, instead of with the physical database. The application does not need to worry about how to connect to the database, how to construct the SQL statements, how to use the proper locking mechanism to ensure concurrency, or how to handle distributed transactions. These database-related activities are handled by ORM.

Entity Framework

Since LINQ to Entities is based on Entity Framework, let's explain what Entity Framework is now.

ADO.NET **Entity Framework (EF)** is a new addition to the Microsoft ADO.NET family. It enables developers to create data access applications by programming against a conceptual application model instead of programming directly against a relational storage schema. The goal is to decrease the amount of code and maintenance required for data-oriented applications. Entity Framework applications provide the following benefits:

- Applications can work in terms of a more application-centric conceptual model including types with inheritance, complex members, and relationships

- Applications are freed from hardcoded dependencies on a particular data engine or storage schema

- Mappings between the conceptual model and the storage-specific schema can change without changing the application code

- Developers can work with a consistent application object model that can be mapped to various storage schemas, possibly implemented in different database management systems

- Multiple conceptual models can be mapped to a single storage schema

- **Language Integrated Query (LINQ)** support provides compile-time syntax validation for queries against a conceptual model

With Entity Framework, developers work with a conceptual data model, an Entity Data Model, or EDM, instead of the underlying databases. The conceptual data model schema is expressed in the **Conceptual Schema Definition Language** (CSDL), the actual storage model is expressed in the **Storage Schema Definition Language** (SSDL), and the mapping in between is expressed in the **Mapping Schema Language** (MSL). A new data-access provider, EntityClient, is created for this new framework, but under the hood, the ADO.NET data providers are still being used to communicate with the databases.

The following diagram shows the high-level architectures of
Entity Framework.

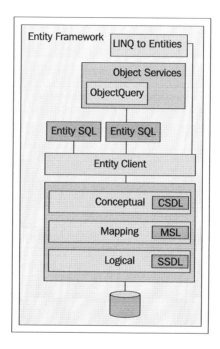

LINQ to Entities

Now let's have a look at what LINQ to Entities is.

LINQ to Entities provides Language Integrated Query (LINQ) support that enables
developers to write queries against Entity Framework conceptual model using
Visual Basic or Visual C#. Queries against the Entity Framework are represented
by command-tree queries which execute against the object context. LINQ to Entities
converts Language Integrated Queries (LINQ) queries to command-tree queries,
executes the queries against Entity Framework, and returns objects that can be
used by both Entity Framework and LINQ.

LINQ to Entities allows developers to create flexible, strongly-typed queries against
the **Entity Data Model (EDM)** by using LINQ expressions and standard LINQ query
operators. To certain degrees, LINQ to Entities is similar to LINQ to SQL, but LINQ
to Entities is a true ORM product from Microsoft and it supports more features than
LINQ to SQL, such as multiple-table inheritance. LINQ to Entities also supports many
other mainstream RDBMS databases such as Oracle, DB2, and MySQL, in addition to
Microsoft SQL Server.

Comparing LINQ to Entities with LINQ to Objects

In the previous chapter, we used LINQ to query in-memory objects. Before we dive further into the world of LINQ to Entities we first need to look at the relationships between LINQ to Entities and LINQ to Objects.

Some key differences between LINQ to Entities and LINQ to Objects are:

- LINQ to Entities needs an Object Context object. The `ObjectContext` object is the bridge between LINQ and the database (we will explain more about `ObjectContext` later). LINQ to Objects doesn't need any intermediate LINQ provider or API.
- LINQ to Entities returns data of type, `IQueryable<T>`, whereas LINQ to Objects returns data of type, `IEnumerable<T>`.
- LINQ to Entities queries are translated to SQL by way of Expression Trees, which allow them to be evaluated as a single unit and translated to appropriate and optimal SQL Statements. LINQ to Objects queries do not need to be translated.
- LINQ to Entities queries are translated to SQL calls and executed on the specified database, while LINQ to Objects queries are executed in the local machine memory.

The similarities shared by all aspects of LINQ are the syntax. They all use the same SQL-like syntax and share the same groups of standard query operators. From the language syntax perspective working with a database is the same as working with in-memory objects.

LINQ to SQL

Before LINQ to Entities Microsoft released another ORM product, LINQ to SQL. Both LINQ to SQL and LINQ to Entities can be used in the data access layer to interact with databases but they are quite different. In this section we will explain what LINQ to SQL is and in the next section we will compare these two technologies.

In short, LINQ to SQL is a component of the .NET framework 3.5 that provides a run-time infrastructure for managing relational data as objects.

In LINQ to SQL the data model of a relational database is mapped to an object model expressed in the programming language of the developer. When the application runs LINQ to SQL translates the language-integrated queries in the object model into SQL and sends them to the database for execution. When the database returns the results LINQ to SQL translates the results back to objects that you can work with in your own programming language.

Unlike LINQ to Entities, with LINQ to SQL developers don't need to create an extra data model between their applications and the underlying database. Under the hood of LINQ to SQL, ADO.NET `SqlClient` adapters are used to communicate with the actual SQL Server databases.

The following diagram shows the use of LINQ to SQL in a .NET application:

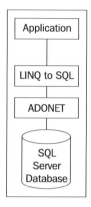

Comparing LINQ to SQL with LINQ to Entities

Now we know what LINQ to Entities is and what LINQ to SQL is. Next in this section, let's compare these two technologies.

As described earlier, LINQ to Entities applications work against a conceptual data model (EDM). All mappings between the languages and the databases go through the new `EntityClient` mapping provider. The application no longer connects directly to a database or sees any database-specific constructs. The entire application operates in terms of the higher level EDM.

This means that you can no longer use the native database query language. Not only will the database not understand the EDM model, but also current database query languages do not have the constructs required to deal with the elements introduced by EDM such as inheritance, relationships, complex-types, and so on.

On the other hand, for developers who do not require mapping to a conceptual model LINQ to SQL enables developers to experience the LINQ programming model directly over existing database schema.

LINQ to SQL allows developers to generate .NET classes that represent data. Rather than map to a conceptual data model these generated classes map directly to database tables, views, stored procedures, and user-defined functions. Using LINQ to SQL, developers can write code directly against the storage schema using the same LINQ programming pattern as was previously described for in-memory collections, Entities, or the Data Set, as well as for other data sources such as XML.

Compared to LINQ to Entities, LINQ to SQL has some limitations, mainly because of its direct mapping against the physical relational storage schema. For example, you can't map two different database entities into one single C# or VB object and if the underlying database schema changes this might require significant client application changes.

In a summary, if you want to work against a conceptual data model use LINQ to Entities. If you want to have a direct mapping to the database from your programming languages use LINQ to SQL.

The following table lists some of the features supported by these two data access methodologies:

Features	LINQ to SQL	LINQ to Entities
Conceptual Data Model	No	Yes
Storage Schema	No	Yes
Mapping Schema	No	Yes
New Data Access Provider	No	Yes
Non-SQL Server Database Support	No	Yes
Direct Database Connection	Yes	No
Language Extensions Support	Yes	Yes
Stored Procedures	Yes	Yes
Single-table Inheritance	Yes	Yes
Multiple-table Inheritance	No	Yes
Single Entity from Multiple Tables	No	Yes
Lazy Loading Support	Yes	Yes

Interestingly some say LINQ to SQL was an intermediate solution. The fact is that LINQ to SQL was made by the C# team instead of the ADO.NET team. It was of great importance for the C# team to release an O/RM mapper together with their new LINQ technology. Without a LINQ to databases implementation the C# team would have had a hard time evangelizing LINQ.

In November 2008 the ADO.NET team announced that Microsoft would continue to make some investments in LINQ to SQL but they also made it pretty clear that LINQ to Entities is the recommended data access solution in future frameworks. Microsoft will invest heavily in the Entity framework. So in this book we will use LINQ to Entities in our data access layer.

Creating a LINQ to Entities test application

Now that we have explained some of the basic concepts of LINQ to Entities let us start exploring LINQ to Entities with some real examples. We will apply the skills we are going to learn in the following two chapters to the data access layer of our WCF service so that from the WCF service we can communicate with the database using LINQ to Entities instead of the raw ADO.NET data adapter.

First we need to create a new project to test LINQ to Entities. Just follow these steps to add this test application to the solution:

1. Open the solution, `TestLINQ`.

2. From Solution Explorer, right-click on the **Solution** item and select **Add | New Project…** from the context menu.

3. Select **Visual C# | Console Application** as the project template, enter **TestLINQToEntitiesApp** as the (project) **Name**, and leave the default value **C:\SOAWithWCFandLINQ\Projects\TestLINQ** as the **Location**.

4. Click on **OK**.

Creating the Data Model

To use LINQ to Entities we need to add a conceptual data model—an **Entity Data Model** or **EDM**—to the project. There are two ways to create the EDM: create from a database, or create manually. Here we will create the EDM from the `Northwind` database. We will add two tables and one view from the `Northwind` database into our project so that later on we can use them to demonstrate LINQ to Entities.

Adding a LINQ to Entities item to the project

To start with let us add a new item to our project: `TestLINQToEntitiesApp`. The new item added should be of the **ADO.NET Entity Data Model** type and named **Northwind.edmx**, as shown in the following **Add New Item** dialog window:

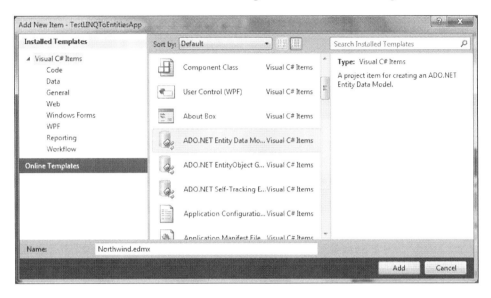

After you click on the **Add** button the Entity Data Model Wizard window will pop up. Follow these steps to finish this wizard:

1. On the **Choose Model Contents** page, select **Generate from database**. Later we will connect to the `Northwind` database and let Visual Studio generate the conceptual data model for us. If you choose the **Empty model** option here you will have to manually create the data model which may be applicable in certain circumstances like when you do not have a physical database while you do the modeling. You can even create your physical database from your model later if you choose this option and have finished your model.

2. Click on the **Next** button on this window.

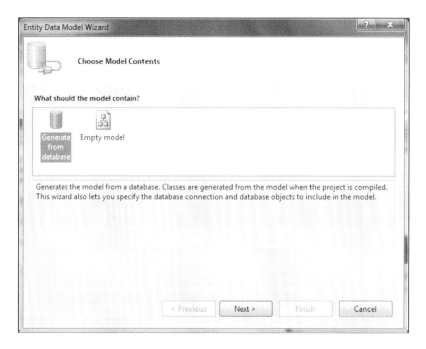

3. Now the **Choose Your Data Connection** window should be displayed. As this is our first LINQ to Entities application there is no existing data connection to choose from, so let's click on the button **New Connection...** and set up a new data connection.

   ○ First choose **Microsoft SQL Server** as the data source and leave **.NET Framework Data Provider for SQL Server** as the data provider. Click on the **OK** button to close this window.

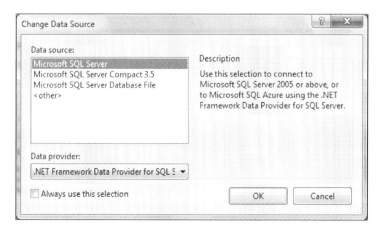

- ○ The **Connection Properties** window should be displayed next on the screen. On this window enter your database server name together with your database instance name if your database instance is not the default one on your server. If it is on your machine you can enter **localhost** as the server name.

- ○ Then specify the login details to your database.

- ○ Click on the **Test Connection** button to test your database connection settings. You should get a **Test connection succeeded** message. If not, modify your server name or login details and make sure your SQL Server service is started. If your SQL Server is on another computer and your firewall is turned on remember to enable the SQL Server port on the SQL Server machine.

- ○ Now select **Northwind** as the database name. If you don't see **Northwind** in the database list you need to install it to your SQL server (refer to the previous chapter for installation details).

The **Connection Properties** window should be like this now:

     °   Click on the **OK** button on the **Connection Properties** window to go back to the **Entity Data Model Wizard**.

The **Entity Data Model Wizard** should be like this now:

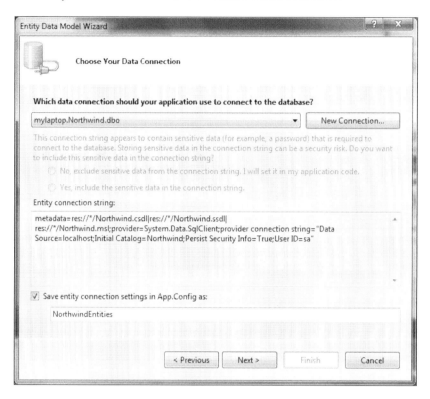

4. On the **Choose Your Database Objects** page, select table **Products**, **Categories** and view **Current Product List**, then click on the **Finish** button:

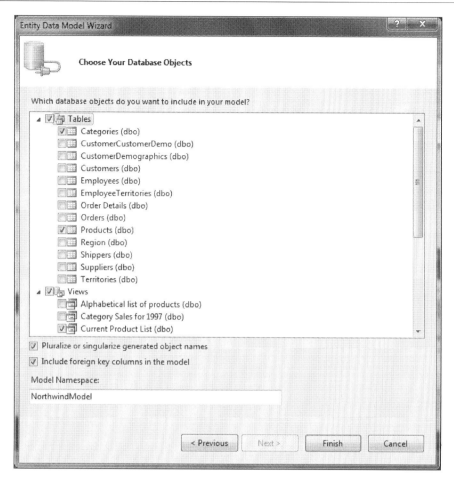

After you click on the **Finish** button the following two files will be added to the project: **Northwind.edmx** and **Northwind.designer.cs**. The first file holds the model of the entities including the entity sets, entity types, conceptual models, and the mappings. The second one is the code for the model which defines the ObjectContext of the model.

At this point the Visual Studio LINQ to Entities designer should be open, as shown in the following image:

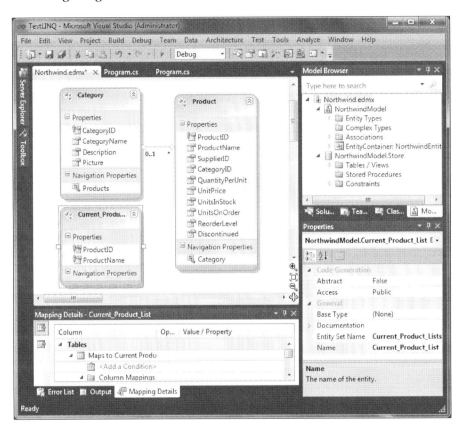

Generated LINQ to Entities classes

If you open the file, `Northwind.Designer.cs` (you need to switch from the Model Browser to Solution Explorer to open this file), you will find that the following classes have been generated for the project:

```
public partial class NorthwindEntities : ObjectContext
public partial class Product : EntityObject
public partial class Category : EntityObject
public partial class Current_Product_List : EntityObject
```

In the above four classes, the `NorthwindEntities` class is the main conduit through which we'll query entities from the database as well as apply changes back to it. It contains various flavors of types and constructors, partial validation methods, and property members for all of the included tables. It inherits from the `ObjectContext` class which represents the main entry point for the LINQ to Entities framework.

The next two classes are for the two tables that we are interested in. They implement the `EntityObject` interface. This interface defines all of the related property changing and property changed event methods which we can extend to validate properties before and after the change.

The last class is for the view. This is a simple class with only two property members. Because we are not going to update the database through this view it doesn't define any property change or changed event method.

Querying and updating the database with a table

Now that we have the entity classes created, we will use them to interact with the database. We will first work with the `products` table to query and update records as well as to insert and delete records.

Querying records

First we will query the database to get some products.

To query a database using LINQ to Entities we first need to construct an `ObjectContext` object, like this:

```
NorthwindEntities NWEntities = new NorthwindEntities();
```

We can then use LINQ query syntax to retrieve records from the database:

```
IEnumerable<Product> beverages = from p in NWEntities.Products
                    where p.Category.CategoryName == "Beverages"
                    orderby p.ProductName
                    select p;
```

The preceding code will retrieve all of the products in the `Beverages` category sorted by product name.

You can use this statement to print out the total number of beverage products in the `Northwind` database:

```
Console.WriteLine("There are {0} Beverages", beverages.Count());
```

Updating records

We can update any of the products that we have just retrieved from the database, like this:

```
// update a product
Product bev1 = beverages.ElementAtOrDefault(10);
if (bev1 != null)
{
    decimal newPrice = (decimal)bev1.UnitPrice + 10.00m;
    Console.WriteLine("The price of {0} is {1}. Update to {2}",
                bev1.ProductName, bev1.UnitPrice, newPrice);
    bev1.UnitPrice = newPrice;
    // submit the change to database
    NWEntities.SaveChanges();
}
```

We used the `ElementAtOrDefault` method, not the `ElementAt` method, just in case there was no product at element 10. We know that there are 12 beverage products in the sample database so we increased the eleventh product's price by 10.00 and called `NWEntities.SaveChanges()` to update the record in the database. After you run the program, if you query the database, you will find that the eleventh beverage's price is increased by 10.00.

Inserting records

We can also create a new product and then insert this new product into the database by using the following code:

```
// add a product
Product newProduct = new Product {ProductName="new test product" };
NWEntities.Products.AddObject(newProduct);
NWEntities.SaveChanges();
Console.WriteLine("Added a new product with name
                'new test product'");
```

Deleting records

To delete a product we first need to retrieve it from the database and then call the `DeleteObject` method, as shown in the following code:

```
// delete a product
IQueryable<Product> productsToDelete =
                from p in NWEntities.Products
                where p.ProductName == "new test product"
```

```
                    select p;
    if (productsToDelete.Count() > 0)
    {
        foreach (var p in productsToDelete)
        {
            NWEntities.DeleteObject(p);
            Console.WriteLine("Deleted product {0}", p.ProductID);
        }
        NWEntities.SaveChanges();
    }
```

Note that here we used a variable of the type, IQueryable<Product>, instead of IEnumerable<Product>, to hold the result of the LINQ to Entities query. Since IQueryable extends the interface, IEnumerable, we can use either one of them though with IQueryable we can do much more, as we will see in next section.

Running the program

The file, Program.cs, has been used so far. Note that we added one method to contain all of the test cases for table operations. We will add more methods later to test other LINQ to Entities functionalities. The following is the content of this file now.

```
using System;
using System.Collections.Generic;
using System.Linq;
using System.Text;

namespace TestLINQToEntitiesApp
{
    class Program
    {
        static void Main(string[] args)
        {
            // CRUD operations on tables
            TestTables();

            Console.WriteLine("Press any key to continue ...");
            Console.ReadKey();
        }

        static void TestTables()
        {
            NorthwindEntities NWEntities = new NorthwindEntities();
            // retrieve all Beverages
            IEnumerable<Product> beverages =
                from p in NWEntities.Products
```

```
            where p.Category.CategoryName == "Beverages"
            orderby p.ProductName
            select p;
        Console.WriteLine("There are {0} Beverages",
            beverages.Count());

    // update one product
    Product bev1 = beverages.ElementAtOrDefault(10);
    if (bev1 != null)
    {
        decimal newPrice = (decimal)bev1.UnitPrice + 10.00m;
        Console.WriteLine("The price of {0} is {1}.
                            Update to {2}",
            bev1.ProductName, bev1.UnitPrice, newPrice);
        bev1.UnitPrice = newPrice;
    }

    // submit the change to database
    NWEntities.SaveChanges();
    // insert a product
    Product newProduct = new Product { ProductName =
                            "new test product" };
    NWEntities.Products.AddObject(newProduct);
    NWEntities.SaveChanges();

        Console.WriteLine("Added a new product");

        // delete a product
        IQueryable<Product> productsToDelete =
                from p in NWEntities.Products
                where p.ProductName == "new test product"
                select p;
        if (productsToDelete.Count() > 0)
        {
            foreach (var p in productsToDelete)
            {
                NWEntities.DeleteObject(p);
                Console.WriteLine("Deleted product {0}",
                        p.ProductID);
            }
            NWEntities.SaveChanges();
        }

        NWEntities.Dispose();
    }
  }
}
```

If you run the program now the output will be:

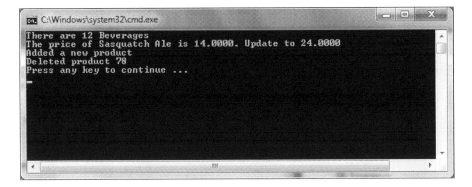

View Generated SQL statements

You may wonder which actual SQL statements are used by LINQ to Entities to interact with the databases. In this section we will explain two ways to view the generated SQL statements used by LINQ to Entities queries.

There are two ways to view the generated LINQ to Entities SQL statements. The first one is to use the `ObjectQuery.ToTraceString` method and the second one is to use SQL Profiler.

View SQL statements using ToTraceString

First let's write a new test method to contain one LINQ to SQL query:

```
static void ViewGeneratedSQL()
{
    NorthwindEntities NWEntities = new NorthwindEntities();

    IQueryable<Product> beverages =
        from p in NWEntities.Products
        where p.Category.CategoryName == "Beverages"
        orderby p.ProductName
        select p;

    NWEntities.Dispose();
}
```

As we have learned from the previous section the variable, beverages, is of the type, IQueryable<Product>, which is a derived class of the type, IEnumerable<Product>. Actually this type is also a subtype of System.Data. Objects.ObjectQuery<Product> which has a method, ToTraceString, we can use to view the generated SQL statements. To make it easier for us to call the ObjectQuery.ToTraceString method we now define an extension method like this:

```
public static class MyExtensions
{
    public static string ToTraceString<T>(this IQueryable<T> t)
    {
        string sql = "";
        ObjectQuery<T> oqt = t as ObjectQuery<T>;
        if (oqt != null)
            sql = oqt.ToTraceString();
        return sql;
    }
}
```

Note that this extension method is inside a non-generic static class, MyEntensions, and we put this class inside the namespace, TestLINQToEntitiesApp, which is the same namespace as our test class so we can use it inside our test method without worrying about importing its namespace.

Now we can print out the SQL statement of the LINQ to Entities query using this statement:

```
// view SQL using ToTraceString method
Console.WriteLine("The SQL statement is:" +
    beverages.ToTraceString());
```

and we also need to add a using statement to import the namespace for the QueryObject class:

```
using System.Data.Objects;
```

The file, Program.cs, should now be like this:

```
using System;
using System.Collections.Generic;
using System.Linq;
using System.Text;
using System.Data.Objects;

namespace TestLINQToEntitiesApp
{
    class Program
```

```
{
    static void Main(string[] args)
    {
        // CRUD operations on tables
        //TestTables();

        ViewGeneratedSQL();

        Console.WriteLine("Press any key to continue ...");
        Console.ReadKey();
    }

    static void TestTables()
    {
        // the body of this method is omitted to save space
    }

    static void ViewGeneratedSQL()
    {
        NorthwindEntities NWEntities = new NorthwindEntities();

        IQueryable<Product> beverages =
            from p in NWEntities.Products
            where p.Category.CategoryName == "Beverages"
            orderby p.ProductName
            select p;

        // view SQL using ToTraceString method
        Console.WriteLine("The SQL statement is:\n" +
            beverages.ToTraceString());

        NWEntities.Dispose();
    }
}

public static class MyExtensions
{
    public static string ToTraceString<T>(this IQueryable<T> t)
    {
        string sql = "";
        ObjectQuery<T> oqt = t as ObjectQuery<T>;
        if (oqt != null)
            sql = oqt.ToTraceString();
        return sql;
    }
}
}
```

Run this program and you will see following output:

View SQL statements using Profiler

With the `ToTraceString` method we can view generated SQL statements for some LINQ to Entities expressions but not all of them. For example when we add a new product to the database or when we execute a stored procedure in the database there is no `IQueryable` object for us to use to view the generated SQL statements. In this case we can use the SQL profiler to view the SQL statements. But if you go to view the generated SQL statements for the above query you may be confused as there is no SQL statement displayed in SQL profiler. We will not explain the steps to view SQL statements in Profiler here but we will explain it in the next section together with the explanation of another important LINQ to Entities feature — deferred execution.

Deferred execution

One important thing to remember when working with LINQ to Entities is the **deferred execution** of LINQ.

Standard query operators differ in the timing of their execution depending on whether they return a singleton value or a sequence of values. Those methods that return a singleton value (for example `Average` and `Sum`) execute immediately. Methods that return a sequence defer the query execution and return an enumerable object. These methods do not consume the target data until the query object is enumerated. This is known as deferred execution.

In the case of the methods that operate on in-memory collections, that is, those methods that extend `IEnumerable<(Of <(T>)>)`, the returned enumerable object captures all of the arguments that were passed to the method. When that object is enumerated the logic of the query operator is employed and the query results are returned.

In contrast, methods that extend IQueryable<(Of <(T>)>) do not implement any querying behavior but build an expression tree that represents the query to be performed. The query processing is handled by the source IQueryable<(Of <(T>)>) object.

Checking deferred execution with SQL profiler

To test the deferred execution of LINQ to Entities, let's first add the following method to our Program.cs file:

```
static void TestDeferredExecution()
{
    NorthwindEntities NWEntities = new NorthwindEntities();

    // SQL is not executed
    IQueryable<Product> beverages =
        from p in NWEntities.Products
        where p.Category.CategoryName == "Beverages"
        orderby p.ProductName
        select p;

    // SQL is executed on this statement
    Console.WriteLine("There are {0} Beverages",
            beverages.Count());

    NWEntities.Dispose();
}
```

Call this method from the Main method of the program and comment out the calls to the two previous test methods, then do the following:

1. Open Profiler (All Programs\Microsoft SQL Server 2005(or 2008)\ Performance Tools\SQL 2005(or 2008) Profiler).

2. Start a new trace on the Northwind database engine.

3. Go back to Visual Studio and set a break point on the first line of the TestDeferredExecution method.

4. Press *F5* to start debugging the program.

The program is now running and the cursor should be stopped on the first line of the method. Press *F10* to move to the next line of code and press *F10* again to step over this line of code:

```
IQueryable<Product> beverages =
    from p in NWEntities.Products
```

```
        where p.Category.CategoryName == "Beverages"
        orderby p.ProductName
            select p;
```

Switch to Profile and you will find that there is nothing in there.

However, when you press *F10* in Visual Studio and before the following statement is executed, you will see from the profiler that a query has been executed in the database:

```
Console.WriteLine("There are {0} Beverages", beverages.Count());
```

The query executed in the database is like this:

```
SELECT
[GroupBy1].[A1] AS [C1]
FROM ( SELECT
    COUNT(1) AS [A1]
    FROM   [dbo].[Products] AS [Extent1]
    INNER JOIN [dbo].[Categories] AS [Extent2] ON [Extent1].[CategoryID]
= [Extent2].[CategoryID]
    WHERE N'Beverages' = [Extent2].[CategoryName]
)  AS [GroupBy1]
```

The Profiler window should look as shown the following image:

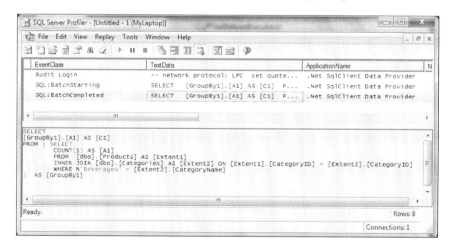

From Profiler we know that, under the hood, LINQ actually first created a sub-query to get the total beverage products count then got this count from the sub-query result. It also used an inner join to get the categories of products.

Note that with LINQ to SQL we can set the `DataContext` object's Log property to `Console.Out` and then view the generated SQL statements from the stand output for all subsequent LINQ to SQL expressions. Unfortunately, with LINQ to Entities, the `ObjectContext` does not have such a property to let us view generated SQL statements. We have to use either `ToTraceString` or Profiler to view the generated SQL statements.

Deferred execution for singleton methods

If the query expression returns a singleton value the query will be executed as soon as it is defined. For example, we can add this statement to our test deferred execution method to get the average price of all products:

```
// SQL is executed on this statement
decimal? averagePrice = (from p in NWEntities.Products
                        select p.UnitPrice).Average();
Console.WriteLine("The average price is {0}", averagePrice);
```

Start SQL Profiler then press *F5* to start debugging the program. When the cursor is stopped on the line to print out the average price, from the Profiler window, we see a query has been executed to get the average price and when the printing statement is being executed no more query is executed in database.

The Profiler window is like this:

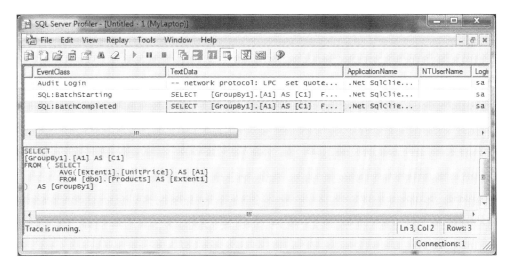

Deferred execution for singleton methods within sequence expressions

However, just because a query is using one of the singleton methods such as `sum`, `average`, or `count`, this doesn't mean that the query will be executed as soon as it is defined. If the query result is a sequence the execution will still be deferred. The following is an example of this kind of query:

```
// SQL is not executed even there is a singleton method
var cheapestProductsByCategory =
    from p in NWEntities.Products
    group p by p.CategoryID into g
    select new
    {
        CategoryID = g.Key,
        CheapestProduct =
            (from p2 in g
            where p2.UnitPrice == g.Min(p3 => p3.UnitPrice)
            select p2).FirstOrDefault()
    };
// SQL is executed on this statement
Console.WriteLine("Cheapest products by category:");
foreach (var p in cheapestProductsByCategory)
{
    Console.WriteLine("category {0}: product name: {1} price: {2}",
                    p.CategoryID, p.CheapestProduct.ProductName,
                    p.CheapestProduct.UnitPrice);
}
```

Start SQL Profiler then press *F5* to start debugging the program. When the cursor is stopped at the beginning of the `foreach` line, from Profiler, we don't see the query statement to get the minimum price for any product. When we press *F10* again the cursor is stopped on the variable, `cheapestProductsByCategory`, in the `foreach` line of code but we still don't see the query statement to get the cheapest products.

Then after we press *F10* again the cursor is stopped on the `in` keyword in the `foreach` line of code and this time, from Profiler, we see the query is executed.

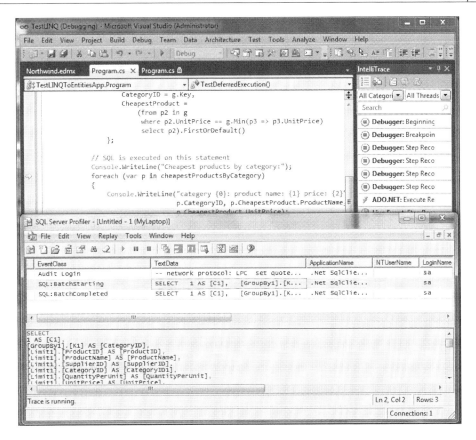

The actual SQL statements for this LINQ to Entities expression are like this:

```
SELECT
1 AS [C1],
[GroupBy1].[K1] AS [CategoryID],
[Limit1].[ProductID] AS [ProductID],
[Limit1].[ProductName] AS [ProductName],
[Limit1].[SupplierID] AS [SupplierID],
[Limit1].[CategoryID] AS [CategoryID1],
[Limit1].[QuantityPerUnit] AS [QuantityPerUnit],
[Limit1].[UnitPrice] AS [UnitPrice],
[Limit1].[UnitsInStock] AS [UnitsInStock],
[Limit1].[UnitsOnOrder] AS [UnitsOnOrder],
[Limit1].[ReorderLevel] AS [ReorderLevel],
[Limit1].[Discontinued] AS [Discontinued]
FROM    (SELECT
  [Extent1].[CategoryID] AS [K1],
  MIN([Extent1].[UnitPrice]) AS [A1]
  FROM [dbo].[Products] AS [Extent1]
  GROUP BY [Extent1].[CategoryID] ) AS [GroupBy1]
```

```
OUTER APPLY  (SELECT TOP (1)
  [Extent2].[ProductID] AS [ProductID],
  [Extent2].[ProductName] AS [ProductName],
  [Extent2].[SupplierID] AS [SupplierID],
  [Extent2].[CategoryID] AS [CategoryID],
  [Extent2].[QuantityPerUnit] AS [QuantityPerUnit],
  [Extent2].[UnitPrice] AS [UnitPrice],
  [Extent2].[UnitsInStock] AS [UnitsInStock],
  [Extent2].[UnitsOnOrder] AS [UnitsOnOrder],
  [Extent2].[ReorderLevel] AS [ReorderLevel],
  [Extent2].[Discontinued] AS [Discontinued]
  FROM [dbo].[Products] AS [Extent2]
  WHERE ((([GroupBy1].[K1] = [Extent2].[CategoryID]) OR (([GroupBy1].
[K1] IS NULL) AND ([Extent2].[CategoryID] IS NULL))) AND ([Extent2].
[UnitPrice] = [GroupBy1].[A1]) ) AS [Limit1]
```

From this output you can see that when the variable, `cheapestProductsByCategory`, is accessed it first calculates the minimum price for each category. Then, for each category, it returns the first product with that price. In a real application you probably wouldn't want to write such a complex query in your code. Instead you may want to put it in a stored procedure which we will discuss in the next chapter.

The test method is like this:

```csharp
static void TestDeferredExecution()
{
    NorthwindEntities NWEntities = new NorthwindEntities();

    // SQL is not executed
    IQueryable<Product> beverages =
        from p in NWEntities.Products
        where p.Category.CategoryName == "Beverages"
        orderby p.ProductName
        select p;

    // SQL is executed on this statement
    Console.WriteLine("There are {0} Beverages",
            beverages.Count());

    // SQL is executed on this statement
    decimal? averagePrice = (from p in NWEntities.Products
                             select p.UnitPrice).Average();
    Console.WriteLine("The average price is {0}", averagePrice);

    // SQL is not executed even there is a singleton method
    var cheapestProductsByCategory =
        from p in NWEntities.Products
        group p by p.CategoryID into g
```

```
            select new
            {
                CategoryID = g.Key,
                CheapestProduct =
                    (from p2 in g
                    where p2.UnitPrice == g.Min(p3 => p3.UnitPrice)
                        select p2).FirstOrDefault()
            };
    // SQL is executed on this statement
    Console.WriteLine("Cheapest products by category:");
    foreach (var p in cheapestProductsByCategory)
    {
        Console.WriteLine(
                "categery {0}: product name: {1} price: {2}",
                p.CategoryID, p.CheapestProduct.ProductName,
                p.CheapestProduct.UnitPrice);
    }
    NWEntities.Dispose();
}
```

If you comment out all other test methods (`TestTables` and `ViewGeneratedSQL`) and run the program you should get an output similar to the following image:

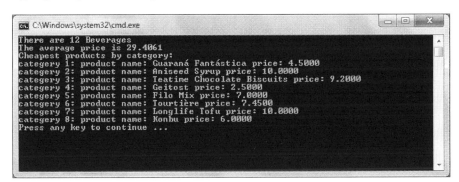

Deferred (lazy) loading versus eager loading

In one of the above examples we retrieved the category name of a product using this expression:

```
p.Category.CategoryName == "Beverages"
```

Even though there is no field called `categoryname` in the `Products` table we can still get the category name of a product because there is an association between the `Products` and `Category` tables. In the **Northwind.edmx** design pane, click on the line that connects the **Products** table and the **Categories** table and you will see all of the properties of the association. Note that its Referential Constraint properties are **Category.CategoryID -> Product.CategoryID**, meaning that category ID is the key field to link these two tables.

Because of this association we can retrieve the category for each product and also retrieve products for each category.

Lazy loading by default

However, even with an association the associated data is not loaded when the query is executed. For example, suppose we use the following test method to retrieve all of the categories, then access the products for each category:

```
static void TestAssociation()
{
    NorthwindEntities NWEntities = new NorthwindEntities();

    var categories = from c in NWEntities.Categories select c;
    foreach (var category in categories)
    {
        Console.WriteLine("There are {0} products in category {1}",
            category.Products.Count(), category.CategoryName);
    }
    NWEntities.Dispose();
}
```

Start SQL Profiler then press *F5* to start debugging the program. When the cursor is stopped on the `foreach` line (after you press *F10* twice to move the cursor to the `in` keyword), from Profiler, we see this SQL statement:

```
SELECT
[Extent1].[CategoryID] AS [CategoryID],
[Extent1].[CategoryName] AS [CategoryName],
[Extent1].[Description] AS [Description],
[Extent1].[Picture] AS [Picture]
FROM [dbo].[Categories] AS [Extent1]
```

When you press *F10* to execute the printout line, from Profiler, we see this SQL statement:

```
exec sp_executesql N'SELECT
[Extent1].[ProductID] AS [ProductID],
```

```
[Extent1].[ProductName] AS [ProductName],
[Extent1].[SupplierID] AS [SupplierID],
[Extent1].[CategoryID] AS [CategoryID],
[Extent1].[QuantityPerUnit] AS [QuantityPerUnit],
[Extent1].[UnitPrice] AS [UnitPrice],
[Extent1].[UnitsInStock] AS [UnitsInStock],
[Extent1].[UnitsOnOrder] AS [UnitsOnOrder],
[Extent1].[ReorderLevel] AS [ReorderLevel],
[Extent1].[Discontinued] AS [Discontinued]
FROM [dbo].[Products] AS [Extent1]
WHERE [Extent1].[CategoryID] = @EntityKeyValue1',N'@EntityKeyValue1
int',@EntityKeyValue1=1
```

From these SQL statements we know that the Entity framework first goes to the database to query all of the categories. Then, for each category, when we need to get the total count of products, it goes to the database again to query all of the products for that category.

This is because, by default, lazy loading is set to `true`, meaning that the loading of all associated data (children) is deferred until the data is needed.

Eager loading the with Include method

To change this behavior we can use the `Include` method to tell `ObjectContext` to automatically load the specified children during the initial query:

```
static void TestEagerLazyLoading()
{
    NorthwindEntities NWEntities = new NorthwindEntities();

    // eager loading products of categories
    var categories = from c
                     in NWEntities.Categories.Include("Products")
                     select c;
    foreach (var category in categories)
    {
        Console.WriteLine("There are {0} products in category {1}",
            category.Products.Count(), category.CategoryName);
    }

    NWEntities.Dispose();
}
```

As you can see, inside this test method, when constructing the LINQ to Entities query, we added an `Include` clause to tell the framework to load all products when loading the categories.

To test it start SQL Profiler and then press *F5* to start debugging the program. When the cursor is stopped on the `foreach` line (at the `in` keyword), from Profiler, you will see this SQL statement:

```
SELECT
[Project1].[CategoryID] AS [CategoryID],
[Project1].[CategoryName] AS [CategoryName],
[Project1].[Description] AS [Description],
[Project1].[Picture] AS [Picture],
[Project1].[C1] AS [C1],
[Project1].[ProductID] AS [ProductID],
[Project1].[ProductName] AS [ProductName],
[Project1].[SupplierID] AS [SupplierID],
[Project1].[CategoryID1] AS [CategoryID1],
[Project1].[QuantityPerUnit] AS [QuantityPerUnit],
[Project1].[UnitPrice] AS [UnitPrice],
[Project1].[UnitsInStock] AS [UnitsInStock],
[Project1].[UnitsOnOrder] AS [UnitsOnOrder],
[Project1].[ReorderLevel] AS [ReorderLevel],
[Project1].[Discontinued] AS [Discontinued]
FROM ( SELECT
  [Extent1].[CategoryID] AS [CategoryID],
  [Extent1].[CategoryName] AS [CategoryName],
  [Extent1].[Description] AS [Description],
  [Extent1].[Picture] AS [Picture],
  [Extent2].[ProductID] AS [ProductID],
  [Extent2].[ProductName] AS [ProductName],
  [Extent2].[SupplierID] AS [SupplierID],
  [Extent2].[CategoryID] AS [CategoryID1],
  [Extent2].[QuantityPerUnit] AS [QuantityPerUnit],
  [Extent2].[UnitPrice] AS [UnitPrice],
  [Extent2].[UnitsInStock] AS [UnitsInStock],
  [Extent2].[UnitsOnOrder] AS [UnitsOnOrder],
  [Extent2].[ReorderLevel] AS [ReorderLevel],
  [Extent2].[Discontinued] AS [Discontinued],
  CASE WHEN ([Extent2].[ProductID] IS NULL) THEN CAST(NULL AS int)
ELSE 1 END AS [C1]
  FROM  [dbo].[Categories] AS [Extent1]
  LEFT OUTER JOIN [dbo].[Products] AS [Extent2] ON [Extent1].
[CategoryID] = [Extent2].[CategoryID]
) AS [Project1]
ORDER BY [Project1].[CategoryID] ASC, [Project1].[C1] ASC
```

As you can see from this SQL statement all products for all categories are loaded during the first query.

In addition to preloading one child entity with the `Include` method you can also traverse multiple child entities together. For example, you can use `Include("Products.Orders")` to preload `products` and `orders` for all `categories`, if `Orders` is also added as an Entity to the model. You can also chain multiple `Includes` to preload multiple child entities on the same level like `Customers.Include("Orders").Include("Contacts")` if there is a `Contacts` table for `customers` and `customers`, `orders`, and `contacts` are all added as entities to the model.

Note that with LINQ to SQL you can set associations and eager loading configurations with `DataLoadOptions` and you can even preload some objects with conditions. With LINQ to Entities, you don't have any other choice. You have to preload an entity entirely.

Another difference between LINQ to SQL and LINQ to Entities is, with LINQ to SQL, you have strong typed load options for eager loading such as `LoadWith<Category>`, but with LINQ to Entities you have to put the entity names in a string expression which might cause a runtime exception if you make a mistake in the entity names.

Joining two tables

Although associations are a kind of join in LINQ we can also explicitly join two tables using the keyword, `Join`, as shown in the following code:

```
static void TestJoin()
{
    NorthwindEntities NWEntities = new NorthwindEntities();
    var categoryProducts =
        from c in NWEntities.Categories
        join p in NWEntities.Products
        on c.CategoryID equals p.CategoryID
        into productsByCategory
        select new {
            c.CategoryName,
            productCount = productsByCategory.Count()
        };

    foreach (var cp in categoryProducts)
    {
      Console.WriteLine("There are {0} products in category {1}",
            cp.productCount, cp.CategoryName);
    }
    NWEntities.Dispose();
}
```

This is not so useful in the above example because the tables, `Products` and `Categories`, are associated with a foreign key relationship. If there is no foreign key association between two tables or if we hadn't added the associations between these two tables this will be particularly useful.

From the following SQL statement we can see that only one query is executed to get the results:

```
SELECT
[Extent1].[CategoryID] AS [CategoryID],
[Extent1].[CategoryName] AS [CategoryName],
(SELECT
   COUNT(1) AS [A1]
   FROM [dbo].[Products] AS [Extent2]
   WHERE [Extent1].[CategoryID] = [Extent2].[CategoryID]) AS [C1]
FROM [dbo].[Categories] AS [Extent1]
```

In addition to joining two tables you can also:

- Join three or more tables
- Join a table to itself
- Create left, right, and outer joins
- Join using composite keys

Querying a view

Querying a view is the same as querying a table. For example you can query the view "current product lists" like this:

```
static void TestView()
{
   NorthwindEntities NWEntities = new NorthwindEntities();

   var currentProducts = from p
                   in NWEntities.Current_Product_Lists
                   select p;
   foreach (var p in currentProducts)
   {
       Console.WriteLine("Product ID: {0} Product Name: {1}",
           p.ProductID, p.ProductName);
   }
    NWEntities.Dispose();
}
```

This will get all of the current products using the view.

Summary

In this chapter, we have learned what an ORM is, why we need an ORM, and what LINQ to Entities is. We also compared LINQ to SQL with LINQ to Entities and explored some basic features of LINQ to Entities.

The key points covered in this chapter include:

- An ORM product can greatly ease data access layer development
- LINQ to Entities is one of Microsoft's ORM products that uses LINQ against a .NET Conceptual Entity Model
- The built-in LINQ to Entities designer in Visual Studio 2010 can be used to model the Conceptual Entity Model
- You can generate the Conceptual Entity Model from a physical database in the Visual Studio 2010 Entity Model designer
- The class, `System.Data.Objects.ObjectContext`, is the main class for LINQ to Entities applications
- LINQ methods that return a sequence defer the query execution and you can check the timing of the execution of a query with Profiler
- LINQ query expressions that return a singleton value will be executed as soon as they are defined
- By default the loading of associated data is deferred (lazy loading). You can change this behavior with the `Include` method
- The `Join` operator can be used to join multiple tables and views
- Views can be used to query a database in LINQ to Entities in the same way as for tables

8

LINQ to Entities: Advanced Concepts and Features

In the previous chapter, we learned some basic concepts and features of LINQ to Entities such as querying and updating databases with tables and views and changing loading behaviors by using the Include method.

In this chapter, we will learn some advanced features of LINQ to Entities such as stored procedure support, concurrency control, and transactional processing. After this chapter, we will rewrite the data access layer of our WCF service to utilize LINQ to Entities technology.

In this chapter we will cover:

- Calling a stored procedure
- Compiled queries
- Direct SQL
- Dynamic querying
- Inheritance support
- Concurrency control
- Transaction support
- Entity class validation
- Debugging LINQ to Entities programs

Calling a stored procedure

Calling a stored procedure is different from calling a table or a view because a stored procedure can't be called directly. A function import has to be added for the stored procedure and its result set has to be mapped. The modeling of a stored procedure is also different from modeling a table or view. In the following sections we will explain how to call a simple stored procedure, how to map the returned result of a stored procedure to an entity class, and how to create a new entity for the result set.

We will reuse the same application that we used in the previous chapter and add more testing methods to the program.

Mapping a stored procedure to a new entity class

First we will try to call a simple stored procedure. In the sample database there is a stored procedure called "Ten Most Expensive Products". We will call this stored procedure to get the top ten most expensive products.

Modeling a stored procedure

Before we can call this stored procedure we need to model it.

1. Open the `Northwind.edmx` designer.
2. Right-click on an empty space of the designer surface and select **Update Model from Database…**.

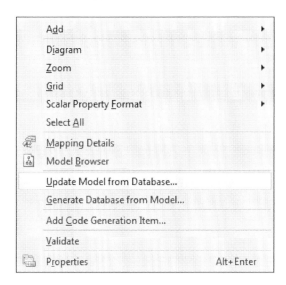

3. From the **Update Wizard | Choose Your Database Objects** window, make sure the **Add** tab is selected, then expand the **Stored Procedures** node, check **Ten Most Expensive Products (dbo)**, and then click on the **Finish** button.

4. On the designer surface, right-click on an empty space, and select **Add** from the context menu, then select **Function Import...**.

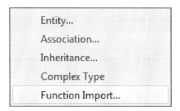

5. On the **Add Function Import** window, select **Ten_Most_Expensive_Products** as the stored procedure name them retype this name as the **Function Import Name**.

6. Click on the **Get Column Information** button to populate the resultant set of the stored procedure.

7. Click on the **Create New Complex Type** button to create a new entity type for the result set of this stored procedure (if the **Create New Complex Type** button is disabled it is because you didn't click on the **Get Column Information** button).

8. **Complex** should be selected as **Returns a Collection Of** and **Ten_Most_Expensive_Products_Result** should be the complex type. Leave this unchanged.

9. Click on the **OK** button.

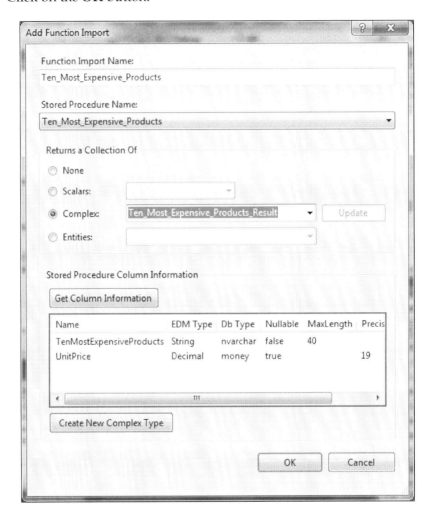

This will add the method, `Ten_Most_Expensive_Products`, to the `NorthwindEntities` class and add a new class, `Ten_Most_Expensive_Products_Result`, as the resultant data type of the stored procedure.

Querying a stored procedure

Now, from `Program.cs`, we can call this stored procedure as follows:

```
var tenProducts = from p in
            NWEntities.Ten_Most_Expensive_Products()
            select p;
```

```
foreach (var p in tenProducts)
{
    Console.WriteLine('"Product Name: {0}, Price: {1}'",
            p.TenMostExpensiveProducts, p.UnitPrice);
}
```

Because we know the return result of the stored procedure we can also replace the `var` data type with the specific return type, as in the following code:

```
IEnumerable<Ten_Most_Expensive_Products_Result> tenProducts =
            from p
            in NWEntities.Ten_Most_Expensive_Products()
            select p;
foreach (Ten_Most_Expensive_Products_Result p in tenProducts)
{
    Console.WriteLine('"Product Name: {0}, Price; {1}'",
            p.TenMostExpensiveProducts, p.UnitPrice);
}
```

The SQL statement is pretty straightforward, like this:

```
exec [dbo].[Ten Most Expensive Products]
```

and the output will look like the following screenshot:

Mapping a stored procedure to an existing entity class

In the above example LINQ to Entities creates a new type for the return result of the stored procedure. It actually just added the word, `Result`, after the stored procedure name to create the name of the return data type. If we know that the return result is a kind of entity we can tell LINQ to Entities to use that specific entity as the return type instead of creating a new type.

For example let us create a stored procedure like this:

```
Create PROCEDURE [dbo].[GetProduct]
    (
    @ProductID int
    )
AS
    SET NOCOUNT ON
    Select * from Products where ProductID = @ProductID
```

You can create this stored procedure in Microsoft SQL Server Management Studio or by right-clicking on the **Stored Procedures** node in Server Explorer of Visual Studio 2010 and selecting **Data Connections | Northwind.dbo | Add New Stored Procedure** from the context menu.

After the stored procedure has been created add it to the Entity data model and add a function import as well.

This time, on the **Add Function Import** window, you can check **Entities** as the **Returns a Collection Of** and choose **Product** as the entity type. Now LINQ to Entities will use the `Product` class as the return type of this stored procedure. The method for this stored procedure will be as follows:

```
public ObjectResult<Product> GetProduct(Nullable<global::System.Int32>
productID)
{
    ObjectParameter productIDParameter;
    if (productID.HasValue)
    {
        productIDParameter = new ObjectParameter('"ProductID'",
                                                 productID);
    }
    else
    {
        productIDParameter = new ObjectParameter('"ProductID'",
                          typeof(global::System.Int32));
```

```
        }

        return base.ExecuteFunction<Product>('"GetProduct'",
                                      productIDParameter);
    }
```

From the signature of the method we know that the return type is of the
`Product` class.

To call this method you can write a statement like this:

```
        Product getProduct = NWEntities.GetProduct(1).FirstOrDefault();
```

The complete test method for the stored procedure should be like this:

```
    static void TestStoredProcedure()
    {
        NorthwindEntities NWEntities = new NorthwindEntities();

        IEnumerable<Ten_Most_Expensive_Products_Result> tenProducts =
                    from p
                    in NWEntities.Ten_Most_Expensive_Products()
                    select p;
        Console.WriteLine('"Ten Most Expensive Products:'");
        foreach (Ten_Most_Expensive_Products_Result p in tenProducts)
        {
            Console.WriteLine('"Product Name: {0}, Price; {1}'",
                    p.TenMostExpensiveProducts, p.UnitPrice);
        }
        // map a stored procedure to an entity class
        Product getProduct = NWEntities.GetProduct(1).FirstOrDefault();
        Console.WriteLine('"\nProduct name for product 1:{0}'",
                                      getProduct.ProductName);

        NWEntities.Dispose();
    }
```

And if you run the program you should have an output like the following:

```
C:\Windows\system32\cmd.exe
Ten Most Expensive Products:
Product Name: Côte de Blaye, Price; 263.5000
Product Name: Thüringer Rostbratwurst, Price; 123.7900
Product Name: Mishi Kobe Niku, Price; 97.0000
Product Name: Sir Rodney's Marmalade, Price; 81.0000
Product Name: Carnarvon Tigers, Price; 62.5000
Product Name: Raclette Courdavault, Price; 55.0000
Product Name: Manjimup Dried Apples, Price; 53.0000
Product Name: Tarte au sucre, Price; 49.3000
Product Name: Ipoh Coffee, Price; 46.0000
Product Name: Rössle Sauerkraut, Price; 45.6000

Product name for product 1:Chai
Press any key to continue ...
```

Interestingly you can add another function for the same stored procedure but with a different function name and, for the new function, you can even create a new complex type for the result of the stored procedure instead of using the `Product` class. LINQ to Entities will automatically create a new class for the return type. If you do so the new method should be as follows:

```
public ObjectResult<GetProduct_Result> GetProduct1(Nullable<global::Sy
stem.Int32> productID)
{
    ObjectParameter productIDParameter;
    if (productID.HasValue)
    {
        productIDParameter = new ObjectParameter('"ProductID'",
                                                     productID);
    }
    else
    {
        productIDParameter = new ObjectParameter('"ProductID'",
                                 typeof(global::System.Int32));
    }
    return base.ExecuteFunction<GetProduct_Result>('"GetProduct1'",
                                             productIDParameter);
}
```

The generated return type class, `GetProduct_Result`, is almost identical to the `Product` class.

Another difference between the `GetProduct` and `GetProduct1` methods is that the product you retrieved using `GetProduct` is managed by the Entity, `ObjectContext`. Any changes you made to it will be committed back to the database if you call `SaveChanges()` later. However the product you retrieved using `GetProduct1` is not managed by the Entity, `ObjectContext`, and thus won't be committed back to the database if you call `SaveChanges()` later.

One thing to keep in mind is Entity Framework version 1.0 only has limited support for stored procedures. For example it can't handle multiple result sets from the same stored procedure, not to mention dynamic result sets (the stored procedure returns different result sets according to different input parameters). Microsoft promises to have better stored procedure support in version 2.0.

 If you really need stored procedure support for multiple result sets or dynamic result sets you can download and install the Entity Framework Extensions at `http://code.msdn.microsoft.com/EFExtensions`.

Compiled query

It is common in many applications to execute structurally similar queries many times. In such cases it is possible to increase performance by compiling the query once and executing it several times in the application with different parameters. This result is obtained in LINQ to Entities by using the `CompiledQuery` class.

The following code shows how to define a compiled query:

```
static void TestCompiledQuery()
{
    NorthwindEntities NWEntities = new NorthwindEntities();

    Func<NorthwindEntities, string, IQueryable<Product>> fn
    = CompiledQuery.Compile((NorthwindEntities NW, string category) =>
        from p in NW.Products
        where p.Category.CategoryName == category
        select p);
    var products1 = fn(NWEntities, '"Beverages'");
    Console.WriteLine('"Total products in category Beverages: {0}'",
        products1.Count());
    var products2 = fn(NWEntities, '"Seafood'");
    Console.WriteLine('"Total products in category Seafood: {0}'",
        products2.Count());

    NWEntities.Dispose();
}
```

As you can see, a compiled query is actually a function. The function contains a compiled LINQ query expression and can be called just like a regular function.

Direct SQL

LINQ to Entities is a part of the ADO.NET family of technologies. It is based on services provided by the ADO.NET provider model. Therefore it is possible to mix LINQ to Entities code with existing ADO.NET applications.

In some cases you might find that the query or submit changes facility of `ObjectContext` is insufficient for the specialized task that you want to perform. In these cases it is possible to use `ObjectContext` to issue raw SQL commands directly to the database.

The `ExecuteStoreQuery()` method lets you execute a raw SQL query and converts the result of your query directly into objects.

The `ExecuteStoreCommand()` method lets you directly execute SQL commands against the database.

For example, the following code will retrieve all discontinued products and update the price for one product:

```
var products = NWEntities.ExecuteStoreQuery<Product>(
    '"SELECT * '" +
    '"FROM Products '" +
    '"WHERE Discontinued = 0 '" +
    '"ORDER BY ProductName;'"
);
Console.WriteLine('"Total discontinued products :{0}'",
    products.Count());

int rowCount = NWEntities.ExecuteStoreCommand(
    '" update products '"
    + '"set UnitPrice=UnitPrice+1 '"
    + '"where productID=35'");
if (rowCount < 1)
    Console.WriteLine('"No product is updated'");
else
    Console.WriteLine('"Product price is updated'");
```

Dynamic query

In addition to using LINQ syntax we can also build queries dynamically. There are two ways to build a query dynamically—using expressions and using parameters. In this section we will explain both of these two methods.

Dynamic query with expressions

First let's build a dynamic query with expressions. The following code will create two method expressions: one for the where clause and one for the order by clause:

```
static void TestDynamicQuery()
{
  NorthwindEntities NWEntities = new NorthwindEntities();

ParameterExpression param = Expression.Parameter(typeof(Product),
'"p'");

Expression left = Expression.Property(param, typeof(Product).
GetProperty('"UnitPrice'"));
Expression right = Expression.Constant((decimal)100.00, typeof(System.
Nullable<decimal>));
Expression filter = Expression.GreaterThanOrEqual(left, right);
Expression pred = Expression.Lambda(filter, param);

IQueryable products = NWEntities.Products;

Expression expr = Expression.Call(typeof(Queryable), '"Where'",
  new Type[] { typeof(Product) }, Expression.Constant(products),
pred);

expr = Expression.Call(typeof(Queryable), '"OrderBy'",
    new Type[] { typeof(Product), typeof(string) }, expr, Expression.
Lambda(Expression.Property(param, '"ProductName'"), param));

IQueryable<Product> query =  NWEntities.Products.AsQueryable().
Provider.CreateQuery<Product>(expr);

foreach (var p in query)
    Console.WriteLine('"Product name: {0}'", p.ProductName);
  NWEntities.Dispose();
}
```

 To simplify our example we save all code in one file. In a real project it might be better to save some common code such as lambda expressions and LINQ queries in a separate file.

To build the first expression we first created a `left` expression and a `right` expression and then used them to create a `filter` expression. The `predicate` expression is then created based on this filter expression.

As the second expression takes the first expression as an argument, it expands the first expression to include an `order by` expression.

The statement with the `CreateQuery` method is the one that creates the query dynamically according to the expressions that we have created before this statement. And, of course, the query won't get executed until the `foreach` statement is executed.

Before running this program you need to add the following `using` statement to the beginning:

```
using System.Linq.Expressions;
```

The output of the above code looks like the following screenshot:

Dynamic query with parameters

In the previous section we created a dynamic query with expressions. Besides expressions we can also build a dynamic query string with parameters and then pass different parameters to query the database at runtime. For example we can build a query string like this:

```
string queryString =
    @'"SELECT VALUE Product
      FROM NorthwindEntities.Products
      AS Product
      WHERE Product.ProductID = @id'";
```

And from this query string we can build a dynamic query to the entity context:

```
ObjectQuery<Product> productQuery =
        new ObjectQuery<Product>(queryString, NWEntities);
```

Then at runtime we can pass in parameters to this query as:

```
productQuery.Parameters.Add(new ObjectParameter('"id'", 1));
```

Now we can query the database using LINQ, just as we did before with a regular LINQ to Entities query:

```
foreach (var p in productQuery)
{
    Console.WriteLine('"Product name: {0}'", p.ProductName);
}
```

Inheritance

LINQ to Entities supports three types of inheritance: **Table Per Hierarchy** (TPH) inheritance, **Table Per Type** (TPT) inheritance, and **Table Per Concrete** (TPC) inheritance. As table per concrete inheritance is not used as often as table per hierarchy and table per type inheritance, in this book we will only cover the first two inheritance types.

LINQ to Entities Table per Hierarchy inheritance

In **Table per Hierarchy inheritance** there is a single database table that contains fields for both parent information and child information. With relational data a discriminator column contains the value that determines which class any given record belongs to.

For example, consider a `Persons` table that contains everyone employed by a company. Some people are employees and some are managers. The `Persons` table contains a column named `EmployeeType` that has a value of 1 for managers and a value of 2 for employees; this is the discriminator column.

In this scenario you can create a child entity of employees and populate the class only with records that have an `EmployeeType` value of 2. You can also remove columns that do not apply from each of the classes.

In our `Northwind` database the `Customers` table contains all of the customers in different countries. Suppose that all customers share some common properties and customers from each country also have some unique properties of their own. We can then define a `BaseCustomer` entity class for all of the common properties of the customers and define a unique child entity class for each country.

We assume that all customers have the following properties:

CustomerID, CompanyName, ContactName, ContactTitle, Address, City, Region, PostalCode.

To simplify the example we will define only two child entity classes in this example: one for customers in USA (called USACustomers) and another for customers in UK (UKCustomers). We assume that a USACustomer has one more property of Phone and a UKCustomer has one more property of Fax.

Modeling the BaseCustomer and USACustomer entities

We will first model these entities with the LINQ to Entities designer.

1. Open the entities conceptual model, Northwind.edmx, right-click on an empty space on the designer surface, then from the context menu choose **Update Model from Database…** and add the **Customers** table to the model, in the same way as we did for the **Products** table in the previous chapter. Change the entity class name from **Customer** to **BaseCustomer** (the **Entity Set Name** should be changed to **BaseCustomer** automatically).

2. Right-click on an empty space on the designer surface, then choose **Add | Entity…** from the context menu.

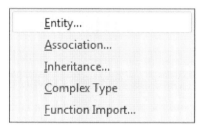

3. On the **Add Entity** window, enter **USACustomer** as the **Entity Name**, and select **BaseCustomer** as the **Base type**. Click on **OK** to close this window.

4. On the entity model designer surface, right-click on the **Phone** property of the **BaseCustomer** entity, and select **Cut** from the context menu.

5. Still on the entity model designer surface, right-click on the **Properties** node of the **USACustomer** entity, and select **Paste** from the context menu.

6. Right-click on the **Country** property of the **BaseCustomer** entity, and select **Delete** from the context menu. We need to delete this property because we will use this property as our discriminator.

7. Now select the **USACustomer** entity on the model designer, and go to the **Mapping Details** window (it should be next to your **Output** window or you can open it from menu **View | Other Windows | Entity Data Model Mapping Details**).

8. On the **Mapping Details** window, click on **<Add a Table or View>**, and select **Customers** from the drop-down list. Make sure **Phone** is mapped to **Phone** and **Country** is not mapped.

9. Again on the **Mapping Details** window, click on **<Add a Condition>**, and select **Country** from the drop-down list. Select = as the operator, and enter **USA** as the **Value / Property**.

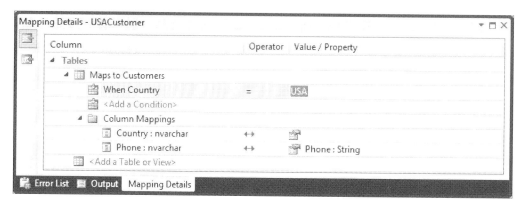

10. Now we have finished modeling the base customer and USA customer entities. If you build the solution now you should see no errors.

Modeling the UKCustomer entity

Next we need to model the UKCustomer entity. This entity will inherit from the BaseCustomer entity but will have an extra property of Fax.

1. On the Northwind.edmx Entity Designer surface, right-click on an empty space, then choose **Add | Entity** from the context menu.

2. On the **Add Entity** window, enter **UKCustomer** as the Entity Name, and select **BaseCustomer** as the **Base type**. Click on **OK** to close this window.

3. On the entity model designer surface, right-click on the **Fax** property of the **BaseCustomer** entity, and select **Cut** from the context menu.

4. Still on the entity model designer surface, right-click on the **Properties** node of the **UKCustomer** entity, and select **Paste** from the context menu.

5. Now select the **UKCustomer** entity on the model designer, and go to the **Mapping Details** window (it should be next to your **Output** window or you can open it from menu **View | Other Windows | Entity Data Model Mapping Details**).

6. On the **Mapping Details** window, click on **<Add a Table or View>**, and select **Customers** from the drop-down list. Make sure **Fax** is mapped to **Fax** and **Country** is not mapped.

7. On the same window, click on **<Add a Condition>**, and select **Country** from the drop-down list. Select = as the operator and enter **UK** as the **Value / Property**.

8. Now the TPH inheritance model is finished. The model for the customer part should be like this image:

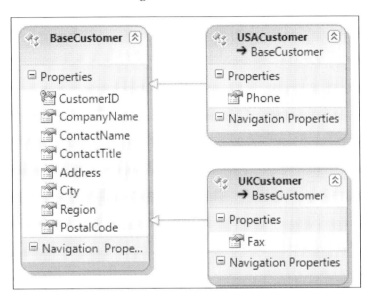

Generated classes with TPH inheritance

Save the model and open the `Northwind.designer.cs` file. You will find that three classes have been added to the model. The first class is the `BaseCustomer` class which has this signature:

```
[EdmEntityTypeAttribute(NamespaceName='"NorthwindModel'",
  Name='"BaseCustomer'")]
[Serializable()]
[DataContractAttribute(IsReference=true)]
[KnownTypeAttribute(typeof(USACustomer))]
[KnownTypeAttribute(typeof(UKCustomer))]
public partial class BaseCustomer : EntityObject
```

Note that its class body neither contains the properties, `Phone` and `Fax`, nor `Country`. This is because `Phone` is now contained in, entity, `USACustomer`, and `Fax` in `UKCustomer`, and `Country` is used as the discriminator for the inheritance. The two `KnownTypeAttribute` attributes are generated from the inheritance properties we set in the model.

The other two classes are for the derived classes; each has only one property:

```
public partial class USACustomer : BaseCustomer
public partial class UKCustomer : BaseCustomer
```

Testing the TPH inheritance

Now we can write a query to show the inheritance between the `BaseCustomer` and the two derived classes.

First we can retrieve all of the USA customers by using the `is` operator like this:

```
var USACustomers1 = from c
                    in NWEntities.BaseCustomers
                    where c is USACustomer
                    select c;
```

We can also use the `OfType` operator to retrieve the same products, as follows:

```
var USACustomers2 = from c
                    in NWEntities.BaseCustomers.OfType<USACustomer>()
                    select c;

Console.WriteLine('"Total number of USA customers: {0}'",
                    USACustomers1.Count());
Console.WriteLine('"Total number of USA customers: {0}'",
                    USACustomers2.Count());
```

Run the program and you will see both queries return **13**.

We can also use the `as` operator to search for all the customers that are USA customers:

```
var USACustomers3 = from c
                    in NWEntities.BaseCustomers
                    select c as USACustomer;
```

In all of the above three queries `Phone` is a property of the returning item which means it is of the `USACustomer` type. Also, all of the `BaseCustomer` properties are available because the returning item's data type is a child of the `BaseCustomer` type.

Similarly we can retrieve all `UKCustomers` and use its `Fax` property, as follows:

```
var UKCustomers = from c
                  in NWEntities.BaseCustomers.OfType<UKCustomer>()
                  select c;
```

The test method should be like this:

```
static void TestTPHInheritance()
{
    NorthwindEntities NWEntities = new NorthwindEntities();

    var USACustomers1 = from c
                        in NWEntities.BaseCustomers
                        where c is USACustomer
                        select c;

    var USACustomers2 = from c
                        in NWEntities.BaseCustomers.OfType<USACustomer>()
                        select c;
    Console.WriteLine('"Total number of USA customers: {0}'",
                        USACustomers1.Count());
    Console.WriteLine('"Total number of USA customers: {0}'",
                        USACustomers2.Count());

    var USACustomers3 = from c
                        in NWEntities.BaseCustomers
                        select c as USACustomer;

    foreach (var c in USACustomers3)
    {
        if (c != null)
        {
            Console.WriteLine('"USA customer: {0}, Phone: {1}'",
                c.CompanyName, c.Phone);
        }
    }
    var UKCustomers = from c
                        in NWEntities.BaseCustomers.OfType<UKCustomer>()
                        select c;

    foreach (var c in UKCustomers)
        Console.WriteLine('"UK customer: {0}, Fax: {1}'",
            c.CompanyName, c.Fax);

    NWEntities.Dispose();
}
```

The output of this is shown in the following screenshot:

LINQ to Entities Table per Type inheritance

In **Table per Type inheritance** there is a parent database table that contains fields for parent information and a separate database table that contains additional fields for child information. With relational data a foreign key constraint links those tables together to provide the detailed information for each entity.

For example, let's consider the same Persons table that contains common properties for everyone employed by a company. Some people are employees and some are managers. All employee-specific information is saved in a separate table, Employees, while all manager-specific information is saved in the table, Managers.

In this scenario you can create a parent entity for people, and two child entities—one for employees and another for managers.

Again in our Northwind database, the Customers table contains all of the customers in different countries. Suppose that all customers share some common properties and customers from each country also have some unique properties of their own. We can then define a BaseCustomer entity class for all of the common properties of the customers and define a unique child entity class for each country.

We assume that all customers have the following properties:

`CustomerID, CompanyName, ContactName, ContactTitle, Address, City, Region, PostalCode`.

To simplify the example we will define only two child entity classes in this example: one for customers in USA (called `USACustomers`) and another for customers in UK (`UKCustomers`). We assume that a `USACustomer` has one more property of `Phone` and a `UKCustomer` has one more property of `Fax`.

However this time we will create those two child entities from two new database tables, not from the same `Customers` table as we did in the last section.

Preparing database tables

We first need to create those two new database tables so that later on we can add them to our model.

1. Open SQL Management Studio and execute the following SQL statements to create two new tables. These two statements also fill in these two new tables with some initial data from the `Customers` table:

    ```
    select CustomerID, Phone
    into USACustomers
    from Customers
    where Country = 'USA'

    select CustomerID, Fax
    into UKCustomers
    from Customers
    where Country = 'UK'
    ```

2. Set `CustomerID` as the primary keys for both tables.

3. Add a foreign key relationship between the USACustomers table and the Customers table. The column, CustomerID, should be used for the foreign key. Do the same for the UKCustomers table. The foreign key mappings for USACustomers should be as shown in the following screenshot:

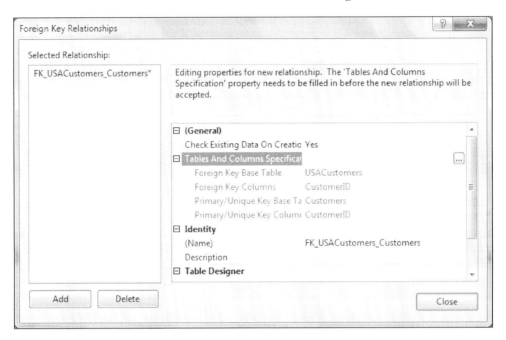

Modeling USACustomer1 and UKCustomer1 entities

Now that we have the database tables ready we need to go to the Entity designer to add them to our model.

1. From Visual Studio, open the Northwind.edmx Entity designer, right-click on an empty space and **select Update Model from Database…**. Add the two new tables USACustomers and UKCustomers, to the model. Note that the entity names for these two tables are USACustomer1 and UKCustomer1 as there are already two entities with the name of USACustomer and UKCustomer.

2. Because of the foreign keys between those two tables and the Customers table, there is an association between USACustomer1 and BaseCustomer as well as between UKCustomer1 and BaseCustomer. Right-click on each of these two associations and delete them.

3. Then right-click on an empty space and select **Add | Inheritance...** from the context menu. Specify **BaseCustomer** as the **base entity** and **USACustomer1** as the **derived entity**. Click on **OK** to close this window. Also add an inheritance between `UKCustomer1` and `BaseCustomer`.

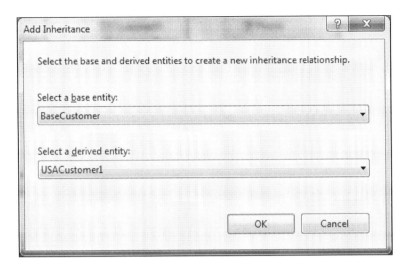

4. Select **CustomerID** from the **USACustomer1** entity and delete it. Also delete **CustomerID** from the **UKCustomer1** entity.

5. Select the **USACustomer1** entity, go to the **Mapping Details** window, and map **CustomerID : nchar** to **CustomerID : String**. Do the same mapping for the **CustomerID** property in the **UKCustomer1** entity.

The finished model should now contain eight entities. The part of the model that contains the two new customer entities should look like the following image:

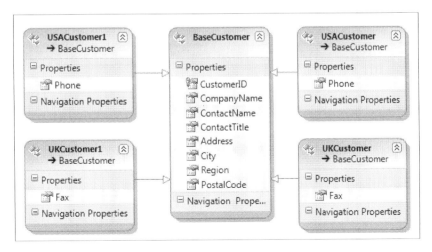

Generated classes with TPT inheritance

Save the model and open the `Northwind.designer.cs` file. You will find that two classes have been added to the model, each having only one property:

```
public partial class USACustomer1 : BaseCustomer
public partial class UKCustomer1 : BaseCustomer
```

You will also find that the class, `BaseCustomer`, now has four `KnownTypeAttribute` attributes instead of two.

Testing the TPT inheritance

Now we can write a query to show the inheritance between `BaseCustomer` and the two new derived classes.

For example, the following code will retrieve the first USA customer from `USACustomers` table, and print out its phone:

```
var usaCustomer1 = (from c
        in NWEntities.BaseCustomers.OfType<USACustomer1>()
        select c).FirstOrDefault();
var phone1 = '"'";
if (usaCustomer1 != null)
{
    phone1 = usaCustomer1.Phone;
    Console.WriteLine('"Phone for USA customer1:{0}'",
        phone1);
}
```

The following code will retrieve and print out the first UK customer's fax:

```
var ukCustomer1 = (from c
    in NWEntities.BaseCustomers.OfType<UKCustomer1>()
    select c).FirstOrDefault();
var fax1 = '"'";
if (ukCustomer1 != null)
{
    fax1 = ukCustomer1.Fax;
    Console.WriteLine('"Fax for UK customer1:{0}'",
        fax1);
}
```

In the same way as with the test result in previous sections when we used TPH inheritance in the previous query to the USACustomer1 entity, Phone is a property of the returning item and all of the BaseCustomer properties are also available because the returning item's data type is a child of the BaseCustomer type. To the UKCustomer1 entity it has all of the properties from the BaseCustomer entity plus the Fax property.

Then what about the Phone column in the BaseCustomer entity? We know that there is a Phone column in database table, Customers, and now USACustomer1 inherits BaseCustomer. Does this mean the Phone property in the child entity overrides the Phone property in the parent entity? The answer is no. Actually there is no Phone property in the parent entity, BaseCustomer, because we have moved it to another child entity, USACustomer.

We can get the Phone value in the database table, Customers, through the USACustomer entity, like in this code:

```
var usaCustomer = (from c
    in NWEntities.BaseCustomers.OfType<USACustomer>()
    where c.CustomerID == usaCustomer1.CustomerID
    select c
    ).SingleOrDefault();
```

There is no compiling error for this code, but if you run the program now, you will get an error like the following:

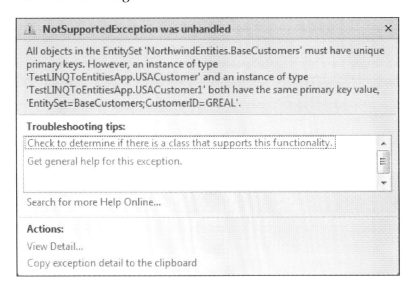

This is because within the same object context there should be only one entity for a primary key. In our model both `USACustomer` and `USACustomer1` share the same primary key, `customerID`. So if two entity objects are pointing to the same record in the database we have a problem. To test this we can change the previous code to compare the `phone` properties of both entities:

```
var usaCustomer = (from c
    in NWEntities.BaseCustomers.OfType<USACustomer>()
    where c.CustomerID == usaCustomer1.CustomerID
    select new { CustomerID = '"new PK'", c.Phone }
    ).SingleOrDefault();
```

If you run the program you will see that both phones for the first USA customer are the same as our two different child entities. If you are not sure if they are all retrieved from the right tables you can go to database, change one of the phones to a different value, run it again, and verify that each child entity is from the correct database table.

The test method should be like this:

```
static void TestTPTInheritance()
{
    NorthwindEntities NWEntities = new NorthwindEntities();
    var usaCustomer1 = (from c
        in NWEntities.BaseCustomers.OfType<USACustomer1>()
        select c).FirstOrDefault();
    var phone1 = '"'";
    if (usaCustomer1 != null)
    {
        phone1 = usaCustomer1.Phone;
        Console.WriteLine('"Phone for USA customer1:{0}'",
            phone1);
    }
    var ukCustomer1 = (from c
        in NWEntities.BaseCustomers.OfType<UKCustomer1>()
        select c).FirstOrDefault();
    var fax1 = '"'";
    if (ukCustomer1 != null)
    {
        fax1 = ukCustomer1.Fax;
        Console.WriteLine('"Fax for UK customer1:{0}'",
            fax1);
    }
    var usaCustomer = (from c
        in NWEntities.BaseCustomers.OfType<USACustomer>()
```

```
                where c.CustomerID == usaCustomer1.CustomerID
                select new { CustomerID = '"new PK'", c.Phone }
                ).SingleOrDefault();

        if (usaCustomer != null)
        {
            var phone = usaCustomer.Phone;
            Console.WriteLine(
              '"Phone for USA customer from Customers table:{0}'",
                    phone);
        }

        NWEntities.Dispose();
    }
```

The output of this is shown in the following screenshot:

Handling simultaneous (concurrent) updates

If two users are updating the same record at the same time a conflict will occur. There are normally three different ways to handle this conflict. The first method is to let the last update win so no controlling mechanism is needed. The second one is to use a pessimistic lock, in which case, before updating a record, a user will first lock the record and then process and update the record. At the same time all other users will have to wait for the lock to be released in order to start the updating process.

The third and most common mechanism in an enterprise product is the optimistic locking. A user doesn't lock a record for update when the data is retrieved but when the application is ready to commit the changes it will first check to see if any other user has updated the same record since that data was retrieved. If nobody else has changed the same record the update will be committed. If any other user has changed the same record the update will fail and the user has to decide what to do with the conflict. Some possible options include overwriting the previous changes, discarding their own changes, or refreshing the record and then reapplying (merging) the changes.

LINQ to Entities supports optimistic concurrency control in two ways. Next we will explain both of them.

Detecting conflicts using a data column

The first way is to use a regular data column to detect the conflicts. We can use the `Concurrency Mode` property for this purpose.

Explaining the Concurrency Mode property

At design time the `Concurrency Mode` property can be set for a column to be one of these two values:

- `Fixed`
- `None`

For a column there are three values to remember: the original value before update, the current value to be updated, and the database value when the change is submitted. For example, consider the case where you fetch a product record from the database with a `UnitPrice` of `25.00` and update it to `26.00`. After you fetched this product, but before you submit your changes back to the database, somebody else may have updated this product's price to `27.00`. In this example, the original value of the price is `25.00`, the current value to update is `26.00`, and the database value when the change is submitted is `27.00`.

When the change is submitted to the database the original value and the database value are compared. If they are different a conflict is detected.

Now let us look at these two settings. The first setting of the property, `Concurrency Mode`, is `Fixed`, which means that the column will be used for conflict detecting. Whenever this column is being changed its current value and database value will be checked to see if it has been updated by other users. If it has been a conflict will be raised.

The second setting, `None`, means that column will not be used for conflict checking. When a change is submitted to the database the application will not check the status of this column. So even if this column has been updated by other users it won't raise an error. This is the default setting of this property. So, by default, no column will be used for conflict detecting.

Adding another Entity Data Model

To test the concurrency of Entity Framework we have to add a second Entity Data Model to the project for the same database. The reason is that, with Entity Framework, each database record has a unique entity key within the Entity Data Model. All entity instances of the same database record will share the same entity key in the data model—even the entities are created within different object contexts.

To explain why this will stop us from testing the concurrency support of Entity Framework let's first list the steps we will take to test the concurrency control.

Below is the list of steps we will make to test the concurrency control of Entity Framework:

1. Retrieve a product from the database.
2. Update its price in memory.
3. Retrieve the same product from the database.
4. Update its price in memory again.
5. Submit the changes made in step 4 to the database.
6. Submit the changes made in step 2 to the database.

Theoretically, with the concurrency control, the commit in step 6 should fail because the product price has been changed by another user/process. However, if we use the same Entity Data Model, the product that is retrieved in step 1 will be cached. So in step 3 the product object from the cache will be returned, thus the update in step 4 will be based on the update in step 2. The commit to the database in step 5 will actually contain both changes in step 2 and step 4, therefore the commit to the database in step 6 will not fail because it really doesn't change anything in the database.

That's why we need to add another Entity Data Model to the project, so we can have two independent entity objects pointing to the same record in the database. The following are the steps to add this new Entity Data Model:

1. From Visual Studio Solution Explorer, right-click on the project, `TestLINQToEntitiesApp`, and select **Add | New Item**.
2. Select **Visual C# Items | ADO.NET Entity Data Model** as the template and change the item name to `Northwind1.edmx`.

3. Select **Generate from database** as the **Model Contents**.

4. Select the existing `Northwind` connection as the **Data Connection**.

5. Choose the table, **Products**, as the **Database Objects**.

6. Click on the **Finish** button to add the model to the project.

7. Open `Northwind1.edmx` and select the entity, **Product**.

8. Change its **Entity Set Name** to **Product1s**.

9. Change its **Name** to **Product1**.

Steps 8 and 9 are essential because there is already a public class the `Product`, in our project. If you leave it unchanged and try to build/run the solution you will find your `Northwind1.designer.cs` file is empty because the designer can't generate it due to the name conflicts.

Writing the test code

Now that we have a new Entity Data Model added to the project we can write the following code to test the concurrency control of Entity Framework:

```
// first user
Console.WriteLine('"First User ...'");
Product product = (from p in NWEntities.Products
                   where p.ProductID == 2
                   select p).First();
Console.WriteLine('"Original price: {0}'", product.UnitPrice);
product.UnitPrice += 1.0m;
Console.WriteLine('"Current price to update: {0}'",
                  product.UnitPrice);
// process more products

// second user
Console.WriteLine('"\nSecond User ...'");
NorthwindEntities1 NWEntities1 = new NorthwindEntities1();
Product1 product1 = (from p in NWEntities1.Product1s
                     where p.ProductID == 2
                     select p).First();
Console.WriteLine('"Original price: {0}'", product1.UnitPrice);
product1.UnitPrice += 2.0m;
Console.WriteLine('"Current price to update: {0}'",
                  product1.UnitPrice);
NWEntities1.SaveChanges();
Console.WriteLine('"Price update submitted to database'");
NWEntities1.Dispose();
```

```
// first user is ready to submit changes
Console.WriteLine('"\nFirst User ...'");
NWEntities.SaveChanges();
Console.WriteLine('"Price update submitted to database'");
```

In this example, we will first retrieve product 2 and increase its price by 1.0. Then we will simulate another user to retrieve the same product and increase its price by 2.0. The second user will submit the changes first with no error. When the first user tries to submit the changes and the price has already been changed by the second user the update will still be saved to the database without any problem. This is because, by default, the concurrency control is not turned on so the later change will always overwrite the previous change.

Testing the conflicts

Now run the program. You will get an output as shown in the following screenshot:

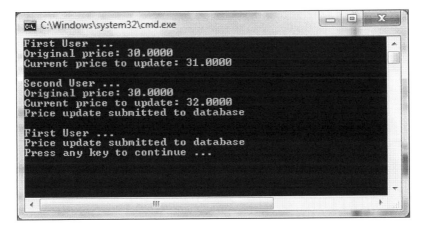

From this image we know both updates have been submitted to the database without any problem. If you query the database you will find the price of product 2 is now 31, not 32, because the first user's update overwrote the second user's update.

Turning on concurrency control

Now open `Northwind.edmx`, click on the **UnitPrice** member of the **Product** entity and change its **Concurrency Mode** to **Fixed**, as shown in following screenshot:

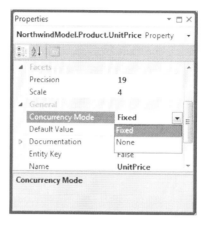

Make sure you open the `Northwind.edmx` model, not the new `Northwind1.edmx` model, because the second user within the new `Northwind1.edmx` model will submit to database first meaning that there will be no conflict for this update.

Run the program again. You will see an exception this time because the price column is now used for conflict detecting. If you query the database now you will find the price for product 2 is now 33 because it hasn't been overwritten by the first user's update, which would have updated its price to 32 if it hadn't failed due to the concurrent conflict.

The output is like this:

```
C:\Windows\system32\cmd.exe

First User ...
Original price: 31.0000
Current price to update: 32.0000

Second User ...
Original price: 31.0000
Current price to update: 33.0000
Price update submitted to database

First User ...

Unhandled Exception: System.Data.OptimisticConcurrencyException: Store update, i
nsert, or delete statement affected an unexpected number of rows (0). Entities m
ay have been modified or deleted since entities were loaded. Refresh ObjectState
Manager entries.
   at System.Data.Mapping.Update.Internal.UpdateTranslator.ValidateRowsAffected(
Int64 rowsAffected, UpdateCommand source)
   at System.Data.Mapping.Update.Internal.UpdateTranslator.Update(IEntityStateMa
nager stateManager, IEntityAdapter adapter)
   at System.Data.EntityClient.EntityAdapter.Update(IEntityStateManager entityCa
che)
   at System.Data.Objects.ObjectContext.SaveChanges(SaveOptions options)
   at System.Data.Objects.ObjectContext.SaveChanges()
   at TestLINQToEntitiesApp.Program.TestSimultaneousChanges() in C:\SOAWithWCFan
dLINQ\Projects\TestLINQ\TestLINQToEntitiesApp\Program.cs:line 489
   at TestLINQToEntitiesApp.Program.Main(String[] args) in C:\SOAWithWCFandLINQ\
Projects\TestLINQ\TestLINQToEntitiesApp\Program.cs:line 56
Press any key to continue . . .
```

To resolve this conflict we can add an exception handling block around the first
user's update, like in this code:

```
// first user is ready to submit changes
Console.WriteLine('"\nFirst User ...'");
try
{
    NWEntities.SaveChanges();
    Console.WriteLine('"Price update submitted to database'");
}
catch (OptimisticConcurrencyException e)
{
    Console.WriteLine('"Conflicts detected. Refreshing ...'");
    NWEntities.Refresh(RefreshMode.ClientWins, product);
    NWEntities.SaveChanges();
    Console.WriteLine('"Price update submitted to database after
refresh'");
}
```

You need to add a `using` block to the `Program.cs` file for the concurrency
exception type:

```
using System.Data;
```

The complete test method should be like this:

```
static void TestSimultaneousChanges()
{
    NorthwindEntities NWEntities = new NorthwindEntities();
    // first user
    Console.WriteLine('"First User ...'");
    Product product = (from p in NWEntities.Products
                        where p.ProductID == 2
                        select p).First();
    Console.WriteLine('"Original price: {0}'", product.UnitPrice);
    product.UnitPrice += 1.0m;
    Console.WriteLine('"Current price to update: {0}'",
                        product.UnitPrice);
    // process more products

    // second user
    Console.WriteLine('"\nSecond User ...'");
    NorthwindEntities1 NWEntities1 = new NorthwindEntities1();
    Product1 product1 = (from p in NWEntities1.Product1s
                        where p.ProductID == 2
                        select p).First();
```

```
        Console.WriteLine('"Original price: {0}'", product1.UnitPrice);
        product1.UnitPrice += 2.0m;
        Console.WriteLine('"Current price to update: {0}'",
                        product1.UnitPrice);
        NWEntities1.SaveChanges();
        Console.WriteLine('"Price update submitted to database'");
        NWEntities1.Dispose();

        // first user is ready to submit changes
        Console.WriteLine('"\nFirst User ...'");
        try
        {
            NWEntities.SaveChanges();
            Console.WriteLine('"Price update submitted to database'");
        }
        catch (OptimisticConcurrencyException e)
        {
            Console.WriteLine('"Conflicts detected. Refreshing ...'");
            NWEntities.Refresh(RefreshMode.ClientWins, product);
            NWEntities.SaveChanges();
            Console.WriteLine('"Price update submitted to database after
refresh'");
        }
        NWEntities.Dispose();
}
```

Run the program now and you will get an output like in following screenshot:

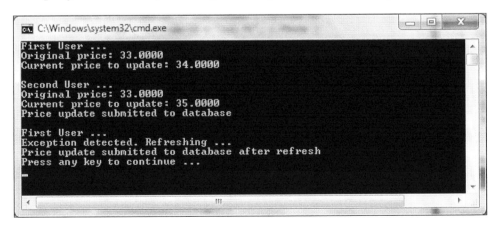

From this output we know the first user's update failed due to the concurrency conflict but, after the refresh, it won the conflict so the final price in the database should be 34— the second user's update has been overwritten by the first user's update.

With this mechanism only the involved column is protected for concurrent updates. All other columns can still be updated by multiple users or processes without causing conflicts. For example, if you change the previous code to update the UnitsInStock property you won't get a concurrency exception because the concurrency mode of UnitsInStock is not set to Fixed and the concurrency setting of UnitPrice doesn't check the UnitsInStock column in the database.

Detecting conflicts using a version column

The second and more efficient way to provide conflict control is to use a **version column**. If you add a column of type, Timestamp or ROWVERSION, when you add this table to the entity model, this column will be marked as a concurrency control version property.

Version numbers are incremented and timestamp columns are updated every time the associated row is updated. Before the update, if there is a column of this type, LINQ to Entities will first check this column to make sure that this record has not been updated by any of the other users. This column will also be synchronized immediately after the data row is updated. The new values are visible after SaveChanges finishes.

Adding a version column

Now let us try this in the `Products` table. First we need to add a new column called `RowVersion` which is of the type, `timestamp`. You can add it within SQL Server Management Studio, as shown in the following image:

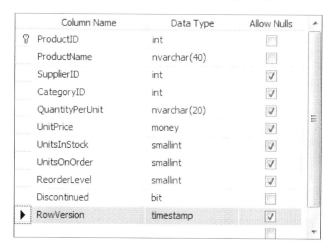

Modeling the Products table with a version column

After saving the changes we need to refresh our data model to take this change to the data model. Follow these steps to refresh the model:

1. From Visual Studio, open the `Northwind.edmx` Entity designer, right-click on an empty space, and select **Update Model from Database...**. Click on the **Refresh** tab and you will see **Products** in the refresh list.

2. Click on the **Finish** button.

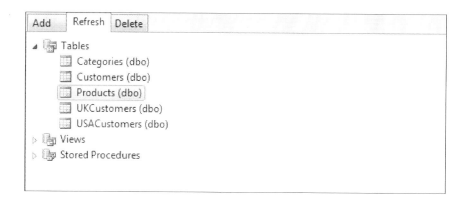

Now a new property, `RowVersion`, has been added to the `Northwind.edmx` data model. However, its **Concurrency Mode** is set to **None** now so you need to change it to **Fixed**. Note that its **StoreGeneratedPattern** is set to **Computed** which is to make sure this property will be refreshed every time after an update. The following screenshot displays the **Concurrency Mode** and **StoreGeneratedPattern** properties of the new `RowVersion` entity property:

Writing the test code

We can write similar code to test this new version controlling mechanism:

```
static void TestVersionControl()
{
    NorthwindEntities NWEntities = new NorthwindEntities();
    // first user
    Console.WriteLine('"First User ..."');
    Product product = (from p in NWEntities.Products
                       where p.ProductID == 3
                       select p).First();
    Console.WriteLine('"Original unit in stock: {0}"',
                    product.UnitsInStock);
    product.UnitsInStock += 1;
    Console.WriteLine('"Current unit in stock to update: {0}"',
```

```
        product.UnitsInStock);
    // process more products

    // second user
    Console.WriteLine('"\nSecond User ...'");
    NorthwindEntities1 NWEntities1 = new NorthwindEntities1();
    Product1 product1 = (from p in NWEntities1.Product1s
                         where p.ProductID == 3
                         select p).First();
    Console.WriteLine('"Original unit in stock: {0}'",
        product1.UnitsInStock);
    product1.UnitsInStock += 2;
    Console.WriteLine('"Current unit in stock to update: {0}'",
        product1.UnitsInStock);
    NWEntities1.SaveChanges();
    Console.WriteLine('"update submitted to database'");
    NWEntities1.Dispose();

    // first user is ready to submit changes
    Console.WriteLine('"\nFirst User ...'");
    try
    {
        NWEntities.SaveChanges();
    }
    catch (OptimisticConcurrencyException)
    {
     Console.WriteLine('"Conflicts detected. Refreshing ...'");
     NWEntities.Refresh(RefreshMode.ClientWins, product);
     NWEntities.SaveChanges();
     Console.WriteLine('"update submitted to database after
refresh'");
    }

    NWEntities.Dispose();
}
```

Testing the conflicts

This time we tried to update `UnitInStock` for product 3. From the output we can see a conflict was detected again when the first user submitted changes to the database.

Transaction support

In the previous section we learned that simultaneous changes by different users can be controlled by using a version column or the `Concurrency Mode` property. Sometimes the same user may have made several changes and some of the changes might not succeed. In this case we need a way to control the behavior of the overall update result. This is handled by transaction support.

LINQ to Entities uses the same transaction mechanism as ADO.NET, that is, it uses implicit or explicit transactions.

Implicit transactions

By default, LINQ to Entities uses an implicit transaction for each `SaveChanges` call. All updates between two `SaveChanges` calls are wrapped within one transaction.

For example, in the following code, we are trying to update two products. The second update will fail due to a constraint. However, as the first update is in a separate transaction, the update has been saved to the database and the first update will stay in the database:

```
static void TestImplicitTransaction()
{
    NorthwindEntities NWEntities = new NorthwindEntities();
```

```
Product prod1 = (from p in NWEntities.Products
                 where p.ProductID == 4
                 select p).First();
Product prod2 = (from p in NWEntities.Products
                 where p.ProductID == 5
                 select p).First();
prod1.UnitPrice += 1;
// update will be saved to database
NWEntities.SaveChanges();
Console.WriteLine('"First update saved to database'");

prod2.UnitPrice = -5;
// update will fail because UnitPrice can't be < 0
// but previous update stays in database
try
{
    NWEntities.SaveChanges();
    Console.WriteLine('"Second update saved to database'");
}
catch (Exception)
{
    Console.WriteLine('"Second update not saved to database'");
}

NWEntities.Dispose();
}
```

The output will look like this:

Explicit transactions

In addition to implicit transactions you can also define a transaction scope to explicitly control the update behavior. All updates within a transaction scope will be within a single transaction. Thus they will all either succeed or fail.

For example, in the following code, we start a transaction scope first. Then, within this transaction scope, we update one product and submit the change to the database. However, at this point, the update has not really been committed because the transaction scope is still not closed. We then try to update another product which fails due to the same constraint as in the previous example. The final result is that neither of these two products has been updated in database.

```
static void TestExplicitTransaction()
{
    NorthwindEntities NWEntities = new NorthwindEntities();
    using (TransactionScope ts = new TransactionScope())
    {
        try
        {
            Product prod1 = (from p in NWEntities.Products
                             where p.ProductID == 4
                             select p).First();
            prod1.UnitPrice += 1;
            NWEntities.SaveChanges();
            Console.WriteLine('"First update saved to database,
                             but not commited.'");

            // now let's try to update another product
            Product prod2 = (from p in NWEntities.Products
                             where p.ProductID == 5
                             select p).First();
            // update will fail because UnitPrice can't be < 0
            prod2.UnitPrice = -5;
            NWEntities.SaveChanges();
        }
        catch (Exception e)
        {
            // both updates will fail because they are wihtin one
            transaction
            Console.WriteLine('"Both updates failed.
                             Rollback the first update.'");
        }
    }
    NWEntities.Dispose();
}
```

Note that `TransactionScope` is in .NET Assembly `System.Transactions`. So you need to add a reference to `System.Transactions` first and then add the following `using` statement to the `Program.cs` file:

```
using System.Transactions;
```

The output of the program is shown below:

 To use `TransactionScope` you need to have **Microsoft Distributed Transaction Coordinator (MSDTC)** configured properly. We will cover distributed transaction in detail in a subsequent chapter, so if you encounter any problem related to MSDTC here you can refer to that chapter to set up your MSDTC environment or you can just skip this section for now and come back later after reading that chapter.

If you start the program in debugging mode, after the first `SaveChanges` is called, you can go to SQL Server Management Studio and query the price of product 4 using the following statement:

```
select UnitPrice from products (nolock) where productID = 4
```

The `nolock` hint is equivalent to READUNCOMMITTED and it is used to retrieve dirty data that has not been committed. With this hint you can see its price has been increased by the first change. Then after the second `SaveChanges` is called, an exception is thrown, and the transaction scope is closed. At this point if you run the query again you will see that the price of product 4 is rolled back to its original value.

After the first call to the `SaveChanges` method you shouldn't use the following statement to query the price value of the product:

```
select UnitPrice from products where productID = 4
```

If you do so you will not get back a result. Instead you will be waiting forever as it is waiting for the transaction to be committed.

Adding validations to entity classes

Validating data is the process of confirming that the values entered into data objects comply with the constraints in an object's schema, in addition to the rules established for your application. Validating data before you send updates to the underlying database is a good practice that reduces both errors and the potential number of round trips between an application and the database.

The Entity designer provides partial methods that enable users to extend the designer-generated code that runs during Inserts, Updates, and Deletes of complete entities and also during and after individual column changes.

These validation methods are all partial methods. Therefore, there is no overhead at all if you don't implement them because unimplemented partial methods are not compiled into IL.

You can implement a validation method in another partial class. In our example we can add the following method to the `Program.cs` file:

```
public partial class Product
{
    partial void OnProductNameChanging(string value)
    {
        if (value.IndexOf('"@'") >= 0)
            throw new Exception('"ProductName can not contain @'");
    }
}
```

You can add this class right after the test methods and before the extension class. You can also add a new file to contain only this class.

Now we can test it using the following code:

```
static void TestValidations()
{
    NorthwindEntities NWEntities = new NorthwindEntities();
    Product product = (from p in NWEntities.Products
                       where p.ProductID == 5
                       select p).First();
    try
    {
        product.ProductName = '"Name @ this place'";
        NWEntities.SaveChanges();
    }
    catch (Exception e)
    {
        Console.WriteLine('"Update failed. Reason: {0}'", e.Message);
    }
    NWEntities.Dispose();
}
```

Run this program and you will get an output as shown in the following screenshot:

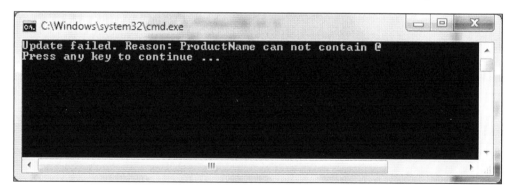

You can implement any of the validation methods for any properties before or after the change.

Debugging LINQ to Entities programs

In Visual Studio 2010, when debugging a LINQ to Entities program, we can use the traditional **Watch** or **Autos** windows to inspect a variable. For example, after the following line is executed, we can go to the **Autos** window to see the contents of the products variable:

```
var products = from p in NWEntities.Products
               where p.CategoryID == 1
               select p;
```

The **Autos** window should look like this:

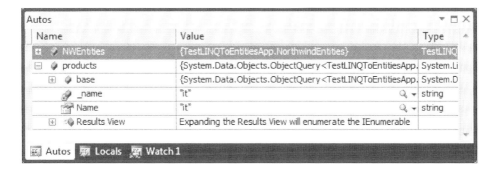

We can also hover our mouse over the **products** variable, wait for the **Quick Info** pop-up window to appear, and then inspect it on the fly. The pop-up **Quick Info** window will appear as shown in the following image:

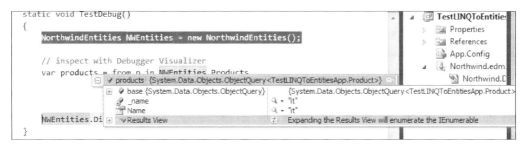

In either of the windows we can inspect the returned result of the variable, its properties, and even its children.

 This inspection may trigger a real query to the database. For example, if you try to open **Results View**, the database will be queried to get all of the products that meet the search criteria. This may have some side effects if you don't expect the query to be executed at this point.

Summary

In this chapter, we have learned some advanced features of LINQ to Entities. At this point we should have a good understanding of LINQ to Entities. In the next chapter, we will apply these skills to the data access layer of our WCF service to connect to databases securely and reliably with LINQ to Entities.

The key points covered in this chapter include:

- LINQ to Entities fully supports stored procedures
- Compiled queries can increase the performance of repeatedly-executed LINQ queries
- LINQ to Entities allows SQL-like queries to the conceptual data model
- Dynamic Queries can be built at runtime using expressions or parameters
- LINQ to Entities supports table per hierarchy, table per type, and table per concrete inheritance
- Concurrent updates can be controlled using a `Concurrency Mode` property or a `Version` column
- By default, LINQ to Entities updates are within one implicit transaction
- Explicit transactions can be defined for LINQ to Entities updates by using `TransactionScope`
- Customized validation code can be added to LINQ to Entities entity classes
- A debugging process may trigger a real query to the database

9

Applying LINQ to Entities to a WCF Service

Now that we have learned all of the features related to LINQ and LINQ to Entities we will use them in the data access layer of a WCF service. We will create a new WCF service very similar to the one we created in the previous chapters but in this service we will use LINQ to Entities to connect to the Northwind database to retrieve and update a product.

In the data access layer we will use LINQ to Entities to retrieve product information from the database and return it to the business logic layer. You will see that with LINQ to Entities we will need only one LINQ statement to retrieve the product details from the database in the GetProduct method and we will no longer need to worry about the database connection or the actual query statement.

In this chapter, we will also learn how to update a product with LINQ to Entities in the data access layer. We will see how to attach an entity object to LINQ to Entities ObjectContext and leave all of the update work to LINQ to Entities and will also see how to control the concurrency of updates with LINQ to Entities.

In this chapter, we will cover:

- Creating the solution
- Modeling the Northwind database in LINQ to Entities designer
- Implementing the data access layer using LINQ to Entities
- Modifying the business logic layer
- Modifying the service interface layer
- Implementing the test client
- Testing the get and update operations of the WCF service
- Testing concurrent updates with LINQ to Entities

Creating the LINQNorthwind solution

The first thing we need to do is to create a test solution. In this chapter we will modify a copy of our last solution, RealNorthwind, to test LINQ to Entities in the data access layer.

Note that you can create the solution from scratch if you like or you can just copy and reuse the RealNorthwind solution without any modification. If you are going to reuse the RealNorthwind solution, wherever you see LINQNorthwind in this chapter, you can just replace it with RealNorthwind and continue.

Here we will make a copy first then rename and change all the words Real to LINQ so that we will have a dedicated solution to test LINQ to Entities.

Now follow these steps to create this solution:

1. Open Windows Explorer and create a new folder, LINQNorthwind, under C:\SOAWithWCFandLINQ\Projects.

2. Copy all files and folders from the RealNorthwind project folder C:\SOAWithWCFandLINQ\Projects\RealNorthwind to the new folder C:\SOAWithWCFandLINQ\Projects\LINQNorthwind.

3. Under the new folder, LINQNorthwind, remove these two subfolders: RealNorthwindService2 and RealNorthwindClient.

4. Change all the folder names under the new folder, LINQNorthwind, from RealNorthwindxxx to LINQNorthwindxxx.

5. Change the solution file name from RealNorthwind.sln to LINQNorthwind. sln and also from RealNorthwind.suo to LINQNorthwind.suo.

The structure and content of the new folder, **LINQNorthwind**, should be as shown in the next screenshot:

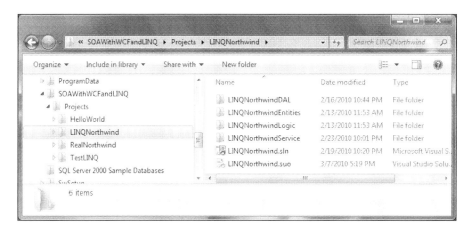

Now we have the file structures ready for the new solution but all the file contents and the solution structure are still for the old solution. Next we need to change them for the new solution.

We will first change all the related WCF service files. Once we have the service up and running we will create a new client to test this new service. Follow these steps to change the service files:

1. Start Visual Studio 2010 and open this solution: `C:\SOAWithWCFandLINQ\Projects\LINQNorthwind\LINQNorthwind.sln`.

2. Click on the **OK** button to close this warning dialog:

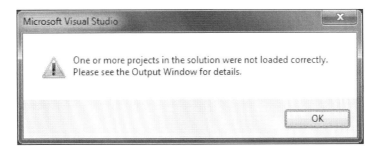

3. Remove all five projects from Solution Explorer (they should all be unavailable).

4. Right-click on the solution item and select **Add | Existing Projects...** to add these four projects to the solution. Note that these are the projects under the `LINQNorthwind` folder, not the ones under the `RealNorthwind` folder:

    `RealNorthwindEntities.csproj, RealNorthwindDAL.csproj, RealNorthwindLogic.csproj, and RealNorthwindService.csproj.`

5. In Solution Explorer, change all of the above four projects' names from `RealNorthwindxxx` to `LINQNorthwindxxx`.

6. In Solution Explorer, right-click on each project, select **Properties** (or select menu **Project | LINQNorthwindxxx Properties**), then change the **Assembly name** from **RealNorthwindxxx** to **LINQNorthwindxxx** and change the **Default namespace** from **MyWCFServices.RealNorthwindxxx** to **MyWCFServices.LINQNorthwindxxx**

The project properties for `LINQNorthwindEntities` are shown here:

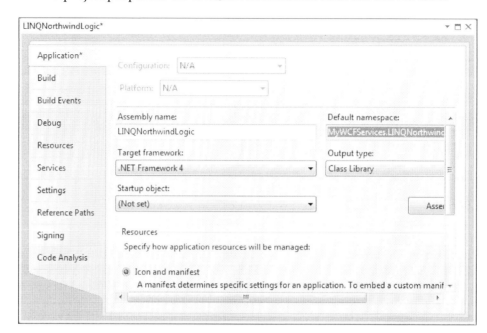

7. Open the following files and change the word, `RealNorthwind` to `LINQNorthwind` in these files:

   `ProductEntity.cs, ProductDAO.cs, ProductLogic.cs, IProductService.cs, and ProductService.cs.`

8. Open the file, `app.config`, in the `LINQNorthwindService` project and change the word, `RealNorthwind` to `LINQNorthwind` in this file.

9. Set the project, `LINQNorthwindService`, as the startup project and you should now be able to run the program. The output should be same as the one we had for the project, `Realnorthwind`.

Modeling the Northwind database

In the previous section we renamed the `RealNorthwind` solution, `LINQNorthwind` solution. Next we will apply LINQ to Entities to this new solution, `LINQNorthwind`.

For the data access layer, we will use LINQ to Entities instead of the raw ADO.NET data adapters. As you will see in the next section, we will use one LINQ statement to retrieve product information from the database and the update LINQ statements will handle the concurrency control for us easily and reliably.

As you may recall, to use LINQ to Entities in the data access layer of our WCF service, we first need to add an Entity data model to the project. The following steps are very similar to those described in the previous chapter. You can refer back to that chapter for more information and screenshots if necessary.

- In Solution Explorer, right-click on the project item, LINQNorthwindDAL, select menu option **Add | New Item...**, and then choose **Visual C# Items | ADO.NET Entity Data Model** as the Template and enter **Northwind.edmx** as the **name**.

- Select **Generate from database**, choose the existing **Northwind** connection, and add the **Products** table to the model.

- The new column, **RowVersion**, should be in the **Product** entity as we added it in the previous chapter. If it is not there, add it to the table with a type of **Timestamp**, and refresh the entity data model.

Just as in the previous chapter, this will generate a file called Northwind.designer. cs which contains the object context for the Northwind database. This file also contains the Product entity class.

There is a standalone project, LINQNorthwindEntities, in the solution. As you may recall, this is the project where we define all of the data entities for the WCF service. However, because the entity classes are all contained inside the LINQ to Entities designer class, this project is no longer needed. We can simply reference the LINQNorthwindDAL project in all three layers and use the Product entity class from the LINQNorthwindDAL project in all three layers. However there is a drawback to this approach, that is, all three layers will have full access to the LINQNorthwindDAL assembly. It is possible for the service interface layer to go to the data access layer directly, bypassing the business logic layer. This is not a good practice as it is against our layering principals. All three layers have to reference the DAL assembly, which makes it impossible to decouple the service layer from the data access layer.

To solve this issue, here we will keep the ProductEntity project and inside the data access layer, after we get a product from the entity model, we will convert it to our ProductEntity type and then still return a ProductEntity object to the business logic layer from the data access layer. In this way we don't need to expose the data access layer at all. We also don't need to change the service interface layer or the business logic layer because the data access method signatures are the same as before. We will explain more when we modify the data access layer later in this chapter.

Copying the connection string to the service layer

In the previous section we added an entity model to the data access layer project. The connection string is stored in the App.config file in the LINQNorthwindDAL project. However this configuration file is only used by the .NET Entity Modeler to retrieve schema information from the database at design time. At runtime the configuration file in the service interface layer is used to get the actual database connection string. So, in this section, we will copy and paste this connection string to the service interface layer project.

The following are the steps to add this connection string to the service interface layer:

1. Open the file, App.config, in the LINQNorthwindDAL project.

2. Copy the connection strings part in this file which should be like this:

```
<connectionStrings>

  <add name="NorthwindEntities" connectionString="metadat
a=res://*/Northwind.csdl|res://*/Northwind.ssdl|res://*/
Northwind.msl;provider=System.Data.SqlClient;provider connection
string=&quot;Data Source=localhost;Initial Catalog=Northwind;User
ID=sa;MultipleActiveResultSets=True&quot;" providerName="System.
Data.EntityClient" />

</connectionStrings>
```

3. Open the file, App.config, in the LINQNorthwindService project.

4. Replace the old connectionStrings node with the above connectionStrings node. Note that the old connection string is using SqlClient but the new connection string is using EntityClient.

5. Open the file, ProductDAO.cs, in the LINQNorthwindDAL project.

6. Remove the following line of code from this file:

```
string connectionString =
    ConfigurationManager .ConnectionStrings["NorthwindConnectionSt
ring"].ConnectionString;
```

The top part of the App.config file in the LINQNorthwindService project should be like this:

```
<?xml version="1.0" encoding="utf-8" ?>
<configuration>

  <connectionStrings>
```

```
    <add name="NorthwindEntities" connectionString="metadata=res://*/
Northwind.csdl|res://*/Northwind.ssdl|res://*/
Northwind.msl;provider=System.Data.SqlClient;provider connection
string=&quot;Data Source=localhost;Initial Catalog=Northwind;
User ID=sa;MultipleActiveResultSets=True&quot;" providerName="System.
Data.EntityClient" />
  </connectionStrings>

  <system.web>
    <compilation debug="true" />
  </system.web>
```

As mentioned at the beginning of this section, the WCF service runtime will look at the service interface layer `app.config` file for the connection string. If you don't put this connection string at the service interface layer you may get this error later when you test this service:

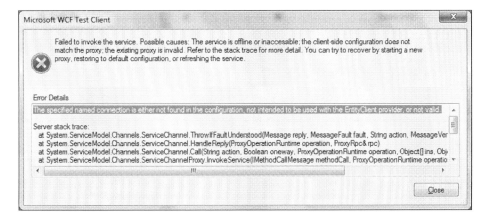

You should leave the original connection string untouched in the `App.config` file in the data access layer project. This connection string is used by the Entity Model Designer at design time. It is not used at all during runtime, but if you remove it, whenever you open the entity model designer in Visual Studio, you will be prompted to specify a connection to your database.

Using LINQ to Entities in the data access layer

Now we have the solution, the Entity model, and the connection string. Next we will modify the data access layer to use LINQ to Entities to retrieve and update products. We will first modify `GetProduct` to retrieve a product from the database and then modify `UpdateProduct` to update a product in the database. In this section the `UpdateProduct` method will not have concurrency control. It will simply commit the changes to the database even though the product has been changed by other users. In the upcoming section, *Adding concurrency support*, we will make further changes to the service so that concurrent updates can be controlled properly.

Modifying GetProduct in the data access layer

We can now modify the `GetProduct` method in the data access layer class, `ProductDAO`, to use LINQ to Entities to retrieve a product from the database. Just as we did in the previous chapter, we will first create an Entity, `ObjectContext`, and then use LINQ to Entities to get the product from `ObjectContext`. The product we get from `ObjectContext` will be a conceptual entity model object. We don't want to pass this product object back to the upper-level layer because we don't want to tightly couple the business logic layer with the data access layer. Therefore we will convert this Entity model product object to a `ProductEntity` object and then pass this `ProductEntity` object back to the upper-level layers.

The modified `GetProduct` method should be like this:

```
public ProductEntity GetProduct(int id)
{
    NorthwindEntities NWEntities = new NorthwindEntities();
    Product product = (from p in NWEntities.Products
                       where p.ProductID == id
                       select p).FirstOrDefault();
    ProductEntity productEntity = null;
    if (product != null)
    {
        productEntity = new ProductEntity()
        {
            ProductID = product.ProductID,
            ProductName = product.ProductName,
            QuantityPerUnit = product.QuantityPerUnit,
            UnitPrice = (decimal)product.UnitPrice,
            UnitsInStock = (int)product.UnitsInStock,
            ReorderLevel = (int)product.ReorderLevel,
```

```
            UnitsOnOrder = (int)product.UnitsOnOrder,
            Discontinued = product.Discontinued,
        };
    }
    NWEntities.Dispose();
    return productEntity;
}
```

You will recall that in the previous chapter, for the `GetProduct` method, we had to create an ADO.NET connection, create an ADO.NET command object with that connection, specify the command text, connect to the `Northwind` database, and send the SQL statement to the database for execution. After the result was returned from the database we had to loop through the `DataReader` and cast the columns to our entity object one by one.

With LINQ to Entities, we only construct one LINQ to Entities statement and everything else is handled by LINQ to Entities. Not only do we need to write less code but now the statement is also strongly typed. We won't have a runtime error like **invalid query syntax** or **invalid column name**. Also, an SQL Injection attack is no longer an issue, as LINQ to Entities will also take care of this when translating LINQ expressions to underlying SQL statements.

Modifying UpdateProduct in the data access layer

In the previous section, we modified the `GetProduct` method in the data access layer to use LINQ to Entities instead of ADO.NET. Now in this section, we will modify the `UpdateProduct` method to use LINQ to Entities instead of ADO.NET. In this section we will update a product in the database using LINQ to Entities but we will not put concurrency control to this update. In a following section, we will turn on concurrency control on the entity model and modify a few more lines of code to utilize LINQ to Entities concurrency control to make sure simultaneous updates are handled properly.

Let's modify the `UpdateProduct` method in the data access layer, as follows:

```
public bool UpdateProduct(ProductEntity productEntity)
{
    // check product ID
    NorthwindEntities NWEntities = new NorthwindEntities();

    Product productInDB =
            (from p
             in NWEntities.Products
```

```
                where p.ProductID == productEntity.ProductID
                select p).FirstOrDefault();
    // check product
    if (productInDB == null)
    {
        throw new Exception("No product with ID " +
                        productEntity.ProductID);
    }
    // update product price
    productInDB.ProductName = productEntity.ProductName;
    productInDB.QuantityPerUnit = productEntity.QuantityPerUnit;
    productInDB.UnitPrice = productEntity.UnitPrice;
    productInDB.Discontinued = productEntity.Discontinued;
    //productInDB.RowVersion = productEntity.RowVersion;

    NWEntities.SaveChanges();
    NWEntities.Dispose();

    return true;
}
```

Inside this method we first retrieve the product from database then check to see if the product to be updated is a valid product in our database. If not, processing will stop, and an exception will be thrown.

Then we update the values of the columns, ProductName, UnitPrice, Discontinued, and QuantityPerUnit to associated properties of the product entity that is passed in from the service interface layer. After we call the SaveChanges method of the entity model these columns are updated in the database.

Testing LINQ to Entities with the WCF Test Client

Now we can run the program to test the GetProduct and UpdateProduct operations with the WCF Test Client.

First set LINQNorthwindService as the startup project and then press *Ctrl + F5* to start the WCF Test Client. Click on **GetProduct**, enter a valid product ID, and click on the **Invoke** button. The detailed product information should be retrieved and displayed on the screen.

Now click on **UpdateProduct**, enter a valid product ID, and specify a name, price, quantity per unit, and then click on **Invoke**. This product will be updated in the database.

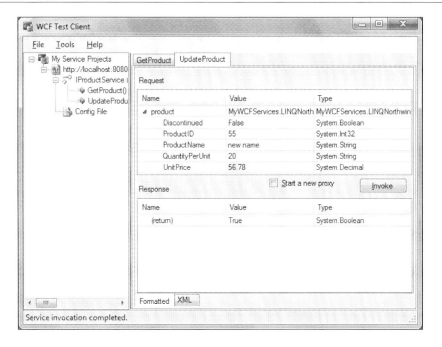

If you get a **False** result make sure the product ID is valid (between 0 and 77), the product name and quantity per unit are not empty, and the unit price is greater than 0. Remember these are the conditions for the `UpdateProduct` operation we added in the business logic layer.

If you get an error like **The specified named connection is either not found in the configuration, not intended to be used with the EntityClient provider, or not valid**, make sure you have copied the entity connection string to your service layer project `App.config` file, as described earlier in this chapter.

Adding concurrency support

You may have noticed that in the section, *Modifying UpdateProduct in the data access layer*, we commented out a line of code about the `RowVersion` in the `ProductDAO.cs` file. This is because in our `ProductEntity` class there is no property for `RowVersion`. Concurrent updates are not supported by this service now. Next we will modify a few classes to add concurrent update control.

Turning on RowVersion concurrency mode

At the beginning of this chapter, when we added the `Products` table to our entity data model, we didn't turn on concurrency mode for the `RowVersion` column, even though its data type is `timestamp`. We just changed the data access layer from ADO.NET to LINQ to Entities without concurrency control. Even if we had turned on concurrency mode for the `RowVersion` column on the Entity data model at that time, we still wouldn't have concurrency control. We need to modify a few more classes to achieve concurrency control. In this section we will explain how to add concurrency control to our service.

To add concurrency support to our WCF service the first thing we need to do is to turn on concurrency mode for the `RowVersion` column on the Entity data model.

To turn it on, just as we did in the previous chapter, open the `Northwind.edmx` model, select the **RowVersion** property, and change its **Concurrency Mode** from **None** to **Fixed**. Note that its **StoreGeneratedPattern** should remain as **Computed**. You can look at the *Turning on concurrency control* section in the previous chapter for a screenshot.

Modifying the ProductEntity class

Next we need to modify the `ProductEntity` class to support concurrent updates. We need to add a new property to this class to hold the `RowVersion` value.

To do this, open the `ProductEntity.cs` file in the `LINQNorthwindEntities` project and add this property to the class:

```
public Byte[] RowVersion { get; set; }
The ProductEntity class should be like this now:
public class ProductEntity
{
    public int ProductID { get; set; }
    public string ProductName { get; set; }
    public string QuantityPerUnit { get; set; }
    public decimal UnitPrice { get; set; }
    public int UnitsInStock { get; set; }
    public int ReorderLevel { get; set; }
    public int UnitsOnOrder { get; set; }
    public bool Discontinued { get; set; }
    public Byte[] RowVersion { get; set; }
}
```

Modifying the ProductDAO class

Then we need to modify the `ProductDAO` class to support concurrent updates. We need to modify both the get and update methods in this layer for concurrency support.

Modifying the GetProduct method

First we need to modify the `GetProduct` method to return the `RowVersion` property from the database. Follow these steps to make this change:

1. Open the `ProductDAO.cs` file in the `LINQNorthwindDAL` project.

2. Add this line of code to the `GetProduct` method, after the line of `Discontinued`:

   ```
   RowVersion = product.RowVersion
   ```

The `GetProduct` method in the `ProductDAO` class should be like this now:

```
public ProductEntity GetProduct(int id)
{
    NorthwindEntities NWEntities = new NorthwindEntities();
    Product product = (from p in NWEntities.Products
                        where p.ProductID == id
                        select p).FirstOrDefault();
    ProductEntity productEntity = null;
    if (product != null)
    {
        productEntity = new ProductEntity()
        {
            ProductID = product.ProductID,
            ProductName = product.ProductName,
            QuantityPerUnit = product.QuantityPerUnit,
            UnitPrice = (decimal)product.UnitPrice,
            UnitsInStock = (int)product.UnitsInStock,
            ReorderLevel = (int)product.ReorderLevel,
            UnitsOnOrder = (int)product.UnitsOnOrder,
            Discontinued = product.Discontinued,
            RowVersion = product.RowVersion
        };
    }
    NWEntities.Dispose();
    return productEntity;
}
```

Modifying UpdateProduct method

To modify the `UpdateProduct` method to support concurrent updates we need to "force" the entity framework to treat the `RowVersion` value from the client as the current `RowVersion` value for the variable `product`, `InDB`. It should not use the cached entity's `RowVersion` value when submitting to the database. Fortunately, with Entity Framework 4.0, we can use the `detach` and `attach` methods to achieve this.

Besides using the client side `RowVersion` value when updating database, we also need to return the new `RowVersion` value back to the client so that the client can do consecutive updates to the same product without causing concurrency exceptions.

The following are the specific steps to make the `UpdateProduct` method support concurrent updates:

1. Retrieve the product from the database.
2. Detach it from the object context so that we can update the `RowVersion` value.
3. Update the product's properties, including `RowVersion`.
4. Attach the product to the object context.
5. Mark the product entity as `Modified`.
6. Submit the product entity to the database.
7. Change the `productEntity` parameter to `ref` type, refresh its `RowVersion` value after the above step so that the client can get the latest `RowVersion` value after an update.

The modified method, `UpdateProduct`, is like this:

```
public bool UpdateProduct(ref ProductEntity productEntity)
{
    // check product ID
    NorthwindEntities NWEntities = new NorthwindEntities();
    // save productID in a variable
    int productID = productEntity.ProductID;

    Product productInDB =
        (from p
         in NWEntities.Products
         where p.ProductID == productID
         select p).FirstOrDefault();
    // check product
    if (productInDB == null)
    {
```

```
            throw new Exception("No product with ID " +
                    productEntity.ProductID);
        }
    // first detach the object
    NWEntities.Detach(productInDB);

    // update product
    productInDB.ProductName = productEntity.ProductName;
    productInDB.QuantityPerUnit = productEntity.QuantityPerUnit;
    productInDB.UnitPrice = productEntity.UnitPrice;
    productInDB.Discontinued = productEntity.Discontinued;
    productInDB.RowVersion = productEntity.RowVersion;

    // now attach the object again
    NWEntities.Attach(productInDB);
    NWEntities.ObjectStateManager.ChangeObjectState(productInDB,
        System.Data.EntityState.Modified);

    NWEntities.SaveChanges();

    //refresh the RowVersion property
    productEntity.RowVersion = productInDB.RowVersion;

    NWEntities.Dispose();

    return true;
}
```

A few notes for the above code:

- You have to save `productID` in a new variable and then use it in the LINQ query. Otherwise you will get an error saying **Cannot use ref or out parameter 'productEntity' inside an anonymous method, lambda expression, or query expression**.

- If `Detach` and `Attach` are not called, `RowVersion` from the database and not from the client, will be used when submitting to database even though you have updated its value before submitting to the database. The update will still succeed but without concurrency control.

- If `Detach` is not called, when you call the `Attach` method you will get an error **The object cannot be attached because it is already in the object context**.

- If `ChangeObjectState` is not called Entity framework will not honor your change to the entity object and you will not be able to save any change to the database.

Modifying the business logic layer classes

Now that we have changed the `UpdateProduct` method in the `ProductDAO` class we need to change the business logic class to call it using the new signature. We also need to change the `UpdateProduct` method in this layer to pass back the new `RowVersion` value to the client:

1. Open the file, `ProductLogic.cs`, in the project, `LINQNorthwindLogic`.

2. Change the `UpdateProduct` function definition to be like this:

   ```
   public bool UpdateProduct(ref ProductEntity product)
   ```

3. Change the last line of the `UpdateProduct` method to be like this:

   ```
   return productDAO.UpdateProduct(ref product);
   ```

Modifying the service interface layer classes

As we have changed the signature of the business logic layer classes we need to change the service interface layer classes to call the business logic layer with the new signature. We also need to change the service interface layer to pass back the new `RowVersion` value after an update to the client so that the client code can use the new `RowVersion` to make consecutive updates.

For the service interface layer classes, we need to make the following changes to support the concurrent updates:

- Open the file, `IProductService.cs`, in the project, `LINQNorthwindService`.

- Add the following property to the `Product` class:

  ```
  [DataMember]
  public Byte[] RowVersion { get; set; }
  ```

- Change the `UpdateProduct` definition to be like this:

  ```
  bool UpdateProduct(ref Product product);
  ```

- Open the `ProductService.cs` file in the same project.

- Add the following line of code to the end of the method, `TranslateProductEntityToProductContractData`:

  ```
  product.RowVersion = productEntity.RowVersion;
  ```

- Add the following line of code to the end of the method, `TranslateProductContractDataToProductEntity`:

```
productEntity.RowVersion = product.RowVersion;
```

- Change the `UpdateProduct` method to be like this:.

```
public bool UpdateProduct(ref Product product)
{
    /*
    // TODO: call business logic layer to update product
    if (product.UnitPrice <= 0)
        return false;
    else
        return true;
    */
    ProductEntity productEntity = new ProductEntity();
    TranslateProductContractDataToProductEntity(product,
productEntity);

    bool result = productLogic.UpdateProduct(ref productEntity);
    if(result == true)
        product.RowVersion = productEntity.RowVersion;

    return result;
}
```

Testing concurrency with WCF Test Client

Now we have concurrent support added to the service let's test it with the built-in WCF Test Client.

Press *Ctrl + F5* to start the program. Click on **GetProduct**, enter a valid product ID, and then click on the **Invoke** button to get the product details. You should have a screen like the following image.

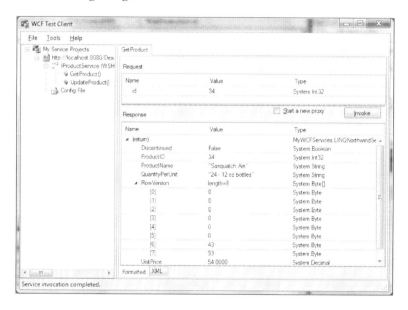

From this image we know the product, `RowVersion`, is returned from the database to the client. It is of the `Byte[]` type.

Now click on **UpdateProduct** and enter the same product ID, a new name, quantity per unit, and unit price. However, you can't enter a value to the `RowVersion` field for this update because it is of the `byte[]` type.

If you click on the **Invoke** button to call the service you will get an exception like this:

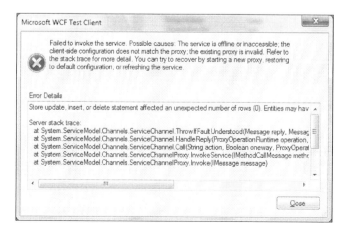

From this image we can see that the update failed due to concurrency control (actually a concurrency exception is thrown in the data access layer). The reason is that we didn't pass in the original RowVersion for the object to be updated and the entity framework thinks this product has been updated by some other user.

Testing concurrency with our own client

Creating the test client

Now that the service is ready we need to create a client to test it. In this section we will create a WinForm client to get the product details and update price for a product.

Follow these steps to create the test client:

- In Solution Explorer, right-click the solution item, and select **Add | New Project...**
- Select **Visual C# | Windows Forms Application** as the template and change the name to **LINQNorthwindClient**. Click on the **OK** button to add the new project.
- On the form designer, add the following five controls:
    - ○ A label named **lblProductID** with text, **Product ID**
    - ○ A textbox named **txtProductID**
    - ○ A button named **btnGetProduct** with text, **&Get Product Details**
    - ○ A label named **lblProductDetails** with text, **Product Details**
    - ○ A textbox named **txtProductDetails** with the **Multiline** property set to **True**

The layout of the form is like this:

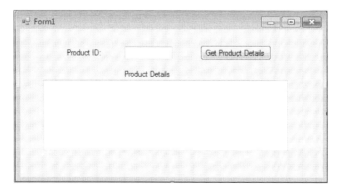

- In Solution Explorer, right-click on the LINQNorthwindClient project and select **Add Service Reference…**.

- On the **Add Service Reference** window, click on the **Discover** button, wait a minute until the service is displayed, then change the **Namespace** from **ServiceReference1** to **ProductServiceRef**, and click on the **OK** button.

The **Add Service Reference** window should be like the next screenshot:

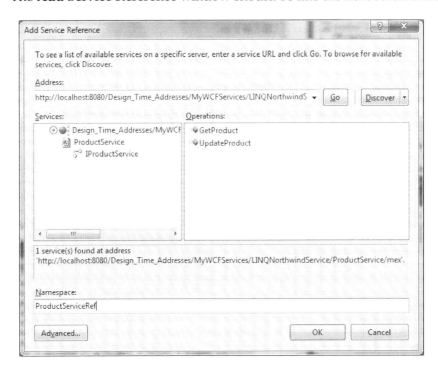

Implementing the GetProduct functionality

Now that we have the test client created we will customize the client application to test the new WCF service.

First we need to customize the test client to call the WCF service to get a product from the database so that we can test the GetProduct operation with LINQ to Entities.

We will call a WCF service through the proxy so let's add the following lines `using` statements to the form class in the file, `Form1.cs`:

```
using LINQNorthwindClient.ProductServiceRef;
using System.ServiceModel;
```

Then on the forms designer, double-click on the **btnGetProductDetails** button and add an event handler for this button, as follows:

```
private void btnGetProduct_Click(object sender, EventArgs e)
{
    ProductServiceClient client = new ProductServiceClient();
    string result = "";

    try
    {
        int productID = Int32.Parse(txtProductID.Text.ToString());
        Product product = client.GetProduct(productID);

        StringBuilder sb = new StringBuilder();
        sb.Append("ProductID:" +
            product.ProductID.ToString() + "\r\n");
        sb.Append("ProductName:" +
            product.ProductName + "\r\n");
        sb.Append("QuantityPerUnit:" +
            product.QuantityPerUnit + "\r\n");
        sb.Append("UnitPrice:" +
            product.UnitPrice.ToString() + "\r\n");
        sb.Append("Discontinued:" +
            product.Discontinued.ToString() + "\r\n");
        sb.Append("RowVersion:");
        foreach (var x in product.RowVersion.AsEnumerable())
        {
            sb.Append(x.ToString());
             sb.Append(" ");
        }
        result = sb.ToString();
    }
    catch (TimeoutException ex)
    {
        result = "The service operation timed out. " +
            ex.Message;
    }
    catch (FaultException<ProductFault> ex)
    {
```

```
            result = "ProductFault returned: " +
                ex.Detail.FaultMessage;
        }
        catch (FaultException ex)
        {
            result = "Unknown Fault: " +
                ex.ToString();
        }
        catch (CommunicationException ex)
        {
            result = "There was a communication problem. " +
                ex.Message + ex.StackTrace;
        }
        catch (Exception ex)
        {
            result = "Other excpetion: " +
                ex.Message + ex.StackTrace;
        }

        txtProductDetails.Text = result;
    }
```

Implementing the UpdateProduct functionality

Next we need to modify the client program to call the `UpdateProduct` operation of the web service. This method is particularly important to us because we will use it to test the concurrent update control of LINQ to Entities.

First we need to add some more controls to the form. We will modify the form UI as follows:

1. Open the file, `Form1.cs,` in the `LINQNorthwindClient` project.
2. Add a label named **lblNewPrice** with text, **New Price**.
3. Add a textbox named **txtNewPrice**.
4. Add a button named **btnUpdatePrice** with text, **&Update Price**.
5. Add a label named **lblUpdateResult** with text, **Update Result**.
6. Add a textbox control named **txtUpdateResult** with **Multiline** property set to **True** and **Scrollbars** set to **Both**.

The form should now appear as shown in the following screenshot:

Now double-click on the **Update Price** button and add the following event handler method for this button:

```
private void btnUpdatePrice_Click(object sender, EventArgs e)
{
    string result = "";
    if (product != null)
    {
        try
        {
            // update its price
            product.UnitPrice =
                Decimal.Parse(txtNewPrice.Text.ToString());

            ProductServiceClient client = new ProductServiceClient();
            StringBuilder sb = new StringBuilder();
            sb.Append("Price updated to ");
            sb.Append(txtNewPrice.Text.ToString());
            sb.Append("\r\n");
            sb.Append("Update result:");
            sb.Append(client.UpdateProduct(ref product).ToString());
            sb.Append("\r\n");
            sb.Append("New RowVersion:");
            foreach (var x in product.RowVersion.AsEnumerable())
            {
                sb.Append(x.ToString());
                sb.Append(" ");
            }
            result = sb.ToString();
```

```
        }
        catch (TimeoutException ex)
        {
            result = "The service operation timed out. " +
                    ex.Message;
        }
        catch (FaultException<ProductFault> ex)
        {
            result = "ProductFault returned: " +
                    ex.Detail.FaultMessage;
        }
        catch (FaultException ex)
        {
            result = "Unknown Fault: " +
                    ex.ToString();
        }
        catch (CommunicationException ex)
        {
            result = "There was a communication problem. " +
                    ex.Message + ex.StackTrace;
        }
        catch (Exception ex)
        {
            result = "Other excpetion: " +
                    ex.Message + ex.StackTrace;
        }
    }
    else
    {
        result = "Get product details first";
    }

    txtUpdateResult.Text = result;
}
```

Note that inside the **Update Price** button event handler listed above we don't get the product from database first. Instead we reuse the same product object from the btnGetProduct_Click method, which means we will update whatever product we get when we click on the **Get Product Details** button. In order to do this we need to move the product variable outside of the private method, btnGetProduct_Click, to be a class variable like this:

```
Product product;
```

Inside the `btnGetProduct_Click` method, we need not define another variable `product`, but use the class member `product` now. The first few lines of code for the class, `Form1`, should be like this now:

```
public partial class Form1 : Form
{
    Product product;

    public Form1()
    {
        InitializeComponent();
    }

    private void btnGetProduct_Click(object sender, EventArgs e)
    {
        ProductServiceClient client = new ProductServiceClient();
        string result = "";
        try
        {
            int productID =
                    Int32.Parse(txtProductID.Text.ToString());
            product = client.GetProduct(productID);
            // More code to follow
```

As you can see, we didn't do anything specific with the concurrent update control of the update, but later in the section, *Testing concurrent update manually*, within this chapter, we will explain how LINQ to Entities inside the WCF service handles this for us.

As in previous chapters, we will also capture all kinds of exceptions and display appropriate messages for them.

Testing the GetProduct and UpdateProduct operations

We can build and run the program to test the `GetProduct` and `UpdateProduct` operations now. Because we are still using the WCF Service Host to host our service, we need to start it first.

1. Make sure the project, `LINQNorthwindService`, is still the startup project and press *Ctrl + F5* to start it. WCF Test Client will also be started. Don't close it or the WCF Service Host will be closed and you will not be able to run the client application.

2. Make the project, `LINQNorthwindClient`, the startup project and press *Ctrl + F5* to start it.

3. Alternatively you can set the solution to start up with multiple projects with the project, `LINQNorthwindService`, to be started up first and the project, `LINQNorthwindClient`, to be started up next. In some cases you may have to do this because as soon as you press *Ctrl + F5* to start the client project, the WCF Service Host (and the WCF Test Client) may be closed automatically, making the client unable to connect to the service. You may also start the service first and then start the client from Windows Explorer by double-clicking on the executable file of the client application.

4. On the Client form, UI, enter **10** as the product ID in the **Product ID** textbox and click on the **Get Product Details** button to get the product details. Note that the **Unit Price** is now **31.0000** and the **RowVersion** is **0 0 0 0 0 0 4 88**, as shown in following screenshot:

5. Now enter **32** as the product price in the **New Price** textbox and click on the **Update Price** button to update its price. The **Update Result** should be **True**. Note that the **RowVersion** has been changed to **0 0 0 0 0 0 90 61**.

6. To verify the new price, click on the **Get Product Details** button again to get the product details for this product and you will see that the unit price has been updated to **32.0000**.

Testing concurrent update manually

We can also test concurrent updates by using the client application, LINQNorthwindClient.

In this section, we will start two clients and update the same product from these two clients at same time. We will create a conflict between the updates from these two clients so that we can test if this conflict is properly handled by LINQ to Entities.

The test sequence will be like this:

1. First client starts.
2. Second client starts.
3. First client reads the product information.
4. Second client reads the same product information.
5. Second client updates the product successfully.
6. First client tries to update the product but fails.

The last step is where the conflict occurs as the product has been updated in between the read and the update by the first client.

The steps are described in detail below:

1. Start the WCF Service Host application in non-debugging mode if you have stopped it (you have to set `LINQNorthwindService` as the startup project first).

2. Start the client application in non-debugging mode by pressing *Control + F5* (you have to make `LINQNorthwindClient` the startup project). We will refer to this client as the first client. As we said in the previous section, you have options such as how to start the WCF service and the client applications at same time.

3. In this first client application, enter **10** in the **Product ID** textbox and click on the **Get Product Details** button to get the product's details. Note that the unit price is **32.0000** and the **RowVersion** is **0 0 0 0 0 0 90 61**.

4. Start another client application in non-debugging mode by pressing *Control + F5*. We will refer to this client as the second client.

5. In the second client application, enter **10** in the **Product ID** textbox, and click on the **Get Product Details** button to get the product's details. Note that the unit price is still **32.0000** and the **RowVersion** is **0 0 0 0 0 0 90 61**. The second client form window should be identical to the first client form window.

6. On the second client form, UI, enter **33** as the product price in the **New Price** textbox and click on the **Update Price** button to update its price.

7. The second client update is committed to the database and the **Update Result** value is **True**. The price of this product has now been updated to 33 and the **RowVersion** has been updated to a new value of **0 0 0 0 0 0 90 62**.

8. In the second client, click on the **Get Product Details** button to get the product details to verify the update. Note that the unit price is now **33.0000** and **RowVersion** is now **0 0 0 0 0 0 90 62**.

9. On the first client form, UI, enter **34** as the product price in the **New Price** textbox and click on the **Update Price** button to update its price.

10. The first client update fails with an error message, **Entities may have been modified or deleted since entities were loaded**.

11. In the second client, click on the **Get Product Details** button again to get the product's details. You will see that the unit price is still **33.0000** and the **RowVersion** is still **0 0 0 0 0 0 90 62**, which means that the first client's update didn't get committed to the database.

The following image is for the second client. You can see the **Update Result** is **True** and the price after the update is **33**.

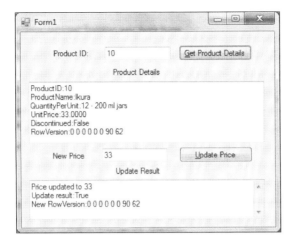

The following image is for the first client. You can see that the price before the update is **32.0000** and the update fails with an error message. This error message is caught as an unknown fault from the client side because we didn't handle the concurrency exception in our service.

From the test above we know that the concurrent update is controlled by LINQ to Entities. An optimistic locking mechanism is enforced and one client's update won't overwrite another client's update. The client that has a conflict will be notified by a fault message.

Concurrent update locking is applied at the record level in the database. If two clients try to update different records in the database they will not interfere with each other. For example, if you repeat the previous steps to update product `10` in one client and product `11` in another client, there will be no problem at all.

Testing concurrent update automatically

In the previous section, we tested the concurrent update control of LINQ to Entities but, as you can see, the timing of the update is fully controlled by our input. We know exactly when the conflict will happen. In a real production a conflict may happen at any time, with no indication as to when and how it will happen. In this section, we will simulate a situation such that a conflict happens randomly. We will add a new functionality to update one product 100 times and let two clients compete with each other until one of the updates fails.

For this test we will put the actual updates in a background worker thread so that the main UI thread won't be blocked.

1. Open the file, `Form1.cs`, in the project, `LINQNorthwindClient`.

2. Add a new class member to the form class for the worker thread like this:

   ```
   BackgroundWorker bw;
   ```

3. Go to `Form1.cs` design mode.

4. Add another button called **btnAutoUpdate** with the text **&Auto Update**.

5. Add the following click event handler for this new button:

   ```
   private void btnAutoUpdate_Click(object sender, EventArgs e)
   {
       if (product != null)
       {
           btnAutoUpdate.Text = "Updating Price ...";
           btnAutoUpdate.Enabled = false;

           bw = new BackgroundWorker();
           bw.WorkerReportsProgress = true;
           bw.DoWork += AutoUpdatePrice;
           bw.ProgressChanged += PriceChanged;
           bw.RunWorkerCompleted += AutoUpdateEnd;
           bw.RunWorkerAsync();
       }
       else
   ```

```
        {
            txtUpdateResult.Text = "Get product details first";
        }
    }

    private void AutoUpdateEnd(object sender,
    RunWorkerCompletedEventArgs e)
    {
        btnAutoUpdate.Text = "&Auto Update";
        btnAutoUpdate.Enabled = true;
    }

    private void PriceChanged(object sender, ProgressChangedEventArgs
    e)
    {
        txtUpdateResult.Text = e.UserState.ToString();
        // Scroll to end of textbox
        txtUpdateResult.SelectionStart = txtUpdateResult.TextLength-4;
        txtUpdateResult.ScrollToCaret();
    }

    private void AutoUpdatePrice(object sender, DoWorkEventArgs e)
    {
        ProductServiceClient client = new ProductServiceClient();
        string result = "";
        try
        {
            // update its price
            for (int i = 0; i < 100; i++)
            {
                // refresh the product first
                product = client.GetProduct(product.ProductID);

                // update its price
                product.UnitPrice += 1.0m;

                StringBuilder sb = new StringBuilder();
                sb.Append("Price updated to ");
                sb.Append(product.UnitPrice.ToString());
                sb.Append("\r\n");
                sb.Append("Update result:");
                bool updateResult = client.UpdateProduct(ref product);
                sb.Append(updateResult.ToString());
                sb.Append("\r\n");
```

```
                sb.Append("New RowVersion:");
                foreach (var x in product.RowVersion.AsEnumerable())
                {
                    sb.Append(x.ToString());
                    sb.Append(" ");
                }
                sb.Append("\r\n");

                sb.Append("Price updated ");
                sb.Append((i + 1).ToString());
                sb.Append(" times\r\n\r\n");

                result += sb.ToString();

                // report progress
                bw.ReportProgress(i+1, result);

                // sleep a while
                Random random = new Random();
                int randomNumber = random.Next(0, 1000);
                System.Threading.Thread.Sleep(randomNumber);
            }
        }
        catch (TimeoutException ex)
        {
            result += "The service operation timed out. " +
                    ex.Message;
        }
        catch (FaultException<ProductFault> ex)
        {
            result += "ProductFault returned: " +
                    ex.Detail.FaultMessage;
        }
        catch (FaultException ex)
        {
            result += "Unknown Fault: " +
                    ex.ToString();
        }
        catch (CommunicationException ex)
        {
            result += "There was a communication problem. " +
                    ex.Message + ex.StackTrace;
        }
```

```
catch (Exception ex)
{
    result += "Other excpetion: " +
            ex.Message + ex.StackTrace;
}

// report progress
bw.ReportProgress(100, result);
}
```

The concept here is that once this button is clicked it will keep updating the price of the selected product 100 times, with a price increase of 1.00 in each iteration. If two clients are running and this button is clicked on both the clients one of the updates will fail as the other client will also be updating the same record.

The sequence of the updates will be as follows:

1. The first client reads the product's details, updates the product, and commits the changes back to the database.

2. The first client sleeps for a while then repeats the above step.

3. The second client reads the product's details, updates the same product, and commits the changes back to the database.

4. The second client sleeps for a while then repeats the above step.

5. At some point these two sets of processes will cross so the following events will happen:

    ° The first client reads the product's details

    ° The first client processes the product in memory

    ° The second client reads the product's details

    ° The first client finishes processing and commits the changes back to the database

    ° The second client finishes processing and tries to commit the changes back to the database

    ° The second client update fails because it finds that the product has been updated while it was still processing the product

    ° The second client stops

    ° The first client keeps updating the product until it has done so 100 times

Now follow these steps to finish this test:

1. Start the WCF Service Host application in non-debugging mode if you had stopped it (you have to set LINQNorthwindService as the startup project first).

2. Make LINQNorthwindClient the startup project and then run it twice in non-debugging mode by pressing *Ctrl + F5*. Two clients should be up and running.

3. From each client, enter **3** in the **Product ID** textbox, and click on **Get Product Details** to get the product details. Both clients should display the price as **10.0000**.

4. Click on the **Auto Update** button on each client.

You will see that one of the clients fails while another one is keeping the updates to the end of 100 times.

The following image shows the results in the successful client. As you can see, the initial price of the product was **10.0000** but, after the updates, it has been changed to **132.0000**. From the source code we know that this client only updates the price 100 times with an increase of 1.00 each time so we know that another client has updated this product 22 times.

The following image shows the results in the failed client. As you can see, the initial price of the product was **10.000**. After updating the price 22 times, when this client tries to update the price again, it fails with the error message **Entities may have been modified or deleted since entities were loaded**. From the results of the other client we also know that this client has updated the product 22 times.

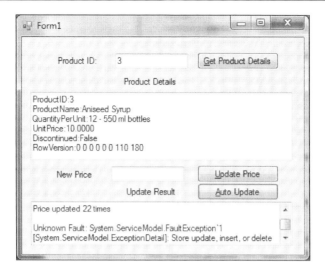

 However if you enter two different product IDs in each client, both client updates will be successful until all 100 updates have been made. This again proves that locking is applied on a record level of the database.

Summary

In this chapter, we have used LINQ to Entities to communicate with the database in the data access layer rather than use the raw ADO.NET APIs. We have used only one LINQ statement to retrieve product information from the database and, as you have seen, the updates with LINQ to Entities prove to be much easier than with the raw ADO.NET data adapters. Now, WCF and LINQ are combined together for our services so we can take advantage of both technologies.

The key points covered in this chapter include:

- The data access layer can be modeled with the LINQ to Entities designer.
- Business entity classes are all located inside the LINQ to Entities designer file within the data access layer.
- It is better to separate our own entities classes from the generated entities classes so we can decouple the data access layer from the service interface layer.

- Client applications still communicate with the service by exchanging messages. The LINQ to Entities objects are not exposed to clients and the technology used in the data access layer is transparent to the clients.

- When updating the database in the data access layer the updated entity has to be attached to a LINQ to Entity `ObjectContext` object.

- Concurrent updates are handled by LINQ to Entities naturally and easily. We just need to add one more column to the database and LINQ to Entities will do the rest for us.

10
Distributed Transaction Support of WCF

In previous chapters we have created a WCF service using LINQ to Entities in the data access layer. Next we will apply settings so that this WCF service will be a distributed service, which means that it can participate in distributed client transactions, if there are any. Client applications will control the transaction scope and decide whether a service should commit or rollback its transaction.

In this chapter, we will first verify that the `LINQNorthwind` WCF service that we built in the previous chapter does not support distributed transaction processing. We will then explain how to enhance this WCF service to support distributed transaction processing and how to configure all related computers to enable distributed transaction support. To demonstrate this, we will propagate a transaction from the client to the WCF service and verify that all sequential calls to the WCF service are within one single distributed transaction. We will also explain the multiple database support of the WCF service and discuss how to configure MSDTC and the firewall for the distributed WCF service.

We will cover the following topics in this chapter:

- Creating the solution files
- Testing the transaction behavior of the `DistNorthwind` WCF service
- Enabling transaction flow in the service bindings
- Modifying the service operation contract to allow transaction flow
- Modifying the service operation implementation to require a transaction scope
- Configuring the Distributed Transaction Coordinator for the distributed WCF service

- Configuring the firewall for the distributed WCF service
- Propagating a transaction from the client to the WCF service
- Testing the multiple database support of the distributed WCF service

Creating the DistNorthwind solution

In this chapter, we will create a new solution based on the `LINQNorthwind` solution. We will copy all of the source code from the `LINQNorthwind` directory to a new directory and then customize it to suit our needs. The steps here are very similar to the steps in the previous chapter when we created the `LINQNorthwind` solution. Please refer to the previous chapter for diagrams.

Follow these steps to create the new solution:

1. Create a new directory named `DistNorthwind` under the existing `C:\SOAwithWCFandLINQ\Projects\` directory.

2. Copy all of the files under the `C:\SOAwithWCFandLINQ\Projects\LINQNorthwind` directory to the `C:\SOAwithWCFandLINQ\Projects\DistNorthwind` directory.

3. Remove the folder, `LINQNorthwindClient`. We will create a new client for this solution.

4. Change all the folder names under the new folder, `DistNorthwind`, from `LINQNorthwindxxx` to `DistNorthwindxxx`.

5. Change the solution files' names from `LINQNorthwind.sln` to `DistNorthwind.sln`, and also from `LINQNorthwind.suo` to `DistNorthwind.suo`.

Now we have the file structures ready for the new solution but all the file contents and the solution structure are still for the old solution. Next we need to change them to work for the new solution.

We will first change all the related WCF service files. Once we have the service up and running we will create a new client to test this new service.

1. Start Visual Studio 2010 and open this solution: `C:\SOAWithWCFandLINQ\Projects\DistNorthwind\DistNorthwind.sln`.

2. Click on the **OK** button to close the **projects were not loaded correctly** warning dialog.

3. From Solution Explorer, remove all five projects (they should all be unavailable).

4. Right-click on the solution item and select **Add | Existing Projects...** to add these four projects to the solution. Note that these are the projects under the DistNorthwind folder, not under the LINQNorthwind folder:

   LINQNorthwindEntities.csproj, LINQNorthwindDAL.csproj, LINQNorthwindLogic.csproj, and LINQNorthwindService.csproj.

5. In Solution Explorer, change all four projects' names from LINQNorthwindxxx to DistNorthwindxxx.

6. In Solution Explorer, right-click on each project, select **Properties** (or select menu **Project | DistNorthwindxxx Properties**), then change the **Assembly name** from LINQNorthwindxxx to DistNorthwindxxx, and change the **Default namespace** from MyWCFServices.LINQNorthwindxxx to MyWCFServices.DistNorthwindxxx.

7. Open the following files and change the word LINQNorthwind to DistNorthwind wherever it occurs:

   ProductEntity.cs, ProductDAO.cs, ProductLogic.cs, IProductService.cs, and ProductService.cs.

8. Open the file, app.config, in the DistNorthwindService project and change the word LINQNorthwind to DistNorthwind in this file.

The screenshot below shows the final structure of the new solution, DistNorthwind:

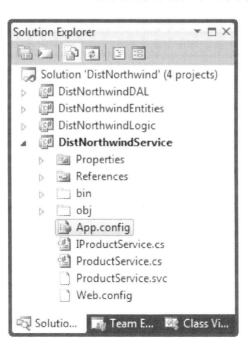

Now we have finished modifying the service projects. If you build the solution now you should see no errors. You can set the service project as the startup project, run the program, and the output should be same as in the last chapter.

Hosting the WCF service in IIS

The WCF service is now hosted within WCF Service Host. You may still remember in the last chapter we had to start the WCF Service Host before we ran our test client. Not only do you have to start the WCF Service Host, you also have to start the WCF Test client and leave it open. This is not that nice. In addition, we will add another service later in this chapter to test distributed transaction support with two databases and it is not that easy to host two services with one WCF Service Host.
So, in this section, we will first decouple our WCF service from Visual Studio to host it in IIS.

As we did in the previous chapter, you can follow these steps to host this WCF service in IIS:

1. In Windows Explorer, go to the directory `C:\SOAWithWCFandLINQ\ Projects\DistNorthwind\DistNorthwindService`.

2. Within this folder create a new text file, `ProductService.svc`, to contain the following one line of code:

    ```
    <%@ServiceHost Service="MyWCFServices.DistNorthwindService.
    ProductService"%>
    ```

3. Again within this folder copy the file, `App.config`, to `Web.config` and remove the following lines from the new `Web.config` file:

    ```
    <host>
      <baseAddresses>
        <add baseAddress="http://localhost:8080/
             Design_Time_Addresses/MyWCFServices/
                DistNorthwindService/ProductService/" />
      </baseAddresses>
    </host>
    ```

4. Now open IIS Manager, add a new application, `DistNorthwindService`, and set its physical path to `C:\SOAWithWCFandLINQ\Projects\DistNorthwind\ DistNorthwindService`. If you choose to use the default application pool, `DefaultAppPool`, make sure it is a .NET 4.0 application pool.
    If you are using Windows XP you can create a new virtual directory, `DistNorthwindService`, set its local path to the above directory, and make sure its ASP.NET version is 4.0.

5. From Visual Studio, in Solution Explorer, right-click on the project item, `DistNorthwindService`, select **Properties**, then click on the **Build Events** tab, and enter the following code to the **Post-build event command line** box:

    ```
    copy .\*.* ..\
    ```

With this **Post-build event command line**, whenever `DistNorthwindService` is rebuilt the service binary files will be copied to the `C:\SOAWithWCFandLINQ\Projects\DistNorthwind\DistNorthwindService\bin` directory so that the service hosted in IIS will always be up-to-date.

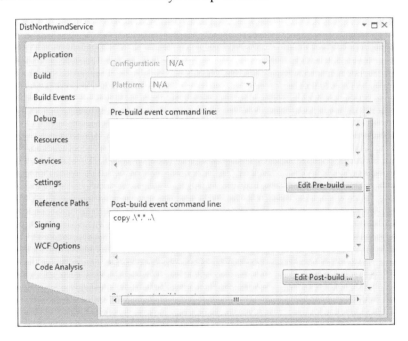

6. From Visual Studio, in Solution Explorer, right-click on the project item, `DistNorthwindService`, and select **Rebuild**.

Now you have finished setting up the service to be hosted in IIS. Open Internet Explorer, go to the following address, and you should see the `ProductService` description in the browser:

```
http://localhost/DistNorthwindService/ProductService.svc
```

Testing the transaction behavior of the WCF service

Before explaining how to enhance this WCF service to support distributed transactions, we will first confirm that the existing WCF service doesn't support distributed transactions. In this section, we will test the following scenarios:

1. Create a WPF client to call the service twice in one method.

2. The first service call should succeed and the second service call should fail.

3. Verify that the update in the first service call has been committed to the database, which means that the WCF service does not support distributed transactions.

4. Wrap the two service calls in one `TransactionScope` and redo the test.

5. Verify that the update in the first service call has still been committed to the database which means the WCF service does not support distributed transactions even if both service calls are within one transaction scope.

6. Add a second database support to the WCF service.

7. Modify the client to update both databases in one method.

8. The first update should succeed and the second update should fail.

9. Verify that the first update has been committed to the database, which means the WCF service does not support distributed transactions with multiple databases.

Creating a client to call the WCF service sequentially

The first scenario to test is that within one method of the client application two service calls will be made and one of them will fail. We then verify whether the update in the successful service call has been committed to the database. If it has been, it will mean that the two service calls are not within a single atomic transaction and will indicate that the WCF service doesn't support distributed transactions.

You can follow these steps to create a WPF client for this test case:

1. In **Solution Explorer**, right-click on the solution item and select **Add | New Project...** from the context menu.

2. Select **Visual C# | WPF Application** as the template.

3. Enter **DistributedWPF** as the **Name**.

4. Click on the **OK** button to create the new client project.

Now the new test client should have been created and added to the solution. Let's follow these steps to customize this client so that we can call `ProductService` twice within one method and test the distributed transaction support of this WCF service:

1. On the WPF `MainWindow` designer surface, add the following controls (you can double-click on the `MainWindow.xaml` item to open this window and make sure you are on the design mode, not the XAML mode):

   ° A label with Content **Product ID**

   ° Two textboxes named **txtProductID1** and **txtProductID2**

   ° A button named **btnGetProduct** with Content **Get Product Details**

   ° A separator to separate above controls from below controls

   ° Two labels with content **Product1 Details** and **Product2 Details**

   ° Two textboxes named **txtProduct1Details** and **txtProduct2Details**, with the following properties:

      ° **AcceptsReturn**: **checked**

      ° **Background**: **Beige**

      ° **HorizontalScrollbarVisibility**: **Auto**

      ° **VerticalScrollbarVisibility**: **Auto**

      ° **IsReadOnly**: **checked**

   ° A separator to separate above controls from below controls

   ° A label with content **New Price**

   ° Two textboxes named **txtNewPrice1** and **txtNewPrice2**

   ° A button named **btnUpdatePrice** with Content **Update Price**

   ° A separator to separate above controls from below controls

   ° Two labels with content **Update1 Results** and **Update2 Results**

   ° Two textboxes named **txtUpdate1Results** and **txtUpdate2Results** with the following properties:

      ° **AcceptsReturn**: **checked**

      ° **Background**: **Beige**

      ° **HorizontalScrollbarVisibility**: **Auto**

      ° **VerticalScrollbarVisibility**: **Auto**

      ° **IsReadOnly**: **checked**

○ Your `MainWindow` design surface should look like the following screenshot:

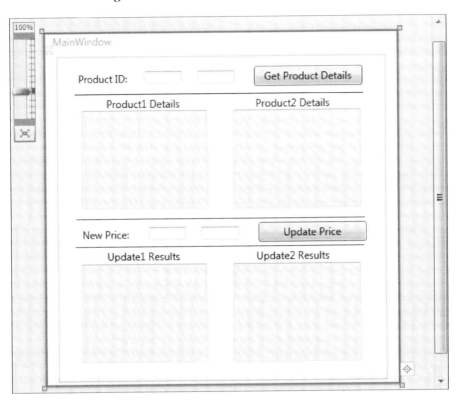

2. In Solution Explorer, right-click on the `DistNorthwindWPF` project item, select **Add Service Reference...** and add a service reference of the product service to the project. The namespace of this service reference should be `ProductServiceProxy` and the URL of the product service should be like this:

```
http://localhost/DistNorthwindService/ProductService.svc
```

 If you get an error saying **An error (Details) occurred while attempting to find service** and the error details are **Metadata contains a reference that cannot be resolved**, you may need to give your IIS identity proper access rights to your windows\temp directory.

3. On the `MainWindow.xaml` designer surface, double-click on the **Get Product Details** button to create an event handler for this button.

4. In the `MainWindow.xaml.cs` file, add the following `using` statement:

```
using DistNorthwindWPF.ProductServiceProxy;
```

3. Again in the `MainWindow.xaml.cs` file, add the following two class members:

```
Product product1, product2;
```

4. Now add the following method to the `MainWindow.xaml.cs` file:

```
private string GetProduct(TextBox txtProductID, ref Product
product)
{
    string result = "";
    try
    {
        int productID = Int32.Parse(txtProductID.Text.ToString());
        ProductServiceClient client = new ProductServiceClient();
        product = client.GetProduct(productID);

        StringBuilder sb = new StringBuilder();
        sb.Append("ProductID:" +
            product.ProductID.ToString() + "\n");
        sb.Append("ProductName:" +
            product.ProductName + "\n");
        sb.Append("UnitPrice:" +
            product.UnitPrice.ToString() + "\n");
        sb.Append("RowVersion:");
        foreach (var x in product.RowVersion.AsEnumerable())
        {
            sb.Append(x.ToString());
            sb.Append(" ");
        }
        result = sb.ToString();
    }
    catch (Exception ex)
    {
        result = "Exception: " + ex.Message.ToString();
    }
    return result;
}
```

This method will call the product service to retrieve a product from the database, format the product details to a string, and return the string. This string will be displayed on the screen. The product object will also be returned so that later on we can reuse this object to update the price of the product.

5. Inside the event handler of the **Get Product Details** button, add the following two lines of code to get and display the product details:

```
txtProduct1Details.Text = GetProduct(txtProductID1, ref product1);

txtProduct2Details.Text = GetProduct(txtProductID2, ref product2);
```

Now we have finished adding code to retrieve products from the database through the Product WCF service. Set `DistNorthwindWPF` as the startup project, press *Ctrl + F5* to start the WPF test client, enter **30** and **31** as the product IDs, and then click on the **Get Product Details** button. You should get a window like this image:

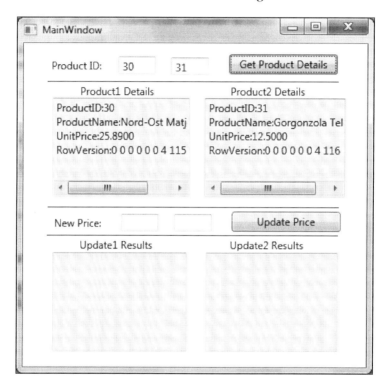

From the preceding image we see product 30's price is now **25.89** and product 31's price is now **12.5**. Next we will write code to update the prices of these two products to test the distributed transaction support of the WCF service.

To update the prices of these two products follow these steps to add the code to the project:

1. On the `MainWindow.xaml` design surface and double-click on the **Update Price** button to add an event handler for this button.

2. Add the following method to the `MainWindow.xaml.cs` file:

```
private string UpdatePrice(
    TextBox txtNewPrice,
    ref Product product,
    ref bool updateResult)
{
    string result = "";

    try
    {
        product.UnitPrice =
            Decimal.Parse(txtNewPrice.Text.ToString());

        ProductServiceClient client =
            new ProductServiceClient();
        updateResult =
            client.UpdateProduct(ref product);
        StringBuilder sb = new StringBuilder();

        if (updateResult == true)
        {
            sb.Append("Price updated to ");
            sb.Append(txtNewPrice.Text.ToString());
            sb.Append("\n");
            sb.Append("Update result:");
            sb.Append(updateResult.ToString());
            sb.Append("\n");
            sb.Append("New RowVersion:");
        }
        else
        {
            sb.Append("Price not updated to ");
            sb.Append(txtNewPrice.Text.ToString());
            sb.Append("\n");
            sb.Append("Update result:");
            sb.Append(updateResult.ToString());
            sb.Append("\n");
            sb.Append("Old RowVersion:");
        }
        foreach (var x in product.RowVersion.AsEnumerable())
        {
            sb.Append(x.ToString());
```

```
            sb.Append(" ");
        }

        result = sb.ToString();
    }
    catch (Exception ex)
    {
        result = "Exception: " + ex.Message;
    }

    return result;
}
```

This method will call the product service to update the price of a product in the database. The update result will be formatted and returned so that later on we can display it. The updated product object with the new RowVersion will also be returned so that later on we can update the price of the same product again and again.

5. Inside the event handler of the **Update Price** button, add the following code to update the product prices:

```
if (product1 == null)
{
    txtUpdate1Results.Text = "Get product details first";
}
else if (product2 == null)
{
    txtUpdate2Results.Text = "Get product details first";
}
else
{
    bool update1Result = false, update2Result = false;

    txtUpdate1Results.Text = UpdatePrice(
        txtNewPrice1, ref product1, ref update1Result);
    txtUpdate2Results.Text = UpdatePrice(
        txtNewPrice2, ref product2, ref update2Result);
}
```

Testing the sequential calls to the WCF service

Let's run the program now to test the distributed transaction support of the WCF service. We will first update two products with two valid prices to make sure our code works with normal use cases. Then we will update one product with a valid price and another with an invalid price. We will verify that the update with the valid price has been committed to the database, regardless of the failure of the other update.

Let's follow these steps for this test:

1. Press *Ctrl* + *F5* to start the program.

2. Enter **30** and **31** as product IDs in the top two textboxes and click on the **Get Product Details** button to retrieve the two products. Note that the prices for these two products are **25.89** and **12.5** respectively.

3. Enter **26.89** and **13.5** as new prices in the middle two textboxes and click on the **Update Price** button to update these two products. The update results are true for both updates, as shown in following screenshot:

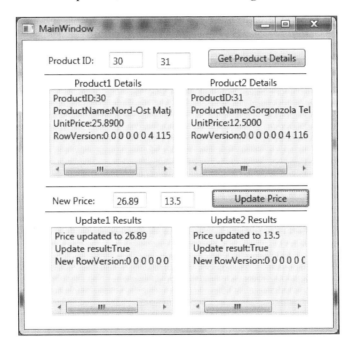

4. Now enter **27.89** and **-14.5** as new prices in the middle two textboxes and click on the **Update Price** button to update these two products. This time the update result for product 30 is still **True** but for the second update the result is **False**. Click on the **Get Product Details** button again to refresh the product prices so that we can verify the update results.

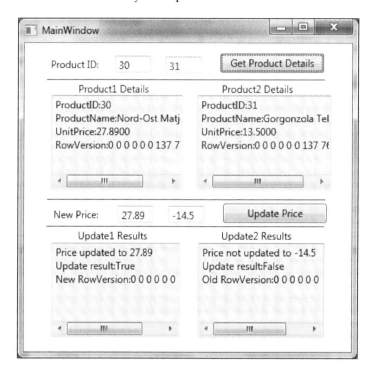

We know that the second service call should fail so the second update should not be committed to the database. From the test result we know this is true (the second product price didn't change). However from the test result we also know that the first update in the first service call has been committed to the database (the first product price has been changed). This means that the first call to the service is not rolled back even when a subsequent service call has failed. Therefore each service call is in a separate standalone transaction. In other words, the two sequential service calls are not within one distributed transaction.

Wrapping the WCF service calls in one transaction scope

This test is not a complete distributed transaction test. On the client side we didn't explicitly wrap the two updates in one transaction scope. We should test to see what will happen if we put the two updates within once transaction scope.

Follow these steps to wrap the two service calls in one transaction scope:

1. Add a reference to `System.Transactions` in the client project.

2. Add a `using` statement to the `MainWindow.xaml.cs` file like this:

   ```
   using System.Transactions;
   ```

3. Add a `using` statement to put both updates within one transaction scope. The click event handler for the **Update Price** button should be like this now:

   ```
   if (product1 == null)
   {
       txtUpdate1Results.Text = "Get product details first";
   }
   else if (product2 == null)
   {
       txtUpdate2Results.Text = "Get product details first";
   }
   else
   {
       bool update1Result = false, update2Result = false;

       using (TransactionScope ts = new TransactionScope())
       {
           txtUpdate1Results.Text = UpdatePrice(
               txtNewPrice1, ref product1, ref update1Result);
           txtUpdate2Results.Text = UpdatePrice(
               txtNewPrice2, ref product2, ref update2Result);
           if (update1Result == true && update2Result == true)
               ts.Complete();
       }
   }
   ```

Run the client program again, still using 30 and 31 as product IDs, and enter 28.89 and -14.5 as new prices and you will find that even though we have wrapped both updates within one transaction scope the first update is still committed to the database—it is not rolled back even though the outer transaction on the client side does not complete and requests all participating parties to roll back. After the updates, product 30's price will be changed to 28.89 and product 31's price will remain as 13.5.

At this point we have proved that the WCF service does not support distributed transactions with multiple sequential service calls. Irrespective of whether the two sequential calls to the service have been wrapped in one transaction scope or not, each service call is treated as a standalone separate transaction and they do not participate in any distributed transaction.

Testing multiple database support of the WCF service

In the previous sections, we tried to call the WCF service sequentially to update records in the same database. We have proved that this WCF service does not support distributed transactions. In this section, we will do one more test, to add a new WCF service—`DistNorthwindRemoteService`—to update records in another database on another computer. We will call the `UpdateProduct` operation in this new service together with the original `UpdateProduct` operation in the old service and then verify whether the two updates to the two databases will be within one distributed transaction.

This new service is very important for our distributed transaction support test because the distributed transaction coordinator will only be activated if more than two servers are involved in the same transaction. For test purposes we can't just update two databases on the same SQL server even though a transaction within a single SQL server that spans two or more databases is actually a distributed transaction. This is because the SQL server manages the distributed transaction internally—to the user it operates as a local transaction.

Creating a new WCF service

First we will add a new WCF service to update a product in a remote database. We will reuse the same WCF service we created for this solution but just change the connection string to point to a remote database in a remote machine.

Follow these steps to add this new service:

1. Discover another machine with the SQL server installed. We will refer to this machine as the remote machine from now on.

2. Install a `Northwind` database to this SQL server on the remote machine. Make sure you add a new column, `RowVersion`, to the `Products` table in this remote `Northwind` database. This is all we need to do on the remote machine in this section.

3. On the local server, in Windows Explorer, create a new folder, `DistNorthwindRemoteService`, under the `DistNorthwind` solution folder: `C:\SOAWithWCFandLINQ\Projects\DistNorthwind`.

4. Copy the following items from the `DistNorthwindService` folder to the new `DistNorthwindRemoteService` folder:

   `Web.config`, `ProductService.svc`, and `bin`.

5. Open the file, `Web.config`, in the new service folder and change the **Data Source** part within the `connectionString` node from **localhost** to the remote machine name with a new `Northwind` database installed.

6. In IIS Manager, add a new application, `DistNorthwindRemoteService`, and set its physical path to the new `DistNorthwindRemoteService` folder. If you are running XP just add a new virtual directory. You can open this address in Internet Explorer to verify that the new service is up and running:

   `http://localhost/DistNorthwindRemoteService/ProductService.svc`

7. To make it easier to maintain this new service, from Visual Studio in Solution Explorer, add a new solution folder `DistNorthwindRemoteService`, to the solution and add the two files and bin folder of this new service to be under the new solution folder.

8. Also from Visual Studio, in Solution Explorer, right-click on the project item, **DistNorthwindService**, select **Properties**, then click on the **Build Events** tab, and add the following to the **Post-build event command line** box, below the original line of the copy command:

   `copy .\*.* ..\..\..\DistNorthwindRemoteService\bin`

Again this **Post-build event command line** will make sure the remote service folder will always contain the latest service binary files.

Calling the new WCF service in the client application

The new service is now up and running. Next we will add a checkbox to the WPF client. If this checkbox is checked when the button, **Get Product Details**, is clicked, we will get the second product from the remote database using the new WCF service. And when the button, **Update Price**, is clicked, we will also update its price in the remote database using the new WCF service.

Now follow these steps to modify the WPF client application to call the new service:

1. From Visual Studio, in Solution Explorer, right-click on the `DistNorthwindWPF` project item and add a service reference to the new WCF service, `DistNorthwindRemoteService`. The namespace of this service reference should be `RemoteProductServiceProxy` and the URL of the product service should be like this:

   `http://localhost/DistNorthwindRemoteService/ProductService.svc`

2. Open the `MainWindow.xaml` file, go to design mode, and add a checkbox to indicate we are going to get and update a product in the remote database using the remote service. Set this checkbox's properties as this:

   ° **Content: Get and Update 2nd Product in Remote Database**

   ° **Name: chkRemote**

3. Open the `MainWindow.xaml.cs` file and add a new class member:

   `RemoteProductServiceProxy.Product remoteProduct;`

4. Still in the `MainWindow.xaml.cs` file, copy the method, `GetProduct`, and paste it as a new method, `GetRemoteProduct`. Change the `Product` type within this new method to be `RemoteProductServiceProxy.Product` and change the client type to `RemoteProductServiceProxy.ProductServiceClient`. The new method should be like this:

```
private string GetRemoteProduct(TextBox txtProductID,
    ref RemoteProductServiceProxy.Product product)
{
    string result = "";

    try
    {
        int productID = Int32.Parse(txtProductID.Text.ToString());
        RemoteProductServiceProxy.ProductServiceClient client =
            new RemoteProductServiceProxy.ProductServiceClient();
```

```
product = client.GetProduct(productID);

StringBuilder sb = new StringBuilder();
sb.Append("ProductID:" +
    product.ProductID.ToString() + "\n");
sb.Append("ProductName:" +
    product.ProductName + "\n");
sb.Append("UnitPrice:" +
    product.UnitPrice.ToString() + "\n");
sb.Append("RowVersion:");
foreach (var x in product.RowVersion.AsEnumerable())
{
    sb.Append(x.ToString());
    sb.Append(" ");
}
result = sb.ToString();

}
catch (Exception ex)
{
    result = "Exception: " + ex.Message.ToString();
}

return result;
}
```

5. Change the method, btnGetProduct_Click, to call the new service if the checkbox is checked, like this:

```
private void btnGetProduct_Click(object sender, RoutedEventArgs e)
{
    txtProduct1Details.Text = GetProduct(
        txtProductID1, ref product1);
    if(chkRemote.IsChecked == true)
        txtProduct2Details.Text = GetRemoteProduct(
            txtProductID2, ref remoteProduct);
    else
        txtProduct2Details.Text = GetProduct(
            txtProductID2, ref product2);
}
```

6. Copy the method, `UpdatePrice`, and paste it as a new method, `UpdateRemotePrice`. Change the `Product` type within this new method to `RemoteProductServiceProxy.Product` and change the client type to `RemoteProductServiceProxy.ProductServiceClient`.

The new method should be like this:

```
private string UpdateRemotePrice(
    TextBox txtNewPrice,
    ref RemoteProductServiceProxy.Product product,
    ref bool updateResult)
{

    string result = "";

    try
    {
        product.UnitPrice =
            Decimal.Parse(txtNewPrice.Text.ToString());

        RemoteProductServiceProxy.ProductServiceClient client =
            new RemoteProductServiceProxy.ProductServiceClient();
        updateResult =
            client.UpdateProduct(ref product);
        StringBuilder sb = new StringBuilder();

        if (updateResult == true)
        {
            sb.Append("Price updated to ");
            sb.Append(txtNewPrice.Text.ToString());
            sb.Append("\n");
            sb.Append("Update result:");
            sb.Append(updateResult.ToString());
            sb.Append("\n");
            sb.Append("New RowVersion:");
        }
        else
        {
            sb.Append("Price not updated to ");
            sb.Append(txtNewPrice.Text.ToString());
            sb.Append("\n");
            sb.Append("Update result:");
            sb.Append(updateResult.ToString());
            sb.Append("\n");
            sb.Append("Old RowVersion:");
```

```
    }
    foreach (var x in product.RowVersion.AsEnumerable())
    {
        sb.Append(x.ToString());
        sb.Append(" ");
    }

    result = sb.ToString();
}
catch (Exception ex)
{
    result = "Exception: " + ex.Message;
}

return result;
}
```

7 Change the method, btnUpdatePrice_Click, to call the new service if the checkbox is checked.

The new method should be like this:

```
private void btnUpdatePrice_Click(object sender, RoutedEventArgs
e)
{
    if (product1 == null)
    {
        txtUpdate1Results.Text = "Get product details first";
    }
    else if (chkRemote.IsChecked == false && product2 == null ||
        chkRemote.IsChecked == true && remoteProduct == null)
    {
        txtUpdate2Results.Text = "Get product details first";
    }
    else
    {
        bool update1Result = false, update2Result = false;
        using (TransactionScope ts = new TransactionScope())
        {
            txtUpdate1Results.Text = UpdatePrice(
                txtNewPrice1, ref product1, ref update1Result);
            if(chkRemote.IsChecked == true)
                txtUpdate2Results.Text = UpdateRemotePrice(
                    txtNewPrice2, ref remoteProduct,
```

```
                        ref update2Result);
              else
                  txtUpdate2Results.Text = UpdatePrice(
                      txtNewPrice2, ref product2, ref
    update2Result);
              if (update1Result == true && update2Result == true)
                  ts.Complete();
          }
      }
  }
```

Testing the WCF service with two databases

Now let's run the program to test the distributed transaction support of the WCF service with two databases.

Follow these steps for this test:

1. Press *Ctrl + F5* to start the client application.

2. Check the checkbox, **Get and Update 2nd Product in Remote Database**.

3. Enter **30** and **31** as product IDs in the top two textboxes.

4. Click on the **Get Product Details** button to get product details for product ID 30 and 31. Note that product 31's details are now retrieved from the remote database. Product 30's price should be 28.89 and product 31's price should be still 12.5 in the remote database.

   If you get an exception like **Exception: An error occurred while executing the command definition. See the inner exception for details.** in the second product details textbox, make sure you have specified the connection string in the `Web.config` file of the new WCF service and make sure you have added the `RowVersion` column in the `Products` table of the remote `North-wind` database.

 If there is a firewall on the remote machine make sure you have the SQL Server port open so that your client application can connect to it through the firewall. The SQL Server port number should be 1433 by default.

   If you see the price for product 31 is not 12.5 but 13.5, it is likely that you didn't check the remote database checkbox. For this test we need to involve the remote database so you need to check the remote database checkbox and again click on the button, **Get Product Details**, before you continue the test.

5. Enter **29.89** and **-14.5** as the new prices in the middle two textboxes and click on the button, **Update Price**.

6. The update result for the first product should be **True** and for the second product should be **False**. This means the second product in the remote database has not been updated.

7. Click on the **Get Product Details** button to refresh the product details so that we can verify the update results.

Just as in the previous test we know that the second service call fails due to the invalid price so the second update is not committed to the database. From the refreshed product details, we know this is true (product 31's price didn't change). However from the refreshed product details we also know that the first update of the first service call has been committed to the remote database (product 30's price has been changed). This means that the first call to the service is not rolled back even when a subsequent service call has failed. Each service call is in a separate standalone transaction. In other words, the two sequential service calls are not within one distributed transaction.

Enabling distributed transaction support

In the previous sections, we verified that the WCF service currently does not support distributed transactions irrespective of whether these are two sequential calls to the same service or two sequential calls to two different services, either with one database or with two databases.

In the following sections, I will explain how to allow this WCF service to support distributed transactions. We will allow the WCF service to participate in the client transaction. From another point of view, I will explain how to flow or propagate a client transaction across the service boundaries so that the client can include service operation calls on multiple services in the same distributed transaction.

> For more information about WCF transaction support you can visit the MSDN MCF transaction support site at `http://msdn.microsoft.com/enus/library/ms730266.aspx`.

Enabling transaction flow in service binding

The first thing that we need to pay attention to is the bindings. As we learned in previous chapters, the three elements of a WCF service end point are the address, the binding, and the contract (WCF ABC). Although the address has nothing to do with the distributed transaction support the other two elements do.

We know that WCF supports several different bindings but not all of these bindings are capable of propagating a transaction across service boundaries. A transaction can only be propagated from a client application into a WCF service with the following bindings: `NetTcpBinding`, `NetNamedPipeBinding`, `WSHttpBinding`, `WSDualHttpBinding`, and `WSFederationHttpBinding`. In this chapter, we will use `WSHttpBinding` as our example.

However using a transaction-aware binding doesn't mean that a transaction will be propagated to the service. The transaction propagation is disabled by default and we have to enable it manually. Unsurprisingly, the attribute to enable transaction flow in the bindings is called `transactionFlow`.

In the following section, we will do the following to enable the transaction propagation:

- Use `WSHttpBinding` on the host application as binding
- Set the value of the `transactionFlow` attribute to `true` on the host application binding configuration

Enabling transaction flow on the service hosting application

In this section, we will enable transaction flow in bindings for both `ProductService` and `RemoteProductService`.

1. In Solution Explorer, open the **web.config** file under the folder **C:\ SOAWithWCFandLINQ\Projects\DistNorthwind\DistNorthwindService**.

2. Change the following line:

   ```
   <endpoint address="" binding="wsHttpBinding"
      contract="MyWCFServices.DistNorthwindService.IProductService">
   ```

   To this line:

   ```
   <endpoint address="" binding="wsHttpBinding"
      contract="MyWCFServices.DistNorthwindService.IProductService"
          bindingConfiguration="transactionalWsHttpBinding">
   ```

3. Add the following node to the `web.config` file inside the node, `system.serviceModel`, and in parallel with node `services`:

   ```
   <bindings>
     <wsHttpBinding>
       <binding name="transactionalWsHttpBinding"
           transactionFlow="true" receiveTimeout="00:10:00"
           sendTimeout="00:10:00" openTimeout="00:10:00"
           closeTimeout="00:10:00" />
     </wsHttpBinding>
   </bindings>
   ```

4. Make the same changes to the **web.config** file under the folder **C:\SOAWithWCFandLINQ\Projects\DistNorthwind\ DistNorthwindRemoteService**.

In the above configuration files we have verified and left the bindings for both `ProductService` and `RemoteProductService` to `wsHttpBinding` and set the attribute, `transactionFlow`, of the binding to `true`. This will enable distributed transaction support from the WCF service binding side.

Modifying the service operation contract to allow a transaction flow

Now the service is able to participate in a propagated transaction from the client application but the client is still not able to propagate a distributed transaction into the service. Before we enable the distributed transaction support from the client side, we need to make some more changes to the service side code, that is, modify the service operation to opt in to participate in a distributed transaction. By default, it is opted out.

Two things need to be done in order to allow an operation to participate in a propagated transaction. The first thing is to enable the transaction flow in operation contracts. Follow these steps to enable this option:

1. Open the `IProductServiceContract.cs` file under the `DistNorthwindService` project.

2. Add the following line before the `UpdateProduct` method:

   `[TransactionFlow(TransactionFlowOption.Allowed)]`

In the above code we set `TransactionFlowOption` in the `UpdateProduct` operation to be `Allowed`. This means a transaction can be propagated from the client to this operation.

The three transaction flow options for a WCF service operation are `Allowed`, `NotAllowed`, and `Mandatory`, as shown in the following table:

Option	Description
NotAllowed	A transaction should not be flowed; this is the default value
Allowed	Transaction may be flowed
Mandatory	Transaction must be flowed

Modifying the service operation implementation to require a transaction scope

The second thing we need to do is to specify the `TransactionScopeRequired` behavior for the service operation. This has to be done on the service implementation project.

1. Open the `ProductService.cs` file under the `DistNorthwindService` project.

2. Add the following line before the `UpdateProduct` method:

```
[OperationBehavior(TransactionScopeRequired = true)]
```

The `TransactionScopeRequired` attribute means that, for the `UpdateProduct` method, the whole service operation will always be executed inside one transaction. If a transaction is propagated from the client application this operation will participate in this existing distributed transaction. If no transaction is propagated a new transaction will be created and this operation will be running within this new transaction.

If you are interested, you can examine the ambient transaction inside the WCF service (`Transaction.Current`), and compare it with the ambient transaction of the client to see if they are the same. You can also examine the `TransactionInformation` property of the ambient transaction object to see if it is a local transaction (`TransactionInformation.LocalIdentifier`) or a distributed transaction (`TransactionInformation.DistributedIdentifier`).

Getting back to our example, we now need to regenerate the service proxy and the configuration files on the client project because we have changed the service interfaces. However, in your real project, you shouldn't change any service interface. Once it goes live you should version your service and allow the client applications to migrate to the new versions of the service. To simplify our example we will just update the proxy and configuration files and recompile our client application.

These are the steps to regenerate the configuration and proxy files:

1. Rebuild the solution. As we have set up the post-build event for the `DistNorthwindService` project to copy all assembly files to two IIS directories, both `ProductService` and `RemoteProductService` now should contain the latest assemblies with distributed transaction support enabled.

3. In Solution Explorer, right-click on `RemoteProductServiceProxy` under the **Service References** directory of the `DistNorthwindWPF` project.

4. Select **Update Service Reference** from the context menu.

5. Right-click on **ProductServiceProxy** under the **Service References** directory of the **DistNorthwindWPF** project.

6. Select **Update Service Reference** from the context menu.

Open the `App.config` file under the `DistNorthwindWPF` project. You will find that the `transactionFlow` attribute is now populated as `true` because the code generator finds that some operations in the service now allow transaction propagation.

Understanding the distributed transaction support of a WCF service

As we have seen, distributed transaction support of a WCF service depends on the binding of the service, the operation contract attribute, the operation implementation behavior, and the client applications.

The following table shows some possible combinations of the WCF-distributed transaction support:

Binding permits transaction flow	Client flows transaction	Service contract opts in transaction	Service operation requires transaction scope	Possible result
True	Yes	`Allowed` or `Mandatory`	True	Service executes under the flowed in transaction
True or False	No	`Allowed`	True	Service creates and executes within a new transaction
True	Yes or No	`Allowed`	False	Service executes without a transaction
True or False	No	`Mandatory`	True or False	SOAP exception
True	Yes	`NotAllowed`	True or False	SOAP exception

Testing the distributed transaction support of the WCF service

Now that we have changed the service to support distributed transaction and let the client propagate the transaction to the service, we will test this. We will propagate a transaction from the client to the service, test the multiple database support of the WCF service, and discuss the Distributed Transaction Coordinator and Firewall settings for the distributed transaction support of the WCF service.

Configuring the Distributed Transaction Coordinator

In a subsequent section, we will call two services to update two databases on two different computers. As these two updates are wrapped within one distributed transaction, **Microsoft Distributed Transaction Coordinator (MSDTC)** will be activated to manage this distributed transaction. If MSDTC is not started or configured properly the distributed transaction will not be successful. In this section, we will explain how to configure MSDTC on both machines.

You can follow these steps to configure MSDTC on your local and remote machines:

1. Open **Component Services** from **Control Panel | Administrative Tools**.

2. In the **Component Services** window, expand **Component Services**, then **Computers**, and then right-click on **My Computer**.

3. Select **Properties** from the context menu.

4. On the **My Computer Properties** window, click on the **MSDTC** tab.

5. If this machine is running Windows XP, click on the **Security Configuration** button.

6. If this machine is running Windows 7, verify that **Use local coordinator** is checked and then close the **My Computer Properties** window. Expand **Distributed Transaction Coordinator** under **My Computer** node, right-click on **Local DTC**, select **Properties** from the context menu, and then from the **Local DTC Properties** window, click on the **Security** tab.

7. You should now see the Security Configuration for DTC on this machine. Set it as in the following screenshot.

8. Remember you have to make these changes for both your local and remote machines.

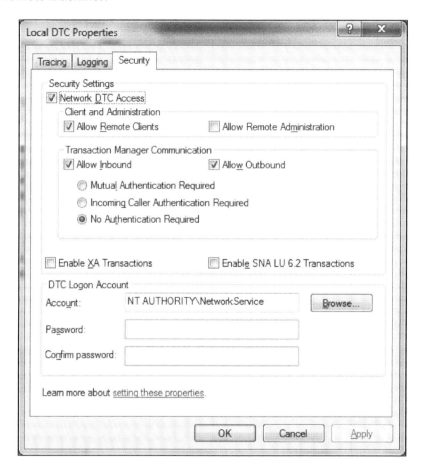

You have to restart the MSDTC service after you have changed your MSDTC settings, for the changes to take effect.

Also, to simplify our example, we have chosen the **No Authentication Required** option. You should be aware that not needing authentication is a serious security issue in production. For more information about WCF security, you can go to the MSDN WCF security website at this address: `http://msdn.microsoft.com/en-us/library/ms735093.aspx.`

Configuring the firewall

Even though Distributed Transaction Coordinator has been enabled the distributed transaction may still fail if the firewall is turned on and hasn't been set up properly for MSDTC.

To set up the firewall for MSTC, follow these steps:

1. Open the **Windows Firewall** window from the **Control Panel**.

2. If the firewall is not turned on you can skip this section.

3. Go to the **Allow a program or feature through Windows Firewall** window (for Windows XP, you need to allow exceptions and go to the **Exceptions** tab on the **Windows Firewall** window).

4. Add **Distributed Transaction Coordinator** to the program list (**windows\ system32\msdtc.exe**) if it is not already on the list. Make sure the checkbox before this item is checked.

5. Again you need to change your firewall setting for both your local and remote machines.

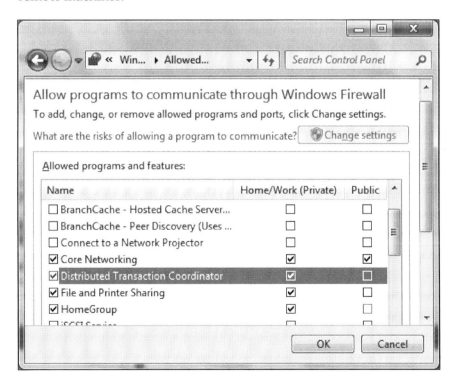

Now the firewall will allow `msdtc.exe` to go through so our next test won't fail due to the firewall restrictions.

 You may have to restart IIS after you have changed your firewall settings. In some cases you may also have to stop and then restart your firewall for the changes to take effect.

Propagating a transaction from the client to the WCF service

Now we have the services and MSDTC ready. In this section, we will rerun the distributed test client and verify the distributed transaction support of the enhanced WCF service.

Testing distributed transaction support with one database

First we will test the distributed transaction support of the WCF service within one database. We will try to update two products (30 and 31). The first update will succeed but the second update will fail. Both updates are wrapped in one client transaction which will be propagated into the service and the service will participate in this distributed transaction. Due to the failure of the second update, the client application will roll back this distributed transaction at the end and the service should also roll back every update that is within this distributed transaction. So, in the end, the first update should not be committed to the database.

Now follow these steps to do this test:

1. Press *Ctrl* + *F5* to start the client application.

2. Enter **30** and **31** as product IDs in the top two textboxes.

3. Make sure **Get and Update 2nd Product in Remote Database** is not checked.

4. Click on the **Get Product Details** button. The prices for these two products should be **29.89** and **13.5**, respectively.

5. Enter **30.89** and **-14.5** as new prices in the middle two textboxes.

6. Click on the **Update Price** button.

7. Click on the **Get Product Details** button to refresh the product details so that we can verify the results.

From the output window we can see that the prices of both products remain the same which proves that the first update has been rolled back. From this output we know that both service calls are within a distributed transaction and the WCF service now fully supports the distributed transaction within one database.

Testing distributed transaction support with two databases

Next we will test the distributed transaction support of the WCF service with two databases or machines involved. As mentioned before, this is a true distributed transaction test as MSDTC will be activated only when the machine boundary is crossed.

In this test, we will try to update two products (product 30 and 31). But this time the second product (product 31) is in a remote database on another machine. As in the previous test the first update will succeed but the second update will fail. Both updates are wrapped in one client transaction which will be propagated into the service and the service will participate in this distributed transaction. Due to the failure of the second update, the client application will roll back this distributed transaction at the end and the service should also roll back every update that is within this distributed transaction. The first update should finally not be committed to the database.

Now follow these steps to carry out this test:

1. Press *Ctrl + F5* to start the client application.

2. Enter **30** and **31** as product IDs in the top two textboxes.

3. Make sure **Get and Update 2nd Product in Remote Database** is checked.

4. Click on the **Get Product Details** button. The prices for these two products should be **29.89** and **12.5**, respectively.

5. Enter **30.89** and **-14.5** as new prices in the middle two textboxes.

6. Click on **Update Price**.

7. Then click on the **Get Product Details** button to refresh the product details so that we can verify the results.

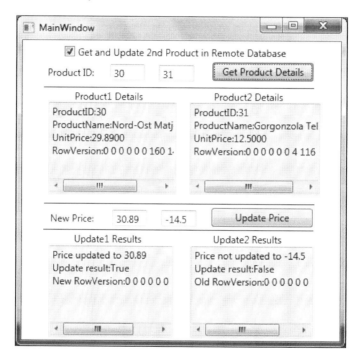

From the output window we can see that the prices of both products remain the same which proves that the first update has been rolled back. From this output we know that both service calls are within a distributed transaction and the WCF service now fully supports the distributed transaction with multiple databases involved.

With the previous tests, you might not get an output as shown here, but instead a message like **Exception: The underlying provider failed to Open** in your **Update Result** textbox. If you debug your code, inside the `UpdatePrice` or `UpdateRemotePrice` method, you may see one of the following error messages:

- **MSDTC on server 'xxxxxx' is unavailable**
- **Network access for Distributed Transaction Manager(MSDTC) has been disabled**
- **The transaction has already been implicitly or explicitly committed or aborted**

This might be because you haven't set your Distributed Transaction Coordinator or firewall correctly. In this case you need to follow the instructions in the previous sections to configure these settings, then come back and redo these tests.

Summary

In this chapter, we have discussed how to enable distributed transaction support for a WCF service. Now we can wrap sequential WCF service calls within one transaction scope and flow the distributed transaction into the WCF services. We can also update multiple databases on different computers all within one single distributed transaction.

The key points discussed in this chapter include:

- Only certain bindings allow transactions to flow from the client to the WCF service using the `transactionFlow` attribute
- A WCF service operation contract can opt to participate in a propagated transaction using the `TransactionFlow` attribute
- A WCF service operation can specify its transaction behavior using the `TransactionScopeRequired` attribute
- MSDTC network access must be enabled for distributed transaction support among multiple computers
- The firewall has to be configured to allow `msdtc.exe` for a distributed transaction to succeed

Index

Symbols

Thank you for buying
WCF 4.0 Multi-tier Services Development with LINQ to Entities

About Packt Publishing

Packt, pronounced 'packed', published its first book "Mastering phpMyAdmin for Effective MySQL Management" in April 2004 and subsequently continued to specialize in publishing highly focused books on specific technologies and solutions.

Our books and publications share the experiences of your fellow IT professionals in adapting and customizing today's systems, applications, and frameworks. Our solution based books give you the knowledge and power to customize the software and technologies you're using to get the job done. Packt books are more specific and less general than the IT books you have seen in the past. Our unique business model allows us to bring you more focused information, giving you more of what you need to know, and less of what you don't.

Packt is a modern, yet unique publishing company, which focuses on producing quality, cutting-edge books for communities of developers, administrators, and newbies alike. For more information, please visit our website: www.packtpub.com.

About Packt Enterprise

In 2010, Packt launched two new brands, Packt Enterprise and Packt Open Source, in order to continue its focus on specialization. This book is part of the Packt Enterprise brand, home to books published on enterprise software – software created by major vendors, including (but not limited to) IBM, Microsoft and Oracle, often for use in other corporations. Its titles will offer information relevant to a range of users of this software, including administrators, developers, architects, and end users.

Writing for Packt

We welcome all inquiries from people who are interested in authoring. Book proposals should be sent to author@packtpub.com. If your book idea is still at an early stage and you would like to discuss it first before writing a formal book proposal, contact us; one of our commissioning editors will get in touch with you.

We're not just looking for published authors; if you have strong technical skills but no writing experience, our experienced editors can help you develop a writing career, or simply get some additional reward for your expertise.

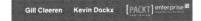

Made in the USA
Lexington, KY
11 April 2011